D0762505

Uncle Dick Wootton

UNCLE DICK WOOTTON

UNCLE DICK WOOTTON

The Pioneer Frontiersman
of the Rocky Mountain Region

By Howard Louis Conard

EDITED BY
MILO MILTON QUAIFE

UNIVERSITY OF NEBRASKA PRESS
Lincoln and London

Reprinted with the permission of R. R. Donnelley & Sons Company, The Lakeside Press.

First Bison Book printing: 1980

Most recent printing indicated by first digit below:

1   2   3   4   5   6   7   8   9   10

Library of Congress Cataloging in Publication Data

Wootton, Richens Lacy, 1816–1893.
    Uncle Dick Wootton, the pioneer frontiersman of the Rocky Mountain region.

    Based on interviews between Wootton and Conard.
    Reprint of the 1957 ed. published by R. R. Donnelley, Chicago, which was issued as no. 55 of the Lakeside classics.
    Includes index.
    1. Wootton, Richens Lacy, 1816–1893. 2. Frontier and pioneer life—The West. 3. The West—History. 4. Indians of North America—The West. 5. Pioneers—The West—Biography. I. Conrad, Howard Louis. II. Quaife, Milo Milton, 1880–1959. III. Title.
[F593.W66 1980]   978′0924 [B]   79–19038
ISBN 0–8032–1408–1
ISBN 0–8032–6306–6 pbk.

Manufactured in the United States of America

CONTENTS

v

ILLUSTRATIONS

HISTORICAL INTRODUCTION

UNCLE DICK WOOTTON (Richens Lacy Wootton) has related his own story in the pages that follow this introduction. That he has told it well, on the whole, and that he led a life well worth recording will be evident to every reader. But no man can see himself as others see him, and apart from this fact the passage of time brings changes in viewpoints and standards of judgment. Chiefly for this reason the "definitive" history so often acclaimed by the book reviewers can never, in fact, be written. Each generation sees life differently than its predecessor has done, and consequently places its own interpretation upon the records of the past.

To orient the reader in the background of Uncle Dick's narrative some editorial comment is required. Born in 1816, his formative years were chiefly passed on his father's tobacco plantation in southern Kentucky. At the age of seventeen, however, he removed to Mississippi, where an uncle owned a cotton plantation. Two years later, moved by a spirit of restless adventure, he journeyed to Independence, Missouri, where he joined an overland caravan bound for Santa Fe.

Henceforth he was never to see his parents nor his boyhood home again. The West of the trapper and the Indian trader had laid its spell upon him. Notably intelligent and enterprising, for over half a century he plied the various roles of trapper and trader, army guide and Indian fighter, freighter and stage operator, pioneer farmer, store-keeper, and road builder. During these years he witnessed and himself shared in the transformation of the Southwest from a domain of savagery under the nominal rule of Mexico to the thriving American civilization of the present day.

Leaving the Santa Fe caravan, Wootton made his way to Bent's Fort, where before long as leader of a party of thirteen men and ten wagons he was dispatched upon an extensive trading expedition to the Sioux Indians who roamed over northern Colorado and Wyoming. Still a mere tenderfoot, and a minor in years, he returned in triumph to Fort Bent several months later with a highly profitable harvest of furs for his employers.

In the autumn of 1838, having meanwhile engaged in several trapping and trading excursions, with attendant encounters with hostile Indians, Wootton joined a party of nineteen trappers who embarked upon a 5000-mile, two-year expedition. From Fort Bent they pushed northward and westward to the valley of the Columbia River, venturing as far as Vancouver. At the time, and for some years to come, ownership of the Oregon country was claimed by both Great Britain and the United States. Turning southward into California, then under Mexican rule, they traversed the present state from north to south when, turning eastward by way of Arizona and Utah, they regained Fort Bent.

It was an astonishing enterprise, undertaken years in advance of the explorations which brought subsequent fame and fortune to John C. Fremont. Although Wootton does not claim to have been its leader, he made himself its only chronicler. Five of the original nineteen members of the party died violent deaths in the course of the expedition. The survivors returned to Fort Bent to learn that the price of beaver skins had taken a sudden and appalling fall. In distant Paris the fashion of making men's hats of silk instead of beaver skins had been set, and along with this fur seal and nutria skins were being used as substitutes for the more expensive beaver. The price of the latter had dropped from the six or eight dollars per pound formerly paid for skins to $1, hardly enough to pay the actual cost of traps and other equipment. The Mountain Men, as they were called, were now compelled to seek other means of livelihood. Kit Carson hired out to Bent and St. Vrain as a hunter to supply the fort with meat. Gordon, one of his long-time associates, migrated to California, where in 1841 he obtained from the Spanish Governor an extensive grant of land northwest of Sacramento, a considerable portion of which is still owned by some of his descendants. Wootton, like Carson, hired out to Bent and St. Vrain as a hunter. From hunting buffaloes (killing as many as thirty in a day) he turned to rearing buffalo calves on a ranch on the site of present-day Pueblo.

In short, Wootton was an enterprising opportunist, ready to embark upon almost any calling which the exigencies of the moment opened to him. Among his contemporary associates were doubtless other men who were no less enterprising than he, but the number of them who were able or fortunate enough to have their life story preserved in a book was painfully small. At the moment, in fact, the Editor can recall but one. Kit Carson's career paralleled in numerous respects the career of Wootton. While still in his mid-career Carson achieved a degree of contemporary renown fairly comparable to that which earlier befell Daniel Boone. Accordingly he was importuned to relate his life story. As a relator of his deeds, however, Carson proved as inept as he was adept in actual life in fighting Indians.

Incomparably a better story-teller than Carson, no one importuned Wootton to relate the story of his life until almost at its close Howard L. Conard, a professional promoter of historical publications, perceived its value and recorded it for the edification of posterity.

Unlike Carson, Wootton possessed the knack for noting and relating details, which is the prime ingredient of the story-teller's art. He knew the Indians no less intimately than did Carson, and detested them no less cordially. During his active career he was an ardent exponent of vigilante justice, and in his old age he defended the custom no less ardently. A veteran of the Indian trade, he does not neglect to supply the reader with a detailed picture of the way it operated. A veteran wagoner across the Plains, also, he has preserved for us an intimate description of the way the commerce of the prairies was conducted. A southern sympathizer during the Civil War, whose activities provoked the repressive measures of the authorities, his old-age narrative, related two decades after the downfall of the "Lost Cause," candidly relates his role in it. The varied roles he played during his active career involved him in so many different activities that his life story constitutes a fair approach to an encyclopaedia of life on the southwestern American frontier.

Quite apart from its informational value, Uncle Dick's story provides grand entertainment for the general reader. The scholar, however, intent upon reconstructing accurately the life of the past, will naturally ask how faithfully Uncle Dick has recorded it. For the scholar, therefore,—perhaps also for the general reader—two further characteristics of Uncle Dick's story must be noted. In the first place, the story as we have it has been ghost-written by a professional interviewer and writer. The calling of the ghost-writer is entirely honorable (the present Editor has practiced it on occasion), but it involves certain consequences which the reader should understand. Uncle Dick, like Henry Ford and other well-known characters, was no adept with the pen. Instead of writing his narrative, therefore, he related it in a series of interviews, which Conard, his interviewer, noted down (whether at the time or later on we are not told) and subsequently recast in the language of the printed book.

How adequately, therefore, we need to know, did Conard perform this important task? For many years Conard was engaged in organizing and publishing local histories on a commercial basis—among others, a two-volume history of Milwaukee, a four-volume encyclopaedia of the history of St. Louis, and a similar historical encyclopaedia of the State of Missouri. As a professional interviewer and writer, therefore, he was adequately qualified to ghost Uncle Dick's narrative. He conceived a great admiration for Wootton, and he assures us that he has given us the pioneer's story "without change or embellishment," save for the rounding off of a rough corner now and then, or the refinement of an expression too forthright to be reproduced in print. Internal evidence of Conard's sincerity is seen in the fact that he made no effort to correct Uncle Dick's sometimes erroneous dates or other misstatements of historical facts. In so far as practicable the present Editor has called attention to these memory slips in the footnotes appended to this edition.

It remains to consider the accuracy of Uncle Dick's old-age memory. We have the testimony of Conard that he was able to recall "not only all the interesting experiences of his own eventful life, but the day and date of almost everything which has happened in the mountain region within the past fifty years which even for the passing moment attracted the attention of the public."

We agree with Conard that Uncle Dick's memory was photostatic and astonishing. In his ability to recreate in ample detail the scenes of his past life consists the great charm, as well as the chief historical value of the book. But Uncle Dick was not omniscient, nor was his memory always infallible, and his errors, whether of omission or of commission, serve to account for the unusual number of editorial footnotes we have appended to his narrative. On occasion he fumbles a date or confuses the sequence of events, and it becomes necessary to supply the required correction. Apart from such frailties, Uncle Dick's ability to recreate the scenes and events of his past life was extraordinary.

How really remarkable it was can best be illustrated, perhaps, by the contrast between his story and Kit Carson's *Autobiography*. Both men had roughly comparable stories to tell. Carson's was recorded while he was still in his physical prime, Wootton's not until in his extreme old age. Yet Carson's story is almost as dry as one of the *Jornadas* of the southwestern deserts. To his journey from Los Angeles to Taos in the spring of 1848 he devotes a single page. Yet the parallel account of George D. Brewerton, his youthful companion on the journey, runs to 150 pages. Brewerton requires seven pages to describe the hazardous crossing of Grand River; Carson disposes of it in a paragraph. Carson describes in four sentences his encounter with several hundred Utes and Apaches whom he overawed and outwitted; Brewerton's account of the same affair consumes six pages. Carson describes in two pages his undertaking of driving several thousand sheep from New Mexico to California. Wootton, who conducted an almost precisely similar venture, consumes twenty-seven pages in relating it. In short, Carson's recital of his experiences is commonly about as arid as a piece of Civil War hardtack. Uncle Dick, on the contrary, remembered and related the many details which not merely endow his story with human interest but afford enlightenment to the reader, who of necessity is a stranger to the by-gone scenes described.

The present edition of Wootton's narrative marks its third appearance in print. The original edition, copies of which are now difficult to obtain, was ghosted by Conard in the summer of 1889 and published at Chicago in 1890, accompanied by a four-page introduction written by Joseph Kirkland, a prominent citizen of Chicago. This has been omitted from the present edition.

In 1950 Long's College Book Company of Columbus, Ohio issued an exact reprint (save for the slight additional information appended to the title page). Wholly unedited, the chief merit of the edition consists in the fact that it made available 500 additional copies of Wootton's book.

In preparing the copy for the present edition I have exercised entire freedom to alter the typographical style of the original edition (chiefly by excising an extraordinary number of commas, paragraph breaks, and quotation marks) and have corrected, where necessary editing, Conard's misspelling of proper names, along with an occasional erroneous date or other historical fact. I have endeavored to verify, whenever possible, Wootton's statements, although in the nature of the case such verification is frequently impossible. Scholarly specialists in the history of the period will no doubt prefer to continue to utilize the original edition of Wootton's narrative. For the general reader, for whom the Lakeside Classics volumes are primarily intended, it is believed that the corrections and the footnote information supplied in the present edition will prove both interesting and helpful. The inclusion of an index and a map of the region identified with the Author's activities should also be found useful.

M. M. QUAIFE

Detroit, February, 1957

"Uncle Dick" Wootton

THE PIONEER FRONTIERSMAN OF THE ROCKY

MOUNTAIN REGION

AN ACCOUNT OF THE ADVENTURES AND THRILLING

EXPERIENCES OF THE MOST NOTED AMERICAN

HUNTER, TRAPPER, GUIDE, SCOUT, AND

INDIAN FIGHTER NOW LIVING

BY

HOWARD LOUIS CONARD

WITH AN INTRODUCTION

BY

MAJ. JOSEPH KIRKLAND

CHICAGO

W. E. DIBBLE & CO

1890

PREFACE

IN presenting to the public the story of Uncle Dick Wootton's life and adventures I have been cautioned by the venerable frontiersman not to embellish a single incident too highly, and to leave out of the work entirely the element of fiction.

"I have observed," said he, "in reading our frontier literature, that the tendency has been to exaggerate and overdraw everything, and the effect of this has been to give the Eastern public a wrong idea of the conditions which existed in this country from twenty-five to fifty years ago, and of the character of the men who found their way into these savage wilds in search of wealth and adventure. Tell my story so that those who care to read it may draw from it correct conclusions as to the kind of lives the mountaineers have really lived, and avoid such coloring of truth as might lead them to think me boasting of my own prowess or exaggerating my own importance."

This admonition, which I could not do otherwise than respect, has restrained me from attempting to build upon a basis of truth a superstructure of fact and fiction ingeniously combined, even had I thought a more attractive book could thereby have been given to the reader.

I am of the opinion, however, that no fiction which could have been devised would have been more replete with thrilling incidents than the plain unvarnished story of one man's life and adventures which is herewith given to the public.

Whether or not this impression of mine is a correct one I leave to the reader to judge, trusting only that the story in its new form may prove not less attractive than when related by Uncle Dick himself in conversation with his friends.

In the absence of a formal dedication, which now-a-days is going out of fashion, I should say, perhaps, that Uncle Dick, half dreaming of the olden time, suggested one day that the story should be dedicated "to the old hunters and trappers." Being reminded, however, that few if any of them were living, it occurred to him that to no one could he with greater propriety pay such compliment than to his son, Hon. R. L. Wootton, Jr., in grateful recognition of his services in connection with the publication of this work.[1]

HOWARD LOUIS CONARD.

[1] R. L. Wootton, Jr. was born in Taos, March 21, 1851. His early years were spent with his grandparents in Kentucky, where he obtained his education. In 1866 he rejoined his parents in Trinidad and for two years served as master of a wagon train engaged in freighting across the Plains. Subsequent occupations included periods of store-keeping, ranching, and real estate and insurance.

In 1872 he married Florence Walker of Trinidad. She died in 1877 and in 1878 he married Lucy M. Huntley, also of Trinidad. In the early nineties he represented his home district in the Colorado Legislature for several terms. He prospered in business, owning in addition to other interests a summer resort and lake near Trinidad. At one period he was Chief of police of El Paso, Texas. He died in a street accident January 24 or 25, 1925. Conard's statement seems to imply that he financed the publication of his father's book. Data condensed from information supplied by Mrs. Laura Elstrom, Assistant Librarian, Colorado State Museum, and Mrs. Ruth A. Justin, Librarian of Carnegie Public Library, Pueblo, Colorado.

Uncle Dick Wootton

The Uncle Dick Wootton Narrative

MAP DRAWN TO ILLUSTRATE

Key ▪▪▪▪▪▪ SANTA FE TRAIL
ooooooooooTAOS TRAIL

Uncle Dick Wootton

CHAPTER I

A Famous Mountaineer

THE man who has been fifty years in active life in any part of the world must necessarily have had some interesting experiences, but the man who has lived for half a century along that border line of civilization which we call in this country the frontier has had fifty years of adventure. It matters little what may have been the temper of the man who has been thus situated, his environments have been such that thrilling incidents and wonderful experiences could not have failed to be prominent features of his everyday life. Even a Quaker, loving above all other things peace and quietude, must have led an eventful life amidst such surroundings.

The western half of the American Continent, which we looked upon in our boyhood days as the sundown land, and of which almost as little was known by those who lived east of the Mississippi River fifty years ago as is now known by the same class of reasonably intelligent people of the Dark Continent, is to-day rapidly throwing off its old time wildness, in fact, has already

3

thrown it off and donned the garb of civilization.

The hunter and the trapper have gone, and in their places we find the farmer and the cattle king; the old-time trader has given way to the modern merchant, and the old-style wares are no longer in demand; the occupation of the stage driver is gone, and trans-continental railways have taken the place of the primitive stage lines. The freighters have gone into retirement along with the stage drivers, and railway freight trains are whirled by strong locomotives over more space in a day then the ox-teams were able to cover in a fortnight.

The old camping grounds have been cut up into town and city lots, magnificent residences and massive business blocks have taken the places of tent and cabin, and the whole face of the country as well as the character of its population has undergone a most complete and remarkable change. Not even the rocks and mountains have preserved their primitive character, and only here and there are to be found undisturbed the old landmarks which were the handiwork of the early mountaineers.

The mountaineers themselves, those brave and hardy adventurers, the path-finders of the Rocky Mountain region, who found their way into the country in advance of the skirmish line thrown westward in the march of civilization, with but few exceptions have long since passed over the trail which ends at the silent camping ground of the dead.

They have been gathered to their fathers, but not in the sense of being carried to the same burying ground. Wherever the battle of life ended they found a burial place, and in widely separated localities those who faced the same dangers, braved the same perils, and shared the same hardships are sleeping to-day, undisturbed by their isolation from old comrades and trusted friends.

Upon most of those who are still living, and their whole number may be counted upon the fingers of one hand, the weight of years rests heavily and like the dismasted and dismantled man-of-war they are little more than a reminiscense of other days. To meet and converse with one of these old-time adventurers, who has borne up under the crush of years and who retains the full and unimpaired use of all his faculties, is to learn the secrets of the hills and hear the very rocks tell tales.

Passing westward over the main line of the Atchison, Topeka & Santa Fe Railroad, one follows from the great bend of the Arkansas River to "the City of the Holy Faith," the line of the old Santa Fe Trail. Just before the line between

Colorado and New Mexico is crossed, the attention of the tourist is always called to one of the most picturesque spots in all the Rocky Mountain region. It is twelve miles from Trinidad, the metropolis of southeastern Colorado, a town noted throughout the West for its extensive coal fields and superior manufacturing facilities.

When the west-bound train reaches Trinidad its motive power is always doubled, and pulled by two strong locomotives it commences to climb a spur of the Rocky Mountain Range, or, perhaps, properly speaking, of the Cimarron Range, known as the Raton Mountains. Slowly the train winds its way upward until it reaches an altitude of eight thousand feet or more, when it enters a long tunnel cut through the backbone of the range, crosses the state line underground, and drops down into New Mexico.

The Raton Mountains were named by the Spanish-speaking natives of that vast territory acquired by the United States from Mexico in 1848. Like all Spanish names, it is supposed to have had, at the time it was given, a significant and appropriate meaning, but traditions differ as to its origin. The word raton means, in English, squirrel or mouse, and some say that the mountains take their name from the grotesque but strikingly squirrel-like shape of one of the principal peaks, while others maintain that it was the large number of squirrels which could always be found in the pine forests and along the wooded ravines and cañons which suggested to the Mexicans the propriety of calling these rugged hills the Raton or Squirrel Mountains.

Less than two miles from the crest of the range, and more than seven thousand feet above the level of the sea, is a charming little valley, not much larger than a good-sized New England garden, through which runs Raton Creek, a mountain stream fed by springs which send their waters rippling down from sun-kissed banks of snow, and fringed on either side by willow, aspen, and cottonwood trees. Rugged peaks surround the little valley, or rather lift themselves up on all sides of it, leaving openings at either end of the level space, through which the creek finds its way in and out of it.

The hills are broken, rock-bound, and rugged. Some are brown and bare; others are covered with a thick growth of scrub oak, piñon, and mesquite, while there are still others crowned with groves of always verdant pine. Between the hills are narrow valleys and wooded cañons which have the appearance of miniature parks, where the shadows chase each other all day long and on moonlight nights through enchanted playgrounds.

Nor are the surroundings of the place lacking in points of geographical and historical prominence. Fisher's Peak, which takes its name from having been the place where Captain Fisher and a party of soldiers got lost in 1846, when on their way through to Santa Fe, towers above the surrounding hills, a few miles south-east of the valley, while Raton Peak rises abruptly a little farther away to the north.

Simpson's Rest, another lofty, rock-ribbed elevation, which is noted as having been the scene of a thrilling adventure and now the burial place of the pioneer whose name it bears, can be plainly seen a dozen miles away, while the Spanish Peaks, Pike's Peak, and the Snowy Range, distant from sixty to one hundred and fifty miles, seem almost near enough to be reached by a few hours walk.

Standing upon the mountain top, the monument which marks the spot where rest the remains of Simpson, the poet mountaineer, is a conspicuous object of interest. It is seldom that even the most ardent lovers of the mountains select as a location for their homes while living one of these rugged peaks, and still more seldom do they exact from loving friends the promise that such shall be their place of burial. The least inquisitive observer never fails, therefore, to inquire what prompted this man to ask for sepulture in a place so isolated and inaccessible. Legend answers the query and informs the curious that once upon a time Simpson found here a friendly shelter from bloodthirsty savages. In after years he expressed the wish to be buried near the scene of his adventure in the following poem.[2]

Taken all in all, the attractive little valley, which is but imperfectly described above, and which seems in some way to have been hewn out of the mountain side, in the beauty of its natural scenery and the interest which attaches to its surroundings is hardly surpassed by any spot which attracts the attention of the tourist in passing over the great ridge of upheaved rock and earth which forms the Continental Divide and separates the Mississippi Valley from the Pacific Slope.

Not less interesting than are his surroundings in this mountain niche, is the man who has for

[2]The page-long poem which Conard printed at this point in his introduction is omitted from the present edition of Wootton's book. George S. Simpson, the reputed discoverer of gold on the site of present-day Denver, was a teamster in the expedition of Captain R. B. Marcy, sent from Fort Union to Fort Bridger in the winter of 1857–58 to procure supplies for General Albert Sidney Johnston's army, then engaged in the expedition to Utah. On May 5, 1858 Marcy's small command encamped at the mouth of Cherry Creek to construct a ferry boat for use in crossing the South Platte. While thus employed, Simpson, who had spent many years in the western country, engaged in

more than a score of years made it his home. In a quaint old adobe house, closely related architecturally to the old style plantation residences of Virginia and Kentucky, lives Uncle Dick Wootton, so well known throughout Kansas, Colorado, and New Mexico that scarcely a citizen of either State or Territory could be found who would be willing to admit that he had not seen or heard of him.

Surrounded by what we ordinarily term the comforts of life and as many of the luxuries as an old timer usually cares for, Uncle Dick, as everybody calls him, is growing old; in fact, has grown old, with but a single untoward circumstance to cloud the afternoon of his eventful life. This was three or four years of almost total blindness, from which he was only relieved by a skillful surgical operation a year or two since.

It was not until his blindness came on that the old hunter laid aside, with the air of a man saying good-bye to the dearest friends he had on

panning for gold in the sands of Cherry Creek. He was rewarded by a small amount of "color," and the report of this discovery, carried to Westport, Mo., is supposed to have started the Pikes Peak' Gold Rush. Simpson, evidently a man of parts, died at Trinidad, September 7, 1885, and in accordance with his instructions to his executors was buried on Simpson's Rest, a peak adjoining Trinidad. See Nolie Mumey, *History of the Early Settlements of Denver* (Glendale, Calif., 1942). Chap. III.

earth, the rifle and hunting knife which had for years been his constant companions. It was this which more than anything else made him chafe under his affliction and regard it as the most severe which could have fallen upon him.

The restoration of his sight was not complete. While it enabled him to look again upon the beauties of nature by which he is surrounded and with which he is in such hearty sympathy, to recognize old friends and look into the faces of new ones, to read the newspapers and attend to his ordinary business affairs, it did not bring back to him that acuity of vision which in former years made his aim unerring and a shot from his rifle always deadly, when fired with that intent.

And so it happens that the celebrated old hunter, trapper, scout, and Indian fighter is now content to point out to his visitors the localities in which game is likely to be found, and entertain them with reminiscences of his palmier days. No longer young, he has hardly yet grown old except in appearance, and this belies his years. With

> "Hair just grizzled
> As in a green old age."

an erect carriage and almost youthful spirits, with intellect unimpaired, a memory never at fault, and vigorous bodily health, time never hangs heavy on his hands or on the hands of those who have the good fortune to be thrown in company with him.

Richens Lacy Wootton, the full name given him by his father, was born in Mecklenburg County, Virginia, on the sixth day of May, 1816. His ancestors were among the early settlers of Virginia, his great-great-grand-father having come over from Scotland, where the head of the family wore a title, in 1726.

David C. Wootton, the father of Richens, was a Virginia planter who removed to Christian County, Kentucky, on the southern border line of the State, when the boy who afterwards became the contemporary of Governor Bent, Colonel Ceran St. Vrain, Lucien B. Maxwell, Kit Carson and other equally famous frontiersmen was seven years old.

Here he grew up, or rather partly grew up, as he was but seventeen years old and had just secured what in those days was considered a fair business education, when he tired of the tobacco plantation and joined an uncle who was at that time in Mississippi. There he spent a little less than two years on a cotton plantation, when he concluded one summer to make a trip to Independence, Missouri.

That was in 1836. At that time all the vast country lying between the western boundary line of Missouri and New Mexico was known as the Indian territory. Ambitious traders and daring adventurers were then just beginning to establish trading posts at various points in this wild and little-known region, peopled entirely by savages. A pathway had been opened up to that very ancient metropolis of New Mexico, the quaint old town of Santa Fe, and Independence was its eastern terminus. This pathway was not called a road or a highway, but was known as the Santa Fe Trail,[3] and traversed eight hundred miles of plain and mountain.

Commerce had begun to travel westward over this afterwards famous trail, and the wagon trains had succeeded the primitive pack mule outfits. When young Wootton reached Independence he found there a wagon train belonging to Bent & St. Vrain, which had been loaded and was ready to start westward to Fort Bent, lo-

---

[3]The classic account of the Santa Fe Trail is Josiah Gregg's *The Commerce of the Prairies*, reprinted as the Lakeside Classics volume for 1926. For more modern accounts see Henry Inman, *The Old Santa Fe Trail. The Story of a Great Highway* (New York, 1897); R. L. Duffus, *The Santa Fe Trail* (New York, 1930); and Archer B. Hulbert, *Southwest on the Turquoise Trail. The First Diaries on the Road to Santa Fe* (Denver, 1933). Both Inman and Hulbert supply maps of the route. Interesting additional information concerning the famous trail is supplied in General Thomas James' *Three Years Among the Indians and Mexicans*, the Lakeside Classics volume for 1953.

cated on the Arkansas River a short distance west of what is now the line between Kansas and Colorado.[4]

It was there that Charles Bent, who was made the first governor of New Mexico when General Kearny took possession of that Territory, in company with Colonel Cerain St. Vrain had established the most noted trading post of the Far West.[5]

To attach himself to the west-bound wagon train which he found at Independence and start

[4]Fort Bent (Bent's Fort) was founded about 1822 on the north bank of the Arkansas some seven or eight miles east of present-day La Junta, Colorado. At first it was named Fort William in honor of William Bent, the founder. Its adobe walls, from two to four feet thick and fifteen feet high, enclosed an area 135 by 180 feet, with bastions at two opposing diagonal corners. Within the enclosure were low earth-roofed rooms, and an adjoining corral housed stock and equipment. Fort Bent became the outstanding trading post of the Southwest, sharing both the mountain trade and the overland trade to Santa Fe. In 1849 Bent abandoned and partially destroyed the famous fort. In 1853 he erected Bent's New Fort some forty miles down the Arkansas, subsequently named Fort Wise and (still later) Fort Lyons. Data adapted from sketch by LeRoy R. Hafen in *Dictionary of American History*; George B. Grinnell, "Old Bent's Fort and its Builders," in *Kansas Hist. Collections*, Vol. XV, 28–88; David Lavender, *Bent's Fort* (New York, 1954); footnote by present Editor in *Kit Carson's Autobiography*, the Lakeside Classics volume for 1935, pp. 33–34.

[5]Cerain St. Vrain, who figures prominently in Wootton's frontier narrative, was a member of the Missouri St. Vrain

on a trip to the Rocky Mountains, where it was thought fortunes were to be had for the seeking, was exactly suited to the adventurous disposition of the Kentucky youth who had started out to see the world, with an ambition to return to his home laden with wealth when he tired of sight-seeing.

There was little formality about the men with whom he was associated after that, and if they had a particularly strong prejudice against any one formality it was against that of calling a man by his full Christian name when it could be abbreviated, or a nickname devised to answer the purpose.

family. His father, Jacques de St. Vrain, was a captain in the French navy who migrated to Louisiana in 1797. One son, Felix (brother of Cerain), agent to the Sauk and Fox tribes, was killed by Sauk Indians at Rock Island in 1832. Another brother, Marcelin St. Vrain, figured for a time in the fur trade of the Southwest. About the year 1848 he returned to Missouri, settled on a farm near New London, and there died in 1871. Cerain St. Vrain, best known of the brothers, was born in 1802. He entered the southwestern fur trade in his early twenties, presently making his home at Taos, where he married a sister of Kit Carson's wife. He died at Mora, his home in his later years, in October, 1870, having been for a generation one of New Mexico's best-known citizens. Of him and his partner William Bent, Kit Carson observed: "I wish I was capable to do Bent and St. Vrain justice for the kindness received at their hands. I can only say that their equals were never seen in the mountains." Data adapted from Edwin L. Sabin, *Kit Carson Days*, I, Chap. 24.

So it happened that the name of Richens Wootton was shortened to Dick Wootton, or rather to Dick Hootton, the surname even, not being quite satisfactory in its original form, and Dick he was always called by the old timers, while to all the boys and girls who have grown up around him of late years, he is Uncle Dick.

With his trip to the mountains the adventures of Uncle Dick began. That was fifty-three years ago, and it is three years more than half a century since he became a frontiersman. He is a frontiersman still, if we have any frontier left in this country, and barring the past few years, not only every year but almost every month of every year has been a period of adventure.

Not all of his adventures were thrilling and blood-curdling as a matter of course, but in all the years of his active life in the mountains I doubt if a week ever passed in which something did not happen which would set the blood tingling in the veins of a healthy man unused to stirring incidents.

If the reader will take a look at the portrait which adorns the frontispiece of this book, and he or she happens to be a reasonably good judge of physiognomy, it will be easy to form a correct idea of the general appearance, character, and truthfulness of the man whose reminiscences have been written down by a summer idler in the mountains as they were related by the gray-haired adventurer to a group of interested listeners.

Here and there the rough corners have been knocked off a peculiar form of expression; now and then a sentence has been more fully rounded out; and occasionally it has been found necessary to temper a frontier phrase to the shorn lambs of polite society, but the substance of the narrative is given to the boys who delight in stories of adventures and the older boys who are always fond of reminiscences, without change or embellishment.

And now that I have fairly introduced him to the reader and said as much as need be said about his early life, Uncle Dick himself shall take the story off my hands and tell of his adventurous career, since he has but to unlock the storehouse of his memory to call to mind not only all the interesting experiences of his own eventful life, but the day and date of almost everything which has happened in the mountain region within the past fifty years, which even for the passing moment attracted the attention of the public.

In this connection I should add that while it has never occurred to the old mountaineer that what he has given to the public in this volume would constitute any important part of the history of the country with which he has been so long identified, the reader will observe that he has thrown much light upon incidents of historic interest which have never received in any former publication, historical or otherwise, the attention to which they were entitled by reason of their importance.

CHAPTER II

Uncle Dick Talks

IF you want to hear something about what an old hunter and trapper who has been in this country more than fifty years has gone through, I reckon I can come as near telling you some things that will make your hair raise up and knock your hat off as anybody you will find, if you travel from one side of this broad land to the other. You might as well understand right now, however, that I wasn't cut out for a smooth story teller, and can't put on any flourishes.

I shall just begin at the beginning and tell you in an off-hand way, which will sound natural to those who know me—and I reckon you will find a good many such people in one place and another—what my experience has been in the mountain region. I shall not try to make it appear that the mountaineers were a lot of highly educated, polished gentlemen, nor shall I make them talk like a pack of savages, as they generally do in frontier stories, because that would be doing all of them a rank injustice.

When I left Independence in the summer of 1836 I was a little under nineteen years of age,[6]

[6]Since he was born May 6, 1816, he was past twenty in the summer of 1836.

19

but I was pretty near full-grown and had been away from home long enough to know how to take care of myself. I could use a gun as well as anybody, knew how to handle a team, and while I was never particularly in love with hard work I wasn't afraid of it, and when there was anything to be done I was always ready to do my share. That was all that was required of me as a wagon man, and I got along first-rate from the start.

We had only seven teams, or rather seven wagons, in the train I started with. We didn't call a pair of mules a team in those days, because it took ten or twelve mules to draw each of the wagons when they were loaded with merchandise and ready to cross the plains. We had to travel all the way through the Indian country, and the redskins were so troublesome that only large parties, or wagon trains accompanied by good-sized bands of well armed men, stood a fair chance of getting through safely.

Two or three days before we started, a wagon train in which there were fifty-seven wagons, and which was accompanied by perhaps a hundred and fifty men, had started for Santa Fe and we were to overtake them before we reached the most dangerous part of the country we had to travel through. Our own train being light, we could travel with greater speed than the Santa

Fe train, and we soon overtook it and were given a place in the long line of wagons.

I learned then, what I did not know before, that all the movements of a big wagon train had to be made with military precision. When we went into camp at night all the wagons were pulled up close together so as to form a sort of circle. Then the mules were unhitched and driven to water, after which they were picketed, that is, hitched by long ropes to stakes driven in the ground outside of the line of wagons, so that they could graze during the night. So many men were detailed every night to stand guard, and they were stationed far enough away from the wagons so that they could see all the stock and prevent any of the mules or horses from being stolen.

The mules were pretty good guards themselves, by the way. If they slept any at all they were very light sleepers, because whenever anything, whether it was a wild animal or an Indian, came near the camp the mules would commence snorting in a way which would at once attract the attention of the guard to the object of suspicion.

While the guards were on the lookout for unwelcome visitors of any kind, the men who were not on duty wrapped themselves in their blankets and lay down on the ground inside the circle of wagons to sleep as soundly as though there was no such thing as danger to be thought of. They slept, however, with their rifles by their sides, and the crack of a sentinel's gun would bring them to their feet full armed in a moment's time.

I remember very well the first night I stood guard. I remember it on account of an occurrence which gave me a good deal of annoyance at the time and furnished every man connected with the train an opportunity to get off a joke at my expense.

We had gotten about one-third of the way across the Indian territory, or what is now the State of Kansas, and although freighting was a new business to me I had managed to get along without making any bad breaks and stood mighty well for a tenderfoot. One night we went into camp on the bank of what was then called Little Cow Creek. It is now called Chavez Creek, and, by the way, I must tell you how the name came to be changed.

A very wealthy Mexican by the name of Chavez was doing business then at Albuquerque, New Mexico, purchasing his goods mainly from St. Louis. Once a year he would make a trip to St. Louis to purchase his goods and make settlements, and on these trips he always carried a large amount of money with him.

He traveled by carriage in the old Spanish style, with outriders and all that sort of thing, and of course attracted a great deal of attention. When he reached the Missouri he proceeded by boat to St. Louis, leaving his splendid carriage and horses to be looked at by the border ruffians of western Missouri, while they speculated as to the amount of his wealth and laid plans to secure a portion of it for themselves.

Along about 1841 a plot to rob him was hatched up by a party of these Missourians. There were nine men in the plot and they all lived at Westport, which is now a part of Kansas City. Some of them were well-known citizens of that place, and one I remember, a doctor, was one of the most prominent men in Jackson County. They found out in some way when Chavez was coming through on one of his trips and went out to meet him in the Indian territory, where there was very little law and where they seem to have thought they could commit any sort of crime with impunity. They met Chavez at Little Cow Creek, where they killed him in cold blood and secured sixty thousand dollars in money as their booty. If Chavez had not been a man of so much prominence they might have escaped punishment, but as it was, the matter was taken up by the government and they were hunted down and all of them either hanged or sent to the penitentiary. On account of its having been the scene of the Chavez murder, Little Cow Creek became known afterwards as Chavez Creek, and it is still called by that name.[7]

Well, as I was going to tell you, it was at this place that I stood guard for the first time over a wagon train. My instructions were to shoot any-

[7]For a brief account of the murder of Don Antonio Jose Chavez on April 10, 1843 see General Thomas James' *Three Years Among the Indians and Mexicans*, the Lakeside Classics volume for 1953, pp. 173–74. As therein noted, the murder was an incidental aftermath of the Texan invasion of New Mexico, whose narrative by George W. Kendall was published as the Lakeside Classics volume for 1929. Embittered by the sorry failure of the expedition, the Texans planned a second invasion of New Mexico, but this eventuated only in an attempt to waylay the overland caravans engaged in the Santa Fe trade, which was by now conducted in large part by Mexicans. Wootton's story of the murder of Chavez errs in several respects. The attackers, fifteen in number, were a band of cutthroats masquerading as Texan soldiers. The seizure of Chavez occurred at the Little Arkansas in Lyons County, Kansas. Seven of the gang who apparently did not wish to engage in murder received their share of the loot and departed. The others took Chavez a little distance aside and killed him. Ten of the number were subsequently brought to trial in St. Louis. Two of them, John McDaniel, leader of the gang, and his brother were convicted and hung. The eight remaining culprits received lesser sentences. The amount of money obtained by the robbers is probably overstated by Wootton. R. L. Duffus (*The Santa Fe Trail*, New York, 1930) states that Chavez left Santa Fe with 2 wagons, 55 mules, a few furs and "over $10,000" in specie and bullion. Most of the animals had died, however, before the robbery occurred. Duffus supplies (pp. 184–88) a general account of the Texan raids upon the Trail, including the murder of Chavez.

thing that I saw moving outside of the line of mules farthest out from the wagons. Nothing had happened so far on our trip to occasion any alarm or anxiety about our safety, and I didn't expect anything was going to happen that night. Still, I didn't feel at all inclined to go to sleep, and kept a sharp lookout.

About one or two o'clock at night I heard a slight noise, and could see something moving about, sixty or seventy-five yards from where I was lying on the ground. I wasn't a coward, if I was a boy, and my hair didn't stand on end, although it may have raised up a little. Of course, the first thing I thought of was Indians, and the more I looked at the dark object creeping along toward the camp, the more it looked to me like a blood-thirsty savage. I didn't get excited, although they tried to make me believe I was afterward, but thought the matter over and made up my mind that whatever the thing was, it had no business out there. So I blazed away at it and down it dropped. The shot roused everybody in camp, and they all came running out with their guns in their hands to see what was up.

I told them I had seen what I supposed was an Indian trying to slip into camp and I had killed him. Very cautiously several of the men crept down to where the supposed dead Indian was lying. I stood at my post and listened for their report, and by and by I heard one of the men say "I'll be cussed if he haint killed Old Jack." Old Jack was one of our lead mules. He had gotten loose and strayed outside the lines, and the result was that he met his death. I felt sorry about it, but the mule had disobeyed orders, you know, and I wasn't to blame for killing him.

The next adventure I had was at Pawnee Fork, just about where it flows into the Arkansas River.[8] This was right in the heart of the Comanche country, and of all the mean Indians I ever had anything to do with, the Comanches were the meanest. Mind I am not saying that there are or ever were any good live Indians. They were all mean then, just the same as they are now, only some were meaner than others.

There was no false alarm about the incident at Pawnee Fork. The Comanches always fought on horseback, and they were good fighters too. It was on a bright moonlight night that they attacked us, although it was not often that they made a night attack. There must have been two hundred and fifty or three hundred of them, and the first thing we knew they swept down on us, yelling like

[8]At present-day Larned, Pawnee County, Kansas. Here Fort Larned was established in 1859, which General Hancock made his base of operations for his Cheyenne campaign of 1867. See General George A. Custer, *My Life on the Plains*, the Lakeside Classics volume for 1952, pp. 31–111. The military establishment was abandoned in 1878.

scared wild cats. A few of them had the old-fashioned fusees, but the most of them had bows and arrows and spears. What we called a fusee was a fire-lock musket with a bore half as big as that of a small cannon, from which either slugs or balls could be shot, although not with any great degree of accuracy.[9] The Indians used sometimes to shoot a copper ball from these guns. Where they got the copper I never knew, but I suppose it came from Old Mexico. They used both flint and steel-pointed arrows, and the spears which they carried were long poles with bayonet-shaped steel points as long as a butcher knife.[10] Among all the

[9]The original fusee was a light flint-lock gun. From it came the terms fusillade and fusilier, the latter still in use in connection with certain British regiments. Apparently Wootton's "fusee" was the type of flint-lock musket long current in the fur trade.

[10]The use of the lance as a weapon, both in hunting and in warfare, was common to the Plains' tribes of Indians, who may have adopted it from the Spaniards of Mexico. The superb horsemanship of both Spaniards and Indians contributed to render the lance a very effective weapon in their hands. General Kearny's crushing defeat by the Californians in the battle of San Pasquale in 1846 was wholly accomplished by their use of the lance. See *Kit Carson's Autobiography*, the Lakeside Classics volume for 1935, pp. 111–14. The official army reports of the mid-century period abound with instances of employment of the lance by the native warriors. For its effective use by the Sioux against General Crook's command in the battle of the Rosebud in 1876 see John F. Finerty, *War Path and Bivouac*, the Lakeside Classics volume for 1955, p. 142.

varmints I have seen since that time, I don't think I have ever seen any that looked as ugly as each of those Comanches did that night.

We heard them before they reached us, and were up in time to give them a warm reception. They didn't try to break into our corral, but their purpose seemed to be to stampede and drive off our stock first. They charged through the camp three or four times, trying to make the mules break loose, and the arrows fell pretty thick inside the corral as well as outside of it. We made it too hot for them though, and when they finally retreated they left three good Indians where they had fallen from their horses. You understand, when I say good Indians that I mean dead ones. Some people may not agree with me on this point, but I think I know what I'm talking about. If I don't I ought to, because I've been among 'em long enough.

That was my first brush with the Indians and I got credit for conducting myself pretty well for a youngster. A few days later we left the Santa Fe train and went up the Arkansas River to Fort Bent, Colonel St. Vrain coming out from the fort with a party of mounted men to meet us. On the way up I shot and killed my first buffalo. By this time my reputation as a frontiersman was pretty well established, and after stopping at the fort a few weeks I was placed at the head of a party of thirteen men and sent north on a trading expedition with the Sioux Indians. These Indians were scattered over what is now the northern part of Colorado, all of Nebraska, and pretty much all of Wyoming.

We started out with ten wagons loaded with beads and other trinkets, hunting knives, powder and bullets, blankets, and a few old guns. When we reached the trading country we would camp outside an Indian village and find out first whether they were in a trading humor. If they were, we would send in a pack mule or two loaded with our wares and establish headquarters at the lodge of some friendly Indian. The Indian at whose lodge we stopped was then authorized to act as a guard to protect our goods from the thieves who were always hanging about to get something without paying for it.

We dressed the guard up in a militia uniform, which we carried for the purpose, made him wear a stove-pipe hat with a red feather in it, put shoulder straps on him, and gave him a sword. We called these fellows Dog Indians, but that made no difference to them. They would put on more style than militia brigadier generals, and always took good care of our goods.[11]

[11]On the subject of military societies among the North American Indians see Frederick W. Hodge, *Handbook of American Indians North of Mexico*, Vol. I. Among many

I reckon you don't know what a lodge of the kind I speak of is. Well, I will tell you. It's an Indian tent, made of white buffalo skins; that is, buffalo skins that have been dressed on both sides. They take three poles about twelve or fifteen feet long and tie them together at the top. Then they are spread apart at the bottom and set on the ground. The buffalo skins are stretched around these poles, with short poles put in between so as to make the tent perfectly round. An opening is left at the top of the tent, through which the smoke from the fire inside passes out. At the top there are also a couple of wings, which can always be so arranged as to break the wind, and keep the smoke from being blown back into the tent.

One of these tents is usually as large inside as a good-sized room, and they're as comfortable as a house. The fire is built in the center of the tent

tribes, military and ceremonial affairs were regulated by societies whose members enforced measures for order when in camp or on the march.

The Dog Men Society among the Cheyennes became notable for its prominence in frontier warfare. Among the Sioux the "soldiers" were chosen by the chiefs from among the most reputable warriors, and they wielded an authority comparable to that of civilized military police. Wootton's account seems to imply (erroneously) that the authority of the Dog Soldiers was conferred upon them by the visiting trader. Obviously the trader upon entering a village would find it to his advantage to seek their protection.

and at night a dozen Indians will sometimes lie down in one of them, sleeping in a circle with their feet to the fire. Generally they sleep on buffalo robes and other undressed skins, but sometimes they have a kind of willow mattress, which makes about as nice a bed as a tired hunter ever stretched himself out on. We don't see many of these lodges among the Indians any more. Buffalo hides have gotten too scarce, and nothing else seems to answer the purpose in putting them up.

Their peltry was piled up inside the lodges, and when we had held a pow-wow with an Indian and arranged to do business at his lodge we unpacked our goods and trading commenced. It was all a matter of barter, and no money value was ever placed on anything. We used to get pretty good bargains in these trades with the Indians, although I suppose everybody understands that.

Their furs, buck-skins, robes, and ponies were what we traded for. For a good butcher-knife they were generally willing to give us a buffalo robe, and for a pound of powder, the gun caps, and about sixty bullets to go with it, we could almost always get two robes. Sometimes when they were disposed to drive hard bargains we had to give them two common butcher-knives for an extra good buffalo robe, but even that, you know, left us a pretty fair profit. A good beaver skin cost us about thirty cents in trade, and it took three bullets and three charges of powder to get a nicely-tanned buckskin.

On this trip we moved about from one Indian village to another until we got away north of Fort Laramie in Wyoming, where we spent a good part of the winter of 1836–37.[12] Finally we traded out and started back to Fort Bent with as fine a lot of peltry as was ever gathered up among the Indians.

The way furs and robes were selling then I am satisfied I had as much as twenty-five thousand

[12]Fort Laramie was established as a trading post at the junction of the Laramie and North Platte rivers in 1832 by William Sublette and Robert Campbell, St. Louis fur-traders. In 1836 the American Fur Company purchased the fort, and in 1841 replaced its log stockade with adobe walls. With the early emigration to Oregon, followed by the California gold-rush of 1849 and later, Fort Laramie became a steadily-increasing center of supply and out-fitting for the emigrants. In June, 1849 it was purchased by the Government, and from this date until 1890 it was a military post. As a center of Indian and military activities it figures prominently in the Lakeside Classics narratives of Mrs. Margaret Carrington, *Absaraka* (1950), John F. Finerty, *War-path and Bivouac* (1955), and others. Here were negotiated the important peace treaties of 1851 and 1868. Near here occurred the Grattan and Harney mas-sacres of 1854 and 1856. At the time of Wootton's trading expedition, the American Fur Company owned the fort. See sketches in *Dictionary of American History*, and LeRoy Hafen and L. M. Young, *Fort Laramie and the Pageant of the West, 1834–1890.*

dollars worth to turn over to my employers when I got into the fort. Just before we got there we were met by Colonel St. Vrain and a party of men with the startling news that Charles Bent and several other Americans had been imprisoned by the Mexicans at Taos, a town about one hundred and fifty miles distant from Fort Bent and across the Mexican line.

I suppose Taos was about as large then as it is now; that is, there were as many people there but not more than half a dozen of them were Americans. Bent had gone over there on business connected with a mercantile establishment which he was about to start in this old Mexican town. The Texas war was going on then, however, and the Mexicans looked upon every American with suspicion. It occurred to them that the little party of Americans who happened to be in the town were spies sent there by the Texans, and Bent and his friends were at once arrested and lodged in jail.

When Colonel St. Vrain heard of it he didn't wait for any diplomatic correspondence to be carried on between Washington and the City of Mexico to bring about the release of his partner, but picked up all the men that could be spared from the fort, armed them with the best guns and pistols in his possession, and started for Taos to liberate the imprisoned Americans at all hazards.

I went along with the party, but before we reached Taos we met Mr. Bent, who had been set at liberty by the Mexicans, they fearing that a party would come to his rescue from the fort and that their town might be burned if they undertook to detain him for any great length of time.

I spent the balance of that winter and the spring at the fort and had little to do but have as good a time as possible. I remember a funny thing that happened there that winter, and I laugh yet when I think of it. We had some visitors at the fort who were from St. Louis and were friends of Bent and St. Vrain.

Among them was the most comical fellow I ever knew, whom we called Belzy Dodd. I don't know what his first name really was, but Belzy was what we called him. His head was as bald as a billiard ball, and by the way, we had the first billiard table brought to Colorado, at the fort that winter.

Dodd wore a wig, and one day when there were a number of Indians hanging about he concluded to have a bit of fun with them. He walked around, eyeing the Indians savagely for some time, and finally, dashing in among them, he gave a series of war-whoops which discounted the Comanche yells, and pulling off his wig he threw it down at the feet of the astonished and terror-stricken red men.

The Indians thought the fellow had jerked off his own scalp, and not one of them waited to see what would happen next. They left the fort running like scared jack-rabbits, and after that none of them could be induced to come near Dodd. They called him "the-white-man-who-scalps-himself," and I think he could have traveled across the Plains alone with perfect safety.

Chapter III

Hunting and Trapping

THE Pawnee Indians gave us a great deal of trouble that summer. They would come around the fort and pretend to be perfectly friendly, but whenever they caught a man away from camp alone, on a hunting expedition or anything of that sort, his life wasn't worth a cent if they could get near enough to him to kill him. Every few days somebody would be run into camp, and now and then a man would be killed. One morning, I remember, two of the herdsmen were killed not more than fifty yards from the fort, and the stock which they were driving out to graze was all stolen.

We got even with them though, soon afterward, when we went out one day with a party of eight men to meet a wagon train, coming through to the fort from the East. At Pawnee Fork, the same place where we had the fight with the Comanches the year before, we struck a band of sixteen Pawnee Indians, watching the trail and seeking an opportunity to rob some small party which could be taken at a disadvantage. There was a strip of country in that region which the Indians always seemed to consider their best fighting ground, and it was a lucky

36

wagon train that got through without being attacked.

Very strong parties, even, were attacked in this locality and sometimes they fared badly. In 1846, in the neighborhood of Pawnee Rock, the Comanches, under the lead of the noted chiefs Little Wolf and Sitting Wolf attacked a considerable force of United States troops who were on their way through to Mexico, and the soldiers got a good deal the worst of the fight. They all had American horses, that is, horses brought from the States, and until they get used to the Indians these horses are as much afraid of them as they would be of any wild animal.

When the Indians swooped down on them, whooping and yelling, as they always did, the horses which the troops were riding got frightened and became entirely unmanageable. They ran away in every direction and the Comanches followed and killed the unfortunate riders who were carried away from the main body of troops. There have been more people killed along that portion of the old trail than have lost their lives at the hands of the Indians in any other spot in the West.[13]

---

[13]Wootton's statements concerning the prevalence of Indian attacks in the vicinity of Pawnee Fork (present-day Larned, Kansas) are not exaggerated. Inman (*The Old Santa Fe Trail*, Chap. XX) describes the adjacent area as

The band of Pawnees that we ran across were on foot and we were on horseback, so that although they outnumbered us two to one the advantage was with us. While we could keep entirely out of reach of their arrows, we could still approach near enough to them to do very effective shooting with our rifles, and we killed thirteen out of the sixteen of them in the fight. The other three escaped by throwing down their tomahawks, bows and arrows and running up to our wagon train, which was in sight at the time.

It wasn't customary to take any prisoners in those days of Indian warfare, but when an Indian came into camp in that way we observed the same unwritten law that governed most of the Indian tribes under similar circumstances. I suppose you would call it observing the law of hospitality, but whatever name you give it, it was a custom of the Indians never to harm the man who came into their camp voluntarily, so long as he remained there, although when he went away they

a no-man's land to which all the tribes resorted for hunting, but which none had the temerity to occupy permanently. The once-famous Pawnee Rock (near the present-day town of Pawnee Rock) has long since vanished, its materials utilized by the settlers for building purposes. Inman narrates a number of raids in the vicinity, "the scene of more sanguinary conflicts between the different Indians of the Plains, perhaps, than any other portion of the Continent." The raid which Wootton describes has not been identified.

might follow and kill him before he had gone half a mile.

Another custom of the Indians was to spare at least one of their conquered enemies when they were at war among themselves. Bloodthirsty and vindicative as they were, and as near as one band sometimes came to exterminating another, one or two of the defeated braves were always left to carry the news of the slaughter to the friends of the slaughtered.

We observed the Indian rule in dealing with the three Pawnees who had made themselves our prisoners. First we gave them as much as they could eat, when we went into camp for the night, and after breakfast in the morning supplied them with food enough to last until they could reach a Pawnee village. Then we told them to go back to their friends and tell them what had happened, giving them fair warning that we intended to kill all the Pawnees if they didn't behave better in the future.

When I got back to the fort after this trip I determined to start out on a hunting and trapping expedition on my own account. I had gotten a pretty good insight into the business by this time, and had learned that furs of all kinds brought good prices, while beaver skins in particular were in great demand. Beaver skins were worth at that time about seven dollars a pound, and as each skin would weigh on an average two pounds, or a little over, we could count on getting fifteen dollars apiece for them. I knew that there were plenty of beaver in nearly all the streams of the country and I thought catching them at fifteen dollars apiece ought to be a speedy way of getting rich.

I got up a party of seventeen men and we started out in June of 1837. We traveled together for the reason that it was not safe for one man or even a small party of men to travel alone, but every man trapped for himself, with two exceptions.

We had two men in the party, one by the name of Briggs and another named Burris, who were in partnership. These men were brothers-in-law, they having married two Indian women belonging to the Snake tribe who were sisters. These two squaws shared the hardships of the trip, traveling along with the party. They did the cooking for their husbands, mended their moccasins and clothes, and took care of themselves quite as well as any of the men. Both Briggs and Burris, with their squaw wives, afterwards went to California and settled in the neighborhood of Sacramento, where they became very wealthy.

I don't suppose any of you ever saw just such a looking lot of fellows as our party of trappers were when we started out. Every man wore a full buckskin suit and a pair of moccasins. In a belt, which he always wore, he carried a couple of pistols, two large knives, and a tomahawk. What we called a tomahawk was a kind of hatchet which we used to chop our meat up with, and in fact to do all the chopping that we had to do. In addition to this, of course, every man carried his rifle and ammunition enough to meet any emergency likely to arise.

Our stock of provisions consisted of coffee, sugar, and tobacco. We didn't try to carry any flour, and never tasted bread from the time we started out until we returned, unless we happened to strike some fort or trading post. Outside of our coffee and sugar we lived altogether on wild game. You might think that this would grow a little monotonous, but it didn't, as there were so many kinds of game in the country then that we could have a change of meat every day. The different varieties of meat that we used to have sometimes in one day would make a famous hotel bill of fare now-a-days.[14]

[14]Kit Carson, in 1859, reminiscing on the golden days of his trapper-life, described the fare of the trappers as follows: "Our ordinary fare consisted of fresh beaver and buffalo-meat without any salt, bread, or vegetables. Once or twice a year, when supplies arrived from the States, we had flour and coffee for one or two meals, though they cost one dollar a pint. During the winter, visiting our traps twice a day, we were often compelled to break the ice

It was no uncommon thing for us to sit down to a meal with a buffalo steak, a piece of roast bear, a hunk of venison, elk or antelope, and a wild turkey before us. There was an abundance of all kinds of small game, such as rabbits, squirrels, pheasants, and partridges, and we got choice roasts out of the beaver, although this is a kind of meat that a great many people never have heard of. These meats were roasted over our camp-fires, and I have never tasted meats cooked any other way which were quite as good as those we used to serve up in the trapper's camp.

It was only when we were in camp at night or moving from one place to another that all the trappers came together. We would locate the camp at a point where it could be reached without difficulty by all the trappers in the company, and then we started out in different directions to trap the various streams within eight or ten miles of the camp. Each man carried eight traps, which was called a set. He started out in the

and wade in water up to our waists. Notwithstanding these hardships sickness was absolutely unknown among us. I lived ten years in the mountains with one to three hundred trappers, and I cannot remember that a single one of them died from disease." Continuing, Carson stated that the flesh of a young horse was better than any other meat. A young mule furnished excellent steaks, but meat from an old one was tough, strong-flavored, and unpalatable. See A. D. Richardson, *Beyond the Mississippi.* . . . , (Hartford, 1873), 257–58.

morning, set and baited his traps, and the next morning went the rounds to see what he had caught.

We trapped altogether for beaver, but every now and then a bear or some other animal would come along and make the mistake of getting caught. When a bear got into a trap he would pull it loose and travel away with it, stopping now and then to pound the ugly thing on the ground and try in other ways to get it off. Poor old Bruin would cry over his bad luck, making a noise almost like the wail of a child, but the strongly made trap would stick to him until we killed him and took it off. Sometimes we would have to follow him a good distance to recover the trap, and a bear was never in good humor when we found him under such circumstances.

The man who has never had an opportunity of studying the habits of the beaver has missed an acquaintance with the most interesting and intelligent animal in the world. In building the dams which constitute their winter homes, they go about the work as systematically as so many men. In forming these dams they sometimes cut down large trees with their teeth, and they never fail to make a tree fall just where they want it. I never knew them to lodge a tree in falling it, and they show the same intelligence in everything they do.

With all their intelligence, however, they fell easy victims to the trapper, who understood his business. Their principal food is the bark and buds of certain kinds of green twigs, and all the bait we used was one of these twigs of trees, stuck down in the ground in such a position that the beaver would have to pass over a trap to get to it when he left his home and started out in search of a meal. That was the bait proper, but in order to persuade the beaver that a particular twig would make a safe and satisfactory lunch we dipped it in the strong smelling castoreum or beaver oil. This led them to believe that other beavers had sampled the tempting bit of wood, and they fell easily into the trap.

Sometimes we would find a queer old beaver living in a lodge by himself. These were always males, and we called them old bachelors. When we had good luck each trapper would come in with four or five beaver skins every night, and it was no light day's work to visit eight traps, take care of the game, and set the traps again.

We had Indian ponies on which we rode from place to place, and on which we packed our provisions. The beaver skins were dried and put up into hundred pound packs, which also had to be carried by the pack animals. Each man started out with as many horses as he thought he should need and if he got more peltry than he could carry he could easily trade with the Indians for more ponies. On this trip we trapped the Rio Grande del Norte, the Arkansas River, and pretty much all the streams of Colorado and Wyoming.

We wintered in Wyoming and were gone about nine months from the time we left Fort Bent. Fifteen of our seventeen trappers got back safely, which made it a pretty lucky trip for those times. Two poor fellows were killed by the Indians, or at least we supposed they were. They left camp one morning as usual and that was the last we ever saw of them. We made a search for their remains, but could find no trace of them and reached the conclusion that they had been killed by the Indians and their bodies devoured by the wolves and coyotes.

We were fortunate on that trip, so far as having any fights with the savages was concerned. Although we were often threatened by them, they only attacked us once. That time it looked very black for us for a while, but we had only one man wounded and his injuries were not serious.

It was when we were coming up Grand River on our way home. We had followed Green River down to its junction with the Grand, and in going up the latter stream had reached Piny Creek when we noticed a large band of the Snake Indians hovering about us. They kept at a considerable distance, but we could see that they were following us and evidently sought an opportunity to take us at a disadvantage.

While we could not tell just how many of the Indians there were, I am certain there were four or five times as many as there were of us. They knew that we had a valuable lot of peltry, and this, along with our horses, was a great temptation to the red robbers. The fact that they delayed making an attack puzzled us a good deal, as we did not understand the purpose of the delay, and thought it more than likely that they were aiming to drive us into an ambuscade. While we could not help getting a little nervous, we knew there was but one thing to do and that was to be prepared to fight at any moment.

We kept on our guard day and night, and it was this constant watchfulness which saved our lives and gave us a very substantial victory over the savages. Just at daybreak one morning they attacked us. They expected to take us by surprise, but in this they were disappointed. They not only found us on our guard, but we had the advantage of being in a thick cottonwood grove, so that we fought them under cover of the trees.

We allowed them to charge almost up to our camp before we fired, and when our guns cracked it seemed that not a trapper missed his mark. We had no time to count the number of Indians who fell at our first fire, but we could see a considerable number of them being dragged away by those who retreated. They made another charge which resulted more disastrously to them than the first, and then they gave up the fight.

I think we must have killed about twenty of them, and we gave them such a whipping that they remembered us and had a great deal of respect for us after that. The next time we went into their country we had no trouble in making peace with them, and we never had a fight with them afterward.

When we got back to Fort Bent we had a splendid lot of peltry and that summer I took a notion to go back to the States to dispose of my share of the beaver and buckskins which we had gotten together. Going back to the States in those days meant going back to Missouri, or some point east of that. I went as far as Westport, now Kansas City, and remained there several weeks. After disposing of my peltry and paying the expenses of the trip, I had about four thousand dollars left as the net proceeds of my nine months' trapping.

I was pretty well satisfied with the venture and like the early gold-hunters I fancied I had a fortune almost within my grasp. A year or two more in the Rockies, I thought, could hardly fail to put me in possession of all the money I needed to live on comfortably in Kentucky, and I wrote to the old folks at home that I should rejoin them in the near future.

Not long since, one of my boys showed me a copy of an old letter that I wrote to my mother about that time, in which I told her that I hoped to come home rich the next year. It brought the tears to my eyes when I looked at it and reflected that I had failed to keep that promise. When the next year came around, although I had made a good deal of money, it had somehow or other gotten away from me and I decided to stay in the mountains a while longer. That's the way I kept putting off going home from time to time, until after awhile my parents died, the ties which bound me to the old homestead were broken, and I have never seen it since the day I left it to go to Mississippi in 1834.

It was about the same way with all the old trappers. When they once got into the mountains they seemed, some way or other, to get chained to the country, and a great many of them became lost entirely to their early friends and associates, and even to their own families.

CHAPTER IV

Five Thousand Miles on Horseback

IN the fall of 1838 I started out on one of the longest trapping expeditions ever made by American trappers. It was in September that we left Fort Bent, and not until nearly two years later did we see it again.

There were nineteen men in the party when we started, and fourteen of them got back, five of our number having fallen by the way, the victims of the Monarch Indians of Oregon and the Pah-Utes, or as they are sometimes called the Piutes, of Utah.

Before I tell you about this trip I should explain to you how the land lay in this far western country in those days, because there were no such divisions into states and territories as we have now.

I have already told you that when I came to the country all the territory lying between Missouri and the Mexican boundary line, was called the Indian territory. A more nearly correct statement in regard to what was considered the Indian territory at that time would have been that it was the vast country bounded on the east by the Mississippi River, on the south and west by Mexico and the Rocky Mountains, and on the north

49

by the British possessions, with the exception of the territory contained in Missouri, Arkansas, and Louisiana. I believe that Congress had declared that territory to be the Indian country in 1834, and it took in what has since been cut up into the states of Kansas, Nebraska, Iowa, Montana, North Dakota, South Dakota, part of Minnesota, a corner of Colorado, about half of Wyoming, and the present Indian territory.

In the early part of 1838 Iowa was made a territory, taking in a good part if not all of the territory now in Minnesota and all of Dakota.[15] All of the territory belonging to the United States which was east of Mexico and the Rocky Mountains, and west of the states of Missouri and Louisiana and the territories of Arkansas and Iowa, was, properly speaking, the Indian territory in 1838.

At the same time all of the country now included in Oregon, Washington, and Idaho was called Oregon, while all the country lying south of the parallel which marks the southern boundary of Oregon and Idaho and west of a line which

[15]Iowa Territory was formally organized July 4, 1838. Its boundaries embraced present-day Iowa and Minnesota and those portions of South Dakota and North Dakota lying east of the Missouri River. It was named for the Iowa River, which in turn derived its name from the Iowa Indians. The Territory, when organized, contained some 23,000 white inhabitants.

followed the Rocky Mountain range south to the source of the Arkansas River, the Arkansas River east to the present eastern boundary of Colorado. the eastern boundary line of Colorado to Texas, and the eastern boundary line of Texas to the Gulf of Mexico, belonged to Mexico, or rather was claimed by the Mexican government, although Texas had at that time declared her independence.

New Mexico and California were Mexican states, the former including in its territory nearly all of what is now Arizona and a considerable portion of what is now Colorado. Only that portion of Colorado lying north of the Arkansas River and east of the Rocky Mountains belonged to the United States prior to the purchase of our Mexican territory.

Utah originally took in all of the present state of Nevada, and when the Mormons went there in 1847 they got outside of the territory of the United States. In 1849, after the region which they claimed had been ceded to the United States, they undertook to set up an independent state, which they called the state of Deseret—the land of the honey bee. The government took a hand in the matter, however, and organized the territory, which took its name from the Ute or Utah Indians, who were natives of the country.[16]

[16]The first party of Mormons, the first settlers of Utah, arrived at Salt Lake City in July, 1847. A provisional

Whether Oregon belonged to the United States or to Great Britain was at that time a question.[17] Both governments claimed it, and it was not until 1846 that the present boundary line of the British possessions was agreed upon. In speaking of what happened on the long trapping expedition I am about to tell you of, I shall use the names of the present geographical divisions of the country,

government was presently set up, and in 1849, following the Mexican cession of the region to the United States, Congress was petitioned to accept the government as the state of Deseret. Instead, the prolonged domestic dispute over slavery and the organization of the country newly-won from Mexico eventuated in the Compromise of 1850, whereby California became a State and Utah Territory was organized, with Brigham Young, the leader of the Mormons, as Governor. Public dislike for Mormon religious and marital practices delayed the admission of Utah to statehood until January 4, 1896.

[17]The long-disputed "Oregon Question" concerned the ownership (whether by Spain, Russia, Great Britain, or the United States) of the Pacific Northwest. By separate treaties with the United States in 1824 and Great Britain in 1825 Russia surrendered all claims to the territory south of 54° 40'. Spain, in 1819 yielded to the United States her claim to the portion of territory lying north of 42°. Meanwhile, in 1818 Great Britain and the United States had agreed upon the 49th parallel, extended westward to the Rocky Mountains as the boundary between the United States and Canada, and being unable to agree upon ownership of the area lying westward of the Rockies mutually consented to its joint occupancy.

Time worked in favor of the United States. Increasing American interest in, and the beginning of settlement of the Oregon Country led to the popular slogan in the although, as I have explained, these divisions have all been made long since that time.

We had six or seven Arapahoe and Shawnee Indians with us on this trip. These Indians were then on good terms with the whites, and as they were good trappers we found it to our advantage to take them with us. Starting with the regulation trappers' outfit, we proceeded up the Arkansas River and followed it to its source in the Rocky Mountains. Then we went north, trapping nearly all the streams of northern Colorado. Passing over into Utah, we struck the Green River and followed it up into Wyoming. After trapping all the smaller streams in that Territory, we followed the Big Horn River into Montana, going north as far as the Yellowstone. Then we turned westward and passed through Idaho, trapping for months along the Snake and Salmon rivers and their tributaries.

Presidential election of 1844 of "Fifty-four forty or fight." Relying upon this popular mandate, President Polk moved aggressively to settle the ownership question. On April 27, 1846 Congress authorized him to give Great Britain notice of the termination of Joint Occupancy of the area. Great Britain at the moment desired no war with the United States, and the controversy eventuated in a compromise whereby the country was divided between the two claimants through the extension of the line of 49° westward from the Rockies to the Pacific, deflecting southward around Vancouver Island and through the Strait of Juan de Fuca. Data condensed from articles on Oregon in *Dictionary of American History.*

It was while we were trapping on the Green River that August Claymore, the oldest trapper in the mountains, who was a member of our party, met with an adventure which we all supposed would end his life, but which he lived to tell of not many years ago when he was the only man in the country who still followed trapping as a business. He fell in one day with a party of Snake Indians, and some way or other they got into a quarrel, the result of which was that the Indians attacked him with their war clubs and beat him until they thought he was dead. Some of the trappers came upon them before they had taken the old fellow's scalp, but his skull had been crushed, the brain had been lacerated, and a portion of it destroyed. We held a sort of trapper's consultation and decided that we would have to bury Claymore before we broke camp. Strangely enough, however, he got well, and used to tell about his living to wear out the suit of clothes that one of the trappers donated for a burial suit.

We reached the Columbia River not long after Claymore's adventure, and followed that magnificent stream up through Washington Territory. Having by this time become pretty well loaded down with peltry, we determined to go to Vancouver and try to dispose of a portion of it. There we succeeded in relieving our pack animals of a part of their burden, and concluding that we had gotten far enough away from home, we turned to the south, and passing through western Washington and Oregon we entered California and struck the Pacific Coast at San Luis Obispo.

Then we went down through southern California, spent some time along the Colorado River, and late in the summer started up through Arizona, following the Gila River some distance and then again going north into Utah.

We were disappointed in southern California and Arizona. We found plenty of beavers in nearly all the streams, but they were not of the fine fur-bearing species. There was about the same difference between the northern and southern beavers that there is between the Alaskan and California seals. The furs which we took along the Colorado and Gila rivers were of little account, and the time we spent there was practically wasted, but we got to see some new country. When we got back to Fort Bent we estimated that we had traveled over five thousand miles.

We didn't know until we got back just how long we had been gone. Like the man who went around the world in eighty days, as the French novelist tells the story, we lost our reckoning.[18]

[18]The allusion is to Jules Verne's immensely popular *Around the World in Eighty Days*, written in 1872 and first published serially (in French) in *Le Temps* soon afterward (1872–73). Book publication and dramatization followed quickly and the novel was greeted with intense interest

When we got out in the mountains we found that nobody in the party had an almanac. A Frenchman by the name of Charlefou agreed to act as timekeeper and recorder of days, his calendar being a square stick upon which he cut a notch every day.

After we had been out some time and had entirely lost the run of dates, so that we couldn't have told to save our lives what day of the month it was without taking a look at Charlefou's stick and figuring up, the Frenchman met with an accident and his calendar was lost. Then we agreed not to make any inquiry about the time until we got home, just to see how far off we would be in our reckoning.

Coming through California, a country with which none of us were acquainted and where the seasons were so different from anything we had been used to, led us to believe it was a month or two later in the year than it really was when we reached Fort Bent, and nearly all of us made wild guesses as to the date of our arrival.

Old Charlefou, as we always called the Frenchman who lost our calendar, had the worst luck of anybody in the party who got back alive, with the

not only in France but also in England and America. See Kenneth Allott, *Jules Verne* (New York, 1941), pp. 169–70; George H. Waltz Jr., *Jules Verne. . . .* (New York, 1943), p. 145.

exception of Claymore. While we were up in eastern Washington, he was out several miles from camp one day when a band of Blackfoot Indians got after him. He was riding a fine Nez Percé horse and kept so far ahead of the Indians that he was out of reach of their arrows. It was a race for life, but he was gaining on his pursuers and had begun to feel sure of reaching the camp safely, when he saw only a few feet in front of him one of those deep fissures in the earth which are characteristic of the Great Plateau. He dared not stop, and if he had turned either to the right or left the Indians would have gained so much on him that he could hardly have escaped being captured or killed.

He put spurs to his horse and undertook to do what it seemed was the only thing for him to do under the circumstances, and that was to make his horse leap across the chasm. The horse made a noble effort to carry out his master's plan of escape, but the distance across the breach was too great and horse and rider went to the bottom together. Charlefou had both legs broken and the horse was instantly killed.

The Indians came up and looked down into the gorge but as neither man nor horse showed any signs of life, and there was no way of getting down to where they were without going to a good deal of trouble, they were left without being molested.

We started out to hunt Charlefou when he did not return to camp as usual, but did not find him for nearly a day after he had met with the accident. He knew that we would make an effort to learn what had become of him, but feared that any signal which he might give to notify us of his whereabouts would bring back the murderous Blackfeet. Finally, however, he made up his mind that he must take the chance of being discovered by the Indians, if he was to be found by his friends. He fired a few shots from his rifle, of which we fortunately heard the report, and after a great deal of hard work we succeeded in rescuing him from his perilous position.

There were no surgeons within five hundred miles of us that we knew of, so we had to set the broken bones ourselves. Then we made a litter out of poles, which we placed on two pack animals, and in this way we carried him from place to place for nearly two months.

This adventure made a great change in the Frenchman's feeling toward the Indians. Before that, he had been inclined to think that the redskins should be shown rather more consideration than we usually gave them. Not a great while before, he had been standing guard one night when he saw something perched in a tree a short distance from him, which changed its position every now and then and appeared to be keeping a close watch on the camp. Without knowing what it was he fired a shot at it, and a dead Indian tumbled out of the branches. The old fellow really seemed to feel a little sorry about having killed the Indian at that time, but after the almost fatal chase of the Blackfeet the naturally kind-hearted old Frenchman became about as vindictive as he had before been charitable.

They used to say several years later that this bitterness cropped out when he was sitting as a juror in a murder case at Taos, New Mexico. An Indian was charged with having killed a white man, and was given a trial by jury. Charlefou was on the jury, and soon after the trial commenced he went to sleep. It didn't last long and they had to wake him up when the jury got ready to retire to one corner of the room in which the trial was held, to agree upon a verdict. Charlefou had slept all the time and hadn't heard either evidence, argument, or the charge of the Court, if there was any, but when they asked him what he thought should be done with the accused, he replied very promptly, "Hang him, of course; if he ain't guilty now he will be."

It was the Blackfoot tribe, or rather the Monarch Indians, who were found in the same section of country and were of pretty much the same character, who killed three of my companions on this trip.

We were encamped on what we called Mussel-shell River, although I do not know that it is still called by the same name, and the Monarch village was not more than a mile distant.[19] It was only a village of tents or lodges, you know, as all these Indians were migratory and never built any permanent villages or had any permanent locations. They were a thieving lot, and one night they stole three ponies belonging to one of the Shawnee Indians who was with us. The next day we went after the horses and found them picketed out with the ponies belonging to the Monarchs. We expected to have a fight if we took them away, but we didn't propose to be robbed, in any event.

There was always just one way of gaining the respect of a tribe of Indians and that was to give them a thorough whipping. They always seemed to have a curiosity to find out what kind of fighting men a party was composed of, before they

[19]The name "Monarch Indians" probably represents Conard's misunderstanding of what Wootton actually said. Apparently he was speaking of the Moachi (variously spelled) Indians, a sub-division of the northern Utes. In *Kit Carson's Autobiography*, the Lakeside Classics volume for 1935, they become the "Muache Utahs." Edwin L. Sabin states (in his *Kit Carson Days*, 1809–1868. . . . New York, 1935) that when Carson was serving as Indian Agent in the fifties they became his especial charges. Wootton, who knew them intimately, can hardly have failed to use the correct name.

could be relied on to keep their promises and cease annoying the party in various ways. As it was certain that we should have to fight the Monarchs sooner or later, we thought we might as well fight for our ponies as anything else. We took the horses back to camp and had just turned them into our corral when a dozen Indians who had followed us dashed in and undertook to drive away some more horses. I don't know who fired the first shot, but I know the fighting commenced just about that time and was kept up for three or four hours. It was about two or three o'clock in the afternoon, and all our men happened to be in camp when the firing commenced.

Everybody turned out and went into the fight on their own account. Nobody ever assumed command of our trapping parties when we got into a rumpus of this sort with the Indians. Each man understood that he had to fight, and keep fighting as long as there were any hostile Indians in sight. There was no choice about the matter. There was no such thing as being taken prisoner and released on parole. We knew if we didn't kill the Indians they would kill us, and all the understanding we had among ourselves was that each man should make every bullet count and that any such thing as a surrender was out of the question.

I may say that we had a further understanding, that not all of us were to shoot at the first fire. It never mattered much how large a band of Indians was, they fell back when fired on. Their next move, however, was to make a charge, let fly a shower of arrows, and perhaps follow this up with an attempt to tomahawk their enemies if they found them with empty guns. As long as they knew that we had loaded rifles, they felt that somebody was going to get killed whenever they got in range of these guns, and they kept at a respectful distance.

The band of Monarchs who had invaded our camp soon retreated to their village. We followed them and kept up a hot fire, picking them off as they ran. The war was carried into their village, and we soon had them scattering in every direction. We pulled down their lodges, and when we got through with our afternoon's work, not an Indian was to be seen in the neighborhood who would ever again go on the war-path, this side the happy hunting grounds.

The first live Indian we saw after that was a very old man named Lone Wolf, who came to us the next day to say that his people wanted to make peace. I suppose this old fellow must have been eighty or ninety years old, and it was on account of his age that they thought it safe to send him to treat with us. He came hobbling along, and of course we allowed him to come into camp. He told us, through an interpreter, that his people had done wrong and that they had been fools for stealing the horses from the white men. It was some of the young men of the tribe, he said, who had brought on the trouble. We had killed many of their people and they had been punished for their wrong doing. The Monarchs wished to make peace with the white men, that they might bury their dead and set up the houses which had been torn down.

We told him we had always wanted to be friendly with them, and through him invited the chief of the tribe, Sitting Buffalo, to come into our camp and talk the matter over. The patriarch of the tribe carried this word back to the chief and a party of his warriors who were in hiding, and by and by they came in carrying a white rag fastened to a pole, as a flag of truce. I don't know how they caught on to this feature of civilized warfare, but that was the way they came into camp. We picked out three of our men to represent us in the long pow-wow which followed, while the rest of us stood around and watched for any manifestation of treachery or bad faith.

Finally the chief and his friends and the three white men who represented the trappers sat down, according to the Indian custom, in a circle, and the old chief lit the pipe of peace. He took a pull at it, and then it was passed around the circle until it reached him again, each of the

Indians and the white men too taking a single puff as it went around. This concluded the ceremony and established a peace which lasted as long as we remained in their country. As I have already said we lost three men in this fight.

There were two other trappers who failed to answer to roll call at the end of this long trip. Both of them were French Canadians and both were killed by the Pah-Utes in Utah. The first one killed was Le Bonte, a noted character among the early trappers. He fell behind one day when we were traveling, and the Indians stole up quietly and killed him without attracting the attention of the rest of the party. Then the miserable cannibals cut off nearly all the flesh from his bones and carried it away to eat. We found the bones and buried them where we found them.

Le Duc, the other Frenchman killed by the Pah-Utes, met with a more horrible death even than poor old Le Bonte. We were sitting around our camp fire one evening just at dusk, when without any previous warning, a shower of arrows fell around us. We sprang to our guns and caught sight of a little band of Indians running away from a thicket in which they had been concealed. We fired on them, but they were soon out of sight and did not return.

Le Duc was the only man who was struck by one of the arrows which dropped into our camp so unexpectedly, and he was only slightly wounded. It was a poisoned arrow, however, which had hit the poor fellow, and he died after suffering terribly for twenty-four hours.[20]

The Pah-Utes were a stoical lot of Indians who paid no more attention to the killing of one of their number than the least intelligent brutes. The Snake Indians used to make war on them frequently and sell their captives to the Mexicans for slaves. It was no uncommon thing to see a party of Mexicans in that country buying Indian slaves in those days, and while we were trapping there I sent a lot of peltry back to Taos by a party of these same slave traders, some of whom I happened to know.

I went from Fort Bent across to Taos to get this peltry in the fall of 1840, and when I was returning to the Fort I did the Arapahoe Indians a good turn, which made them my warm friends ever afterward. The Utes and the Arapahoes had been at war and the Arapahoes had been defeated. A great many of them had been killed, and some of the Arapahoe women and children had been carried away as prisoners. I had gotten into a place in the mountains where there was a good deal of snow and was picking my way along

[20]On the use of poisoned arrows by the Indians, and the method employed in poisoning them see Wootton's narrative, *post*, 124–25.

carefully when I saw something floundering about in a big drift. I raised my gun to shoot, when I saw that it was an Indian woman.

I knew something of the Arapahoe language and she made me understand that she belonged to that tribe and had been taken captive by the Utes. She had managed to escape, and without moccasins and with scarcely any clothing she had made her way through the mountains until, exhausted by hunger and fatigue, she had fallen in the snow where I found her. She was badly frozen and would have perished in a short time had I not picked her up. I put her on one of my ponies and carried her along until we went into camp for the night.

The camp-fire and something to eat soon had the effect of restoring her to her normal condition, and after a day or two she left us and made her way to one of the Arapahoe villages, where she told her friends how she had been rescued and cared for by a white man. They came out to meet me, and with a great deal more warmth and enthusiasm than I had ever thought them capable of manifesting they thanked me for what I had done. There was something substantial about their thanks too, for they made me a present of two ponies before they left me, and would not be satisfied until I accepted them. They were always my friends after that, and I never had any kind of trouble with them. I think every member of the tribe who was old enough to know anything was told about the Indian woman's rescue, because they all seemed to know me, and looked upon me as an exceptionally good white man.

CHAPTER V

Buffalo Farming

TRAPPING had by this time become less profitable than it was formerly. The prices of peltry of all kinds had gone down, and from that time on I paid less attention to it. Now and then I made a short trip, but for the next two or three years I was engaged mainly in a new line of business.

It required a large amount of meat to supply Fort Bent, and I took a contract to furnish what was needed. Buffalo meat was what I was expected to supply, with deer or bear thrown in when a change of meat was wanted. In this I combined business with pleasure, because the finest sport a man ever had was hunting buffaloes.

There were millions of them on the Plains at that time. I say millions at a venture, although the fact is it was impossible to make even an approximate estimate of the number we could sometimes see at one time. You might as well have tried to make an estimate of the number of ants in a big Colorado anthill. As far as the eye could reach I have seen the Plains black with them, and it would actually look as though the prairies themselves were on the move.

68

When the emigrants commenced traveling across Kansas a few years later, the buffaloes used to get mixed up with their cattle, and sometimes the herds of cattle would get stampeded and half of them would be lost.

I remember when I was freighting I was in camp one night and my ox teams were grazing under the care of a Mexican herder. About twelve o'clock at night I rode out to see that everything was all right, and just about that time a big band of buffaloes came along. One of my oxen took it into his head to join the buffaloes and quit the freighting business. I undertook to drive him back, and the whole band started to run. The steer had either determined to desert me or else gotten it into his head that he was a buffalo, because I never had a bigger chase than I had to get him back among the other cattle.

It never occurred to me then that I should live long enough to see all the buffaloes killed off. I never expected to see the time when I could not go out and shoot a buffalo, butcher him, and have the meat ready for use, with about as little trouble as a ranchman has in getting a beef out of his herd of cattle.

They were hardly as wild in those days as range cattle are now, and I have killed thirty buffaloes in a day when I was supplying Fort Bent with meat. Now, the best informed sportsmen say that there are not two hundred buffaloes in the United States, and these are in small bands scattered about in the West, the largest band being in Yellowstone Park.[21]

The Indians killed a great many of these animals, but as a rule they only killed what they needed for food. The skin hunters were the fellows who were mainly responsible for the extermination of the buffaloes. As long as they were killed only for the purpose of supplying the people on the frontier and the Indians with food, we could not notice that their number was decreasing, but when an army of men came into the country to kill them for the purpose of supplying the eastern market with robes, they didn't last long.[22]

[21]Dr. William T. Hornaday of the National Museum directed public attention to the impending extinction of the buffaloes. In 1889, the year when Wootton was relating his memories to Conard, Dr. Hornaday conducted a census which disclosed 1091 living animals in the entire world. Another census taken in 1903 disclosed 969 animals in 41 herds in the United States and a world total of 1644. Thirty years later (1933) 4404 were reported in the United States and 17043 in Canada. With the danger of extinction eliminated, the increase in numbers is regulated by controlled slaughter of animals from time to time. Census figures adopted from sketch in *Dictionary of American History*.

[22]It is axiomatic that two objects cannot occupy the same space at the same time. However much one may deplore the extinction of the buffaloes, the fundamental reason for it was the occupation of the Plains country by

I used to enjoy seeing the Indians hunt buffaloes; that is, when the Indians were friendly and were not hunting white men at the same time. A large party of them would start out on horseback and when they had picked out a band of buffaloes they would form a circle around the game and gradually close in on it. Then they started their horses on a run, bending their bows and adjusting their arrows as they neared the animals marked for the slaughter.

They did not shoot until they ran alongside the game, and then their arrows were quite as effective as the bullets of the white hunters. The little Indian boys who followed the hunters took part in the chase, and the buffalo calves were left for them to practice on.

When I went out after buffaloes I took a good saddle horse, the best I could find in the country, one or two men to do the butchering, and a lot of pack animals or a wagon to carry the meat. I never rode my saddle horse until I got ready

white settlers, whose economy was incompatible with their continued occupation by the buffalo. Today the cattle on a thousand hills provide a far greater economic resource than the buffaloes, if left to thrive in their primitive paradise, could possibly supply. Probably the best account ever written of the activities of the "skin hunters" is John R. Cook's *The Border and the Buffalo*, reprinted as the Lakeside Classics volume for 1938. For a popular, more recent account see Marie Sandoz, *The Buffalo Hunter, The Story of the Hide Men* (New York, 1954).

for the chase, because it took a good horse, and a fresh one, to catch a buffalo when he started to run, and there was nothing sportsmanlike about killing without giving him a chance to escape in a fair race.

About a month after I commenced hunting in the fall of 1840, I was waiting one day, after having killed about twenty buffaloes, for the butchers to get through with their work, when I noticed a pair of twin buffalo calves, and it occurred to me that I might take them back to the fort alive and raise them.

They were easily captured but how they were to be fed was not so easily determined. When I got back to the fort, however, I tried an experiment which proved entirely successful. I persuaded a good-natured and kindly disposed cow to adopt the kidnapped young buffaloes, and they seemed to do quite as well as they would have done roaming over the Plains with the herd to which they originally belonged. Satisfied with that experiment, I then commenced buffalo farming, and although I am not the only man who has tried the experiment in the United States, I have never heard of anyone who made as much of a success of it as I did.

I succeeded in picking up about forty milch cows and located my farm where the city of Pueblo has since been built. That was twenty years before the town was started, and I suppose few people now living there know that the city is located on the site of the only buffalo farm Colorado ever had.[23]

I fitted up a corral there, and got together forty-four buffalo calves, which I turned in with the cows, after taking away from them their own calves. They were not inclined to look with much favor on the hump-backed, ugly-looking little animals in the start, but by and by they began to think better of it, and in a short time they were getting along as well together as if they had belonged to the same family. When they were able to take care of themselves, the buffaloes and the cattle were herded together, and one appeared to be about as much of a domestic animal as the other.

I kept them until they were three years old and then sold them to a man who took them to New York. There they were parceled out to showmen,

[23]Wootton's enterprise of rearing buffaloes in captivity was by no means unique. George Washington tried rearing buffaloes at Mount Vernon, and at his death a buffalo cow was listed among his assets. Walter Havighurol, *Wilderness for Sale* (N. Y., 1956), 95–96. The capture by hunters of buffalo calves for subsequent sale or rearing was more or less commonplace. As one illustration, John C. Fremont on July 11, 1843 met a hunter who had been out in pursuit of buffalo calves, "a number of which I saw among some domestic cattle near his lodge." *Memoirs of My Life* (Chicago, 1887) I, 182.

and some of them, I think, were put into the Central Park Zoological Gardens. I delivered them to the purchaser at Kansas City, driving them across the Plains along with a few cows just as I would have driven a band of cattle. I had two or three pairs of them broke to work like oxen and they made first class teams.

The meanest enemy the buffalo ever had, aside from the skin hunters, was the grey wolf. The wolves followed the buffaloes and lived on them. Their killing of the calves has had a great deal to do with the disappearance of the finest game animal we have ever had in America.

Their slaughter was not confined to the buffalo calves either. I have seen a pack of hungry wolves single out a full-grown bull, drag him down, and tear him to pieces in about as little time as it takes me to tell of it. A single buffalo could not defend himself against them, because while some of the wolves charged him in front other would fasten their sharp teeth in his hind parts, cut the ham-strings as we used to say, and the poor bull dropped down and was entirely at the mercy of his enemies.

The buffaloes were intelligent enough to know that in union there was strength, in a fight with wolves. When a band of them lay down at night it was usually in a circle, inside of which were the calves. Then if they were attacked by wolves, standing side by side with their heads down, they presented a solid fighting front and could take care of themselves.

When hunting buffaloes, I have sat many a time all night by a blazing fire, throwing the red-hot brands every now and then at a pack of wolves to keep them from stealing the game which I had slaughtered. One night, I remember, when I was alone there must have been hundreds of the vicious brutes in the pack that kept me company all night. They would come so close that I could see their eyes shining like balls of fire in the darkness, and all the time they kept up a snapping and snarling which would have set a man crazy who did not know what cowardly brutes they were.

I didn't care to waste much ammunition on them, but I killed three or four during the night and the dead wolves were at once torn to pieces and devoured by the balance of the dirty gang of cannibals. They sneaked away just before daylight came in the morning, but they had given me a mighty lively all-night serenade.

With as much game as there was in the country it would seem that we never ought to have suffered for anything to eat, but we did now and then get into a tight place. I remember about the time I have been speaking of, I went up one time to where the town of Greeley is now to trade with the Arapahoe Indians. While I was there a terrible snow-storm came on and lasted so long that the Indians ran out of food, because they could not get out to kill any game. I got about as hungry that time as a man ever gets, and swam the South Platte River one morning when it was full of melting ice to get a wild goose that I had shot on the opposite bank.

The Arapahoes, by the way, saved me from the Pawnee Indians that winter. I have told you how I made them my friends by returning to them one of their squaws, who had been carried away by the Utes. The three chiefs, Roman Nose, Buffalo Billy, and Big Mouth, had gotten their bands together, and had a village of about six hundred lodges at the mouth of Crow Creek.[24]

That was only a year or two before Buffalo Billy and eighteen or twenty of his braves were killed in a drunken brawl on Cherry Creek, about a dozen miles from the present city limits of

[24]Wootton, who had excellent reasons for knowing, calls Roman Nose an Arapahoe. Various other authorities believed him to be a Cheyenne. The confusion may perhaps be explained by the fact that for over half a century the two tribes lived in close alliance. Whatever his tribal identity, Roman Nose was a notable leader of his race until his death in the celebrated Beecher Island battle of Sept. 17–25, 1868. See Hodge, *Handbook of American Indians North of Mexico* (who calls him a Cheyenne); Baker and Hafen (Eds.), *History of Colorado* (Denver, 1927), I, 381 and II, 407–409.

Denver. The quarrel which resulted in the killing was all their own affair, as it was entirely among the Indians, although the white man who traded them the firewater was in a sense responsible for it.

I started out to tell you, however, that on one of my trips from the fort to the Indian village my horse gave out and I had to turn him loose. There was a deep snow on the ground and I buried my saddle where I thought I could find it when I came back, and then started for the village on foot. I had thirty miles to travel, but I shouldn't have minded the walk particularly had it not been in a country where I was likely to run into a band of hostile Indians at any moment.

The Pawnees were the sneaking, murderous scoundrels that I was most afraid of, but I began to feel reasonably safe when I had gotten within a few miles of the end of my journey without seeing any signs of the hostiles.

About the middle of the afternoon I was jogging along at a pretty good pace because I wanted to reach the village before night, when I happened to cast my eye toward a low ridge which was perhaps four or five hundred yards to one side of me, and saw moving objects which at once attracted my attention. What I saw was something coming up over the crest of the hill from the opposite side, and at first I thought it a

band of antelope just coming in sight. I stopped
and took a good look at them, and then the things
began to look like Indians.

That's what they were too, and Pawnee Indians at that. They were on foot and saw me about
the same time that I caught sight of them. There
was but one thing for me to do, and that was to
run for the Arapahoe village, six miles away. I
knew that if I could reach it I should be as safe as
I would be in Fort Bent, but the question was
whether or not I could keep a safe distance
ahead of the Pawnees in a foot race.

As soon as they discovered that I had caught
sight of them they commenced brandishing their
tomahawks, and with one of those yells which
will always make a man's hair jump straight up,
no matter how often he has heard it, they started
after me. I had no time to count them, but as I
started to run, I reached the conclusion that
there were about twenty Indians in the band.
Two of the Pawnee bucks shot ahead of the
others at the beginning of the race, and as I
glanced over my shoulder from time to time I
saw that they were gaining on me. The others
soon fell away behind, and I made up my mind
that I could escape if I got rid of the two Indians
nearest to me. One of them was by this time
within two hundred yards of me and the other
about a hundred yards behind him.

Exhausted as I was by a run of two or three miles, I was by no means certain that my aim would be steady enough to kill him if I turned and fired at that distance from the foremost of my pursuers, and if I missed, with an empty rifle and the two Indians so close to me, the chances would be very much against me. Fortunately, just at that time I had to run over a little hill which hid me for a moment from the Indians as they were coming up on the other side.

At the foot of the hill I stopped, raised my gun to my shoulder, and waited until the foremost Indian reached the crest of the hill. That brought him within a hundred yards of me and when my gun cracked he dropped. I knew from the way he fell that he was a dead savage and that there was no danger of his following me any farther. I ran on, loading my gun for the other Indian as I ran, but when I looked back again he had fallen so far behind that he was out of reach of a bullet. He waited until the balance of the band came up, and then they all followed me until they caught sight of the Arapahoe village for which I was headed.

Before I reached the village the Arapahoes saw me and knew from the way I ran that I was being pursued. About forty warriors mounted their horses and came galloping out to meet me. I was so near exhausted by the long run that I couldn't mount the horse which they offered me, to go with them in pursuit of the Pawnees, when I told them what was up, but they went back without me while I made my way into the village.

Being mounted on good horses they soon overtook the Pawnees, and when they came back that night they told me that but one of the band which had given me such a chase had been left alive, and his life was only spared in accordance with the Indian custom, that he might carry the news of the killing to his friends and inform them that his comrades had fallen at the hands of the Arapahoe braves.

They brought in seventeen scalps, and as one of the Pawnees escaped the slaughter there must have been eighteen in the party. I never saw a band of Indians so much elated over anything as the Arapahoes were over this killing of the Pawnees. They were pleased because they had saved the life of a white man to whom they thought themselves under great obligations, and still more pleased over having taken the scalps of so many of their inveterate enemies, the Pawnees.

I was in high favor among the Arapahoes at that time, and if I had had a fancy for it I think they would have made me a big chief without hesitation. My shooting used to astonish them, and when a difficult shot was to be made at game or any of the wild animals which came near the village they would call on me to do the shooting.

I became very thoroughly acquainted with the Arapahoes that winter, and learned more of their habits and customs than I had ever known before, although I had at that time been among them more or less for several years.

When they came back from their fight with the Pawnees I noticed for the first time how each Indian kept the record of those he had slain. In one place on the handle of his tomahawk he cut a notch for each scalp he had taken. In another place he cut a notch for each enemy found lying upon the battlefield after the fight was won, whom he had been the first to approach and strike with his tomahawk. It was looked upon by the Arapahoes, Cheyennes, and some other Indians as an evidence of great courage for a warrior to be the first to strike an enemy who had fallen in battle, their idea being that the prostrate enemy might be only feigning death, and if wounded he would fight more desperately than under any other circumstances.

They called these notches on the tomahawk handles coups, and in addition to those which indicated the number of scalps taken and the number of killed or disabled enemies struck they had another row of notches which indicated the number of horses captured, when they fought with mounted enemies. The Indian who grew up to manhood without being able to exhibit any coups was looked upon by the tribe as a very worthless and good-for-nothing Indian, and he stood no show of securing any kind of preferment. On the other hand, the Indian who could show a long string of coups was looked up to and loaded with savage honors.

I had a little experience that same winter in the dangerous business of traveling back and forth between Fort Bent and Fort St. Vrain, carrying money and other valuables which had to be transported from one post to the other.[25]

Fort St. Vrain had been built by the owners of Fort Bent in the Arapahoe country, north of where Denver is now, and a weekly express was established in 1842 between the two posts. A portion of the time I filled the position of expressman, and have carried as much as sixty thousand dollars in silver at a time from one point to the

[25]Fort St. Vrain was established in 1837 or 1838 by Bent and St. Vrain on the east bank of the South Platte, about a mile or more below the mouth of St. Vrain Creek. A fourteen-foot wall enclosed an area of 100 by 125 feet. In 1846, when Francis Parkman visited the place he described it as "abandoned and fast falling into ruin." In 1911 a granite monument marking the site was erected by the Daughters of the American Revolution. See LeRoy R. Hafen, "The Early Fur Trade Posts on the South Platte," in *Mississippi Valley Historical Review*, XII, 340–41 (December, 1925).

other. It was carried on pack animals and every dollar was delivered safely to the parties to whom it was consigned. I made several trips of this character, at one time and another, not only between Forts Bent and St. Vrain, but between Fort Bent and Taos, New Mexico, where Bent and St. Vrain carried on a large business. I was always fortunate enough to get through safely and never lost a dollar entrusted to my care.

CHAPTER VI

Among the Utes and Apaches

TRADING with the Indians had its attractions, the chief of which was, of course, the very handsome profits which we made out of the business, but it was always a perilous vocation.

When we started out to trade with a band of peaceable Indians we never knew how many hostiles we should find roving about in the country we had to travel over. In the winter of 1843 I got together a lot of goods and took out a license to trade with the Utes. It was always necessary, before starting out on one of these expeditions, to take out a license which was issued by the Indian Agent having charge of the band or tribe with whom the trader wished to do business. We had to give bond in the sum of two thousand dollars, conditioned on observance of the law in our conduct of the Indian traffic. That is, we bound ourselves not to sell or trade them intoxicating liquors of any kind, or anything which we knew it to be unlawful to put them in possession of. Although we generally found the Utes on Mexican territory, they occasionally came across the line and then we had to deal with them on the same terms as with other Indians we found within the United States.

84

We were not having any trouble with the Utes at that time, but the Apaches were at war with us, and while we were looking for Ute villages we had to steer clear of every Apache camp. I had a big stock of vermilion and other cheap paints, beads, knives, ammunition, and guns which I carried on pack animals, and had gotten so well acquainted with the country by that time that I thought I could get through without taking a party of men along with me.

With only one man, and he a Delaware Indian, to accompany me, I started out to find a band of Utes that I knew were moving about from place to place, and finally found them in the Canadian River country, in the Panhandle of Texas. I came down through Trinidad, or rather through the pass in which Trinidad is now located—there wasn't any such place then—followed Raton Creek up past the place where I am now living, climbed the Raton Mountains, and went over into New Mexico. On the other side of the mountains I started down Sugarite Creek and not more than eight or nine miles from my present home I came to an Indian village.

Supposing it to be a Ute village we rode in, stopped under the shade of some cottonwood trees, and as it was getting along toward night we began to make preparations to go into camp. There were perhaps thirty or forty lodges in the village, but it was some time before we saw any Indians, or anyone took notice of us. Then we saw only two or three old men, and so confident were we of being among friendly Indians that we did not think to look at them closely, and it was not until we saw a group of squaws peering at us intently that we began to think it necessary to make sure of our whereabouts.

All Indians look pretty much alike to one unaccustomed to meeting members of the different tribes, but there were always some distinguishing features or characteristics which enabled a frontiersman, even when he did not understand their language, to determine without much difficulty what tribe an Indian belonged to, no matter where he might turn up.

So when we began to look about us in the village into which we had found our way, we were not long in reaching the conclusion that we were surrounded by the hostile Apaches instead of the friendly Utes. You may be sure that there was nothing very pleasant about this discovery, but we had to make the best of the situation. It was evident that there was a reason for our not being disturbed, and the small number of men about the village indicated that the band was out on a hunting expedition. We knew there was no danger of our being attacked by the few old men and squaws about the place, and thought if we could get a good distance away before the hunters returned we would be safe.

We lost no time in mounting our horses and riding as far as we could before night overtook us. Then we selected a camping place in a thickly wooded spot and prepared to defend ourselves the best we could if the Apaches followed us. I had about fifty guns in my stock of goods and plenty of ammunition. I got out all of these guns, loaded each one carefully, and put them all where they could be handled as rapidly as we could shoot, in case we were attacked; then my companion and I stood guard all night. We saw none of the Apaches, however, until the next morning, when a few of them came down to where we were and wanted to come into camp. They did not show any disposition to be hostile, but we refused to allow them to come close to us, and after some parleying they went away, and as we traveled rapidly when we moved on again, we saw nothing more of them.

If we had happened to strike this village at a time when the fighting men of the band were at home, instead of being out after game, it is not at all likely that we should ever have gotten out of it alive. As it was, however, there happened to be nobody to interfere with us, or prevent our hurried departure, and when we happened to strike a favorable camping ground and got our guns loaded, we could have defended ourselves to pretty good advantage, even if they had attacked us. I think one reason they did not follow us was that they were very much afraid of the Utes, who were not far away, and whom they knew to be our friends for the time being.

I reached the Ute village a day or two later and there I had the misfortune of finding the chief of the band, whose name I have forgotten, very sick. This was unfortunate for several reasons. In the first place, the Indians were all greatly distressed, and it was difficult to get them to trade. In the second place, as the old chief had been sick some time and none of the Indians had been allowed to go out to kill game, they had very little either to eat themselves, or give to a stranger; and in the third place, there were some peculiar customs among the Utes in connection with the obsequies of a dead chieftain which made it an exceedingly unpleasant time for a stranger to be in their immediate neighborhood.

What purpose it was designed to subserve I never knew; but the Utes considered it incumbent upon them to kill the first stranger found in their village after the death of a chief. Possibly they thought the spirit of the dead chief might more readily gain admission to the happy hunting grounds if accompanied by the captive spirit of a stranger, or it may have been the design to furnish the prince of darkness with the stranger's spirit and thereby persuade him to relax his grip upon the chief's immortal soul; but whatever the poetic idea of the thing, the unpleasant fact impressed itself upon me that there might be a demand for the taking off of a stranger at almost any moment, and that myself and my companion were in a position to be available should such an emergency arise.

I felt sure that the poor old chief could not live a week, and I was exceedingly anxious to get through with my business and get away. They came to me and insisted that I should give the sick Indian some of the white man's medicine, but this I refused to do, first because I knew it would not do him any good, and second, because if he died they would just as likely as not think my medicine killed him, and then they would very promptly send me over the same road.

I determined to dispatch my business as quickly as possible, and decided to remain right in the village and make use of every artifice I was master of to force the trading. In order to do this it was necessary that I should live on such food as the Indians could supply me with. They had but one kind of meat, and I ate that without asking any questions. I knew it was no kind of game with which I was familiar, and I had a very strong suspicion that it was the flesh of a domestic animal which is about the last thing a man usually thinks of butchering. Before I had been long in the village I happened to see the Indians slaughter one of these animals, and then, as I suspected, found out that we had been eating dog meat, and very poor dogs they were at that.

It was three days before I could get the Utes in the notion of trading, and in the meantime the old chief was growing weaker all the time. Two or three times I was half inclined to move out without doing any business, thinking that I ran too great a risk in remaining in the village. I finally got them worked up to the trading point, however, and when we once commenced bartering it did not take long to get through. I got a number of mules and ponies and a fine lot of peltry, and you may be sure I lost no time in loading the furs and robes on my pack horses and starting for home. I learned afterward that the chief died two days after I left the village.

I carried my goods back to Pueblo where a fort had been built by the trappers.[26] It had become a

[26]Fort Pueblo was established in 1842 by some independent trappers. Wootton ascribes his present visit to the place to the following year (*ante*, 84). He subsequently spent much of his time here for a period of several years, (*post*, 266 ff). John C. Fremont visited the post in 1843 and reported that is was "principally" inhabited by American mountaineers with Spanish wives. Francis Parkman visited and described the post in 1846, and George

sort of trading post by that time, and there I entered into a kind of partnership with a man by the name of Tharp, who was going back to Kansas City to dispose of a lot of peltry. I furnished him with ten or twelve mules and he was to take my buffalo robes, buckskins, and furs back East, sell them, and return me the money.

F. Ruxton, in the winter of 1847, shortly following the Taos Massacre of January 19. He found it "a small square fort of adobe with circular bastions at the corners, no part of the walls being more than eight feet high, and round the inside of the yard or corral [were] some half-dozen little rooms inhabited by as many Indian traders, *coureurs des bois*, and mountain men. They live entirely upon game, and the greater part of the year without even bread, since but little maize is cultivated. As soon as their supply of meat is exhausted they start to the mountains with two or three pack-animals and bring them back in two or three days loaded with buffalo or venison. . . . Three or four Taos women and as many squaws of every nation comprised the female society on the upper Arkansas, giving good promise of peopling the River with a sturdy race of half-breeds, if all the dusky buffalo-fed urchins who played about the corral of the fort arrived scatheless at maturity." See *Adventures in Mexico and the Rocky Mountains* (New York, 1855), 217–18, 271.

The decline of the fur-trade, chiefly occasioned by a ruinous fall in the price of beaver skins, spelled the decline of Fort Pueblo, whose inmates were slaughtered in the frightful massacre of Christmas Day, 1854, described by Wootton, *post*, Chap. 19. The modern city was founded on the site by a group of American settlers in the winter of 1859–60. The original fort, Ruxton states, was on the left bank of the Arkansas a few hundred yards above the mouth of the Fontaine-qui-bouille or Boiling Spring River.

It was an unfortunate trip for me and still more unfortunate for poor Tharp. While he was crossing Kansas he fell into the hands of the Comanches. He was killed, all the horses were captured, and the entire train-load of goods either carried off or destroyed.[27] I lost a good deal of money through the capture of that wagon train, but nobody was to blame, and it couldn't have been helped. Soon after that I made a trip up into Northern Colorado and traded with old Yellow Wolf's band of Cheyennes, but didn't get into any dangerous places or have any particularly interesting experiences.

I put in the next summer hunting and furnishing supplies of game for the fort, and in the fall traded again with the Utes, going over the line into New Mexico.

The Indians were at war with the Mexicans about that time, and that was a good time for an American to trade with them. That was the time when they always had plenty of mules and ponies. That they ran a great many of them away from the ranches of the Mexicans I had no doubt,

[27]George F. Ruxton, the English traveler, had planned to cross the Plains this summer in Tharp's company, but because Tharp was delayed in starting Ruxton went ahead with a government wagon train. His narrative fixes the date of Tharp's death as the summer of 1847. See *Adventures in Mexico and the Rocky Mountains*, 275–76.

but they were shrewd horse thieves and had a way of effacing the brands, so that I had no means of knowing what animals rightfully belonged to them and what ones were stolen. Even if I had known I could not have refused to trade for anything that they wished to dispose of without giving them great offense and perhaps getting into serious trouble. They didn't set a very high price on either their mules or the ponies. The mules usually cost me ten or twelve dollars apiece in trade, and the ponies a little less.

Sometimes when we had concluded a trade they would say to me that I should come again after so many moons, or half moons, and they would have more ponies, or furs, or robes. That meant that I should visit them again at the end of so many months or fortnights. It is well known that all Indians reckon time by suns and moons, but not so well known, I think, that the Indians of the Rocky Mountain region reckon also by snows. If you ask one of these Indians how old he is, he will tell you how many snows he has seen, and that means the number of years he has lived. His snows are years, his suns are days, and as I have already said, his moons and half moons are months and half months.

After telling me when I should come back they would tell me where I should find them at that time, and they were always there on time, unless they went on the war-path or something happened to make it impossible for them to keep their engagement. If I failed to find their village the understanding was that when I got in the neighborhood of the meeting place which had been agreed upon I should kindle a fire and when they saw the smoke they would come out and find me.

I have been asked a good many times how we managed, when we understood but a few words of the Indian language, to reach an understanding as to the basis of exchange in bartering articles differing very materially in value. I will tell you how I traded with the Utes, which illustrates fairly well how all Indian trading was conducted. They knew nothing about money, and when they occasionally got hold of a silver dollar they used it to make some kind of an ornament of. They knew, however, that a pony was worth more than a buckskin, and that a rifle was more valuable than a butcher-knife.

The trader always fixed the prices and the first thing to do was to arrange the schedule, if such a term can be used in connection with anything so primitive in style as Indian trading. I got together a parcel of sticks, each representing one of the articles I had to dispose of. The Indian laid down a buffalo robe, for instance, and then I commenced laying down the sticks, representing different things, that he wanted to trade for. When I had put down sticks enough to represent, in my line of goods, what I thought was the value of the robe, I waited to see if the Indian was satisfied. As a rule he wasn't. I don't know whether or not the Indian has descended from the Jew, but I know he has some of the same instincts in trade. He would insist on having sticks representing other articles added to the pile, and sometimes it would take a good while to reach an agreement.

When the agreement was reached, however, it fixed the price on buffalo robes, and as fast as they were transferred to my side of the lodge in which the trading was carried on I dealt out the articles traded for. In the same manner the prices were fixed on all the other Indian commodities, and we got through with our business very rapidly. In this way I have traded to the amount of a thousand dollars or two in a half day, after we once got started.

That fall and winter I put in trading with the Indians and hunting about the fort was a very prosperous one in a business way, and I scarcely had an adventure more thrilling than one which was a little out of the usual order, and very amusing. I was up at old Fort St. Vrain, something like forty miles north of Denver, and there was a party of fellows there who had come out from St.

Louis to see the Wild West, and teach the old timers how to fight Indians. They were loud talkers, and almost every time they went out of the fort would have a story of Indian killing to tell when they got back.

Some of us had doubts about their ever having seen any real live fighting Indians, and one day we concluded to find out how they would act in case they had reason to think themselves in danger. We heard them talking about going out to gather wild cherries in a thicket some distance from the fort, and knowing that it was a good place for an Indian ambuscade I took a companion along with me and rode out in advance of them to the thicket, where we secreted ourselves, after having picketed our horses where they would not be seen.

The eastern Indian slayers came along by and by, hitched their horses, laid down their guns, and then went into the thicket after the cherries. About the time they had gotten interested in their work we commenced shooting off our pistols and yelling like Comanche Indians; and then you ought to have seen those Indian fighters run. They never fired a shot, and didn't even stop to pick up their guns, but made the best possible time in getting back to the fort. When they got in they reported that they had been attacked by a large force of Indians; they had killed a good many of them and had only sought safety in flight when they found that they could not contend against the overwhelming numbers of the savages. To account for the loss of their guns, they said they had to swim the Platte River and had been compelled to leave their weapons behind them.

My companion and I rode in shortly after they had finished the story of their thrilling adventure, and in a day or two the facts leaked out. Then those St. Louis braves wanted to go home, and they embraced the earliest opportunity afforded them of making a safe trip to the East.

Chapter VII

Indian Tribes of the Far West

I SUPPOSE I ought to tell you something about the Indian tribes of the far West, to give you a correct idea of where they were located when they were at home. That is, where you might expect to find them when they were not on the warpath or away on some kind of stealing expedition. Of course I can't tell you just what territory each band claimed, but at one time and another I have seen and had something to do with all of them, and know in a general way where they lived and what kind of Indians they were.

To begin then at the western border line of Missouri, coming west we traveled through the territory claimed by the Sacs and Foxes, or if we kept farther south, through the country claimed by the Cherokees, Choctaws, Creeks, Senecas, and other bands of what is now the Indian Territory proper.[28]

[28]The Indian Territory, in 1889 when Wootton was talking, comprised all of present-day Oklahoma save for its western extension known as the Panhandle. The area had been set aside as a home for the Five Civilized Tribes (Cherokee, Creek, Choctaw, Chickasaw, and Seminole) who were removed chiefly in the 1830's from their homes east of the Mississippi to this section. In 1866 they ceded the western half of the area to the United States as a home

98

The Pawnees and one or two other tribes who spoke the same language were in the country at the mouth of the Platte, on the Missouri River, although they wandered pretty much all over Kansas.

The Comanches were scattered all over central and western Kansas and along the upper Arkansas River. North of them were the Cheyennes and Arapahoes, and then came the Sioux, who roamed over Nebraska, northern Colorado, and Wyoming, and were considered at home anywhere along the upper Platte River. There were more of the Sioux in the country when I first came West than there were of any other Indians. I think I must have known as many as thirty different bands of them, and possibly more.

In the country northwest and west of the Sioux were the Blackfoot and Monarch Indians, who lived together, the Nez Percés, the Crows, and the Flatheads, spreading over Montana, Idaho, Oregon, and Washington Territory. The Blackfoot Indians could always be found along the upper Missouri River and in the Yellowstone Park.

In the Salt Lake region and other portions of Utah were the Utes and Pah-Utes. There were

for other tribes. A portion of this ceded area was opened to white settlement in 1889, and was organized as Oklahoma Territory in 1890. In 1907 the two areas, reunited, were admitted to Statehood under the name of Oklahoma. Data condensed from *Dictionary of American History.*

Utes farther south and east too, in New Mexico and Colorado, and they frequently got a long way east and north on their marauding excursions. The Snakes and Shoshones, who spoke the same language, had about the same customs and traditions, and belonged to the same family, were scattered over a great deal of the country between the Rocky Mountains and the Sierra Nevadas, and could be found almost any place in that region.

The Apaches belonged in lower New Mexico and Arizona, and the Navahoes in northern New Mexico.

When you went west from Arizona, of course, you came to the California tribes, of which there were so many that it would take up a good deal of time and space to enumerate them. The Yumas, the Pimas, the Maricopas, and the Mojaves were the southern tribes that I knew most about.

There were some Delaware and Shawnee Indians and a band or two of the Kiowas in the same country as the Cheyennes and Arapahoes, along the Upper Platte and Upper Arkansas rivers.

There were subdivisions of the tribes I have mentioned, and scores of different names for them, but I have given you, I think, a pretty good general idea of the names and locations of the different bands. Now I am going to tell you what kind of terms they were on with each other, and farther along what kind of Indians they were.

Some of those people who have never seen an Indian more hostile than those with Buffalo Bill's Wild West Show, or more dangerous than the wooden Indian in front of a cigar store, are always talking about the extermination of the unfortunate natives of this country, by the Whites.[29] I want to tell these soft-hearted, well-meaning, but not well-informed people that if there are fewer Indians in America to-day than there were when the Continent was discovered, the white man is not to blame for it. All the Indians who have ever been killed by white settlers, traders, trappers, hunters, and soldiers between the Atlantic and Pacific oceans within the past two hundred years would not be a corporal's guard in comparison with the army of red skins slaughtered in wars, quarrels, and brawls of various kinds which they have had among themselves.

[29]William F. Cody (Buffalo Bill), famed as a scout and hunter, turned his attention to the stage as early as 1872, alternating for some years between acting and scouting. In 1883 he started his Wild West Show which toured the country for thirty years or more, to the vast delight of bug-eyed citizens and youngsters. Cody died January 10, 1917 at Denver; his body was taken to the State Capitol, where it was viewed by "immense throngs" of people. It was finally buried on the top of Lookout Mountain, near Golden, June 3, 1917. For a sketch of Cody's career see the *Dictionary of American Biography*.

It is not true either, as some people seem to think, that their treachery, cruelty, and vindictiveness have been the result of the treatment which they have received from the Whites. Long before a white man had found his way into this country the tribes which had never seen a white man, and possibly never heard of one, had the same distinguishing characteristics which they have had ever since the Whites came in contact with them. Before there were Whites to rob and plunder and steal from, they robbed and stole from each other. Before there were white men in the country to kill, they killed each other. Before there were white women and children to scalp and mutilate and torture, the Indians scalped and mutilated and tortured the women and children of their enemies of their own race. They made slaves of each other when there were no pale faces to be captured and sold or held for ransom, and before they commenced lying in ambush along the trails of the white man to murder unwary travelers the Indians of one tribe would set the same sort of death traps for the Indians of another tribe.

My opinion is—and I think I have as thorough a knowledge of the Indian character as any man living, and have seen as much of them in their dealings with each other—that we only use the proper form of expression in speaking of Indians when we call them savages. They are about as wild by nature as any other animal found roaming through forest and jungle, hiding in caves, and climbing over rocks and mountains. They have never recognized any law but the law of force, and the difference between a wild Indian and a civilized Indian is about the difference between the tiger at large and the tiger in a cage. As we find them now, on their reservations and under proper restraints, they are as harmless as the caged animal; but they were under no such restraints when I first came West, and we had to deal with them in a different way.

The Creek, Cherokee, Choctaw, Delaware, Shawnee, and other Indians that I used to have more or less to do with were the thoroughly tamed, or you might call them, perhaps, the domesticated animals. They did very little fighting among themselves, and we had no trouble in getting along with them.

The other tribes however, were always fighting with each other, and I have personal knowledge of thousands of them having been killed in these wars. The Arapahoes and the Cheyennes were closely related to each other and were always allies. Among their inveterate enemies were the Kiowas, a tribe which used to make its headquarters about where Pueblo now is. They kept up a war with the Arapahoes and Cheyennes until there was but a remnant of their tribe left, and then they joined the Comanche band and, I think, have remained with them ever since.

The Arapahoes and Comanches, and the Arapahoes and Utes, were always at war. When they fought the Comanches on their own ground, that is in the mountain region, the Arapahoes were generally the victors, but on the Kansas prairies, where the Comanches were at home, the Arapahoes were badly worsted in several encounters.

There were bloody battles within my recollection between the allied Arapahoes and Cheyennes and the Utes on Apishapa Creek above Trinidad, on the Sugarite in New Mexico, and at one or two other places. Both bands were good fighters and neither seemed to gain much advantage in either of these battles.

The Utes and mountain Apaches were never on good terms. They quarreled on all occasions and killed each other whenever opportunity offered.

The Comanches and Utes were always hostile to each other and had a great many fights at one time and another. The Utes and prairie Apaches —not the mountain Apaches—were allies once in fighting the Comanches and Kiowas.[30] They

[30]The Kiowas figure largely in General Custer's *My Life on the Plains*, the Lakeside Classics volume for 1952. Conquered in the mid-seventies, in large part through Custer's efforts, they were permanently settled near Fort Sill, Oklahoma.

met at Cimarron City, and left about as many dead Indians on the field as were ever left on a western battlefield.

The Sioux were continually fighting among themselves. As I have told you, there were many different bands of these Indians, and while they spoke the same language, looked alike, and made common cause in fighting other tribes, they seemed to have some differences which were always breeding trouble, and they hardly ever got together without having a row of such proportions that it might very properly be called a battle.

The Navahoes did less fighting with their neighbors, perhaps, than most of the other Indians, but their thieving propensities would every now and then get them into trouble. They fought well when they did go to war, and had a sort of Spartan courage which made them prefer death to capture. A Navaho Indian who allowed himself to be taken prisoner was discarded by his tribe, if he chanced to return to it alive.

The Crows and the Cheyennes were the best warriors of all the Indian tribes of the West. The Comanches and Pawnees always sought to have the odds largely in their favor, and would sometimes hover for days around an enemy waiting for an opportunity to kill without taking any chances of being killed. They were very skillful in preparing an ambush as they could stretch themselves out on the Plains and cover themselves with sand or hide themselves so completely in the tall grass that it was not an uncommon occurrence for them to fall upon unwary travelers as suddenly and unexpectedly as though they had come up out of the ground.

Nothing better illustrates the Comanche character than his queer notion about killing rattlesnakes. The only time they kill the rattlesnake is when they find him in that sluggish condition in which he fails to rattle when approached. Judging the snake instinct by his own, the Comanche says, when the snake fails to warn the Indian of his presence, "he is on the warpath"; that is, he is lying in ambush for an enemy and wants to bite him. There was never any such thing as honor among the Comanches, and it was on account of their stealing that they were in trouble so much of the time with other Indians.

The Arapahoes and Cheyennes were good hunters, had plenty of game in their country, and were better Indians than any of the Far West tribes, with the exception of the Delawares and Shawnees. When I say Far West, I mean the mountain and prairie Indians. We never had much serious trouble with them for a long time after I came West, I think about the only battle we had with them being down on the Arkansas River at the point where the old Santa Fe Trail crossed it. We gave them a terrible whipping at that time and it was a good many years before they forgot it and went on the warpath again.

The Sioux would steal a few horses now and then when they happened to take a fancy to those belonging to the mountaineers or to some other tribe of Indians, but they were fairly honest and didn't give us serious trouble. We could always get along well trading with them, although now and then they acted a little war-like in their intercourse with the white men.

The Apaches were always just what they are now; a dirty, thieving lot of cut-throats, who would rather steal than live by any other means. They lived on horses and mules stolen from the Mexicans and other Indians because they were too lazy to hunt game, although there were always plenty of deer in their country.

The Utes were more honest than the Apaches, but they were sometimes bad tempered, quarrelsome, and vindictive to a remarkable degree, even for Indians. You could never tell when they would take offense at some trivial thing and go on the warpath. As a rule, however, they killed to satisfy revenge rather than for the purpose of plunder.

The most degraded Indians I have ever seen, that is those who seemed to me to be lower down in the scale of humanity than any others, were the Pah-Utes, the Yumas, and the Mojaves. The

Pah-Utes, as I have said in the account of my long trapping expedition to the Northwest, were to some extent cannibals, while the Mojaves and Yumas went naked, were more filthy in their habits than an average lot of hogs, and lived on ants, lizards, and anything else they could get without exerting themselves.

This reminds me of an amusing thing which happened when I was trapping on the Colorado River. There was a Yuma village near our camp, and one night some of the trappers went into the village and brought back with them, what they thought was some kind of bread. Without noticing it very particularly they commenced eating, but it was not long before they discovered that if they were eating bread it was a different kind from any they had ever tasted before. They made an examination of the stuff then, and found that what they had supposed were biscuits were small cakes made of red ants, crushed together and dried in the sun.

The Maricopas located on the Gila River were a good-looking, industrious, and rather thrifty lot of Indians, who were generally well behaved and so far as I know always friendly to the Whites. The Pimas were also a peaceable and well disposed band.

The Navahoes were always rather better than the average run of Indians, although they never knew what it meant to be honest. They were industrious, however, and while other bands were roaming about over the country they stayed most of the time where they belonged, made the blankets which we used to like to get hold of and which have since become famous all over the country, manufactured water-tight baskets to sell, and cultivated the soil to a considerable extent. Outside of the Pueblo Indians, the Navahoes are the only mountain Indians that I have ever seen doing anything of consequence in the way of planting and raising crops of any kind.

The Pueblo Indians were an entirely different kind of Indians from the roving tribes. They have always been called Pueblo Indians, because they built permanent villages or pueblos. They were all natives of the Mexican country and several of the pueblos may be seen in New Mexico, where some thousands of this peculiar class of Indians still live. The pueblo was a building, or group of buildings, designed, when they were built, to subserve the purpose of domiciles and places of refuge at the same time.

As a general rule they were built of adobe or sun-dried bricks. These are the same kind of bricks, by the way, that the Israelites were making for Pharaoh down in Egypt when he cut off the supply of straw which has to be mixed with the adobe mortar and raised such a row among them that they went on a strike.

I have seen several ruins of pueblos, and you can still see them down along the Rio Puerco in the Arizona country, which are built of stone and are several stories high. The first story is always without any entrance from the ground. The second story is narrower than the first and this makes a terrace, the floor of which constitutes the roof of the first story. This terrace is reached by ladders, and then the first story is entered through trap doors, while doors opening out on the terrace are the entrances to the second stories. These tightly closed rooms on the ground floor, or rather on the first floor, because all the floors were ground floors, made a very safe retreat from an enemy when the ladders leading to the entrance were drawn up and hidden away, in the days of bow and arrow warfare.

Some of the pueblos still in existence are very ancient, it being claimed that the Pueblo de Taos and the Acoma Pueblo were built before the advent into the country of Coronado, the Spanish explorer, in 1540.[31] They are queer buildings, and the people we found in them and those found in them today are queer Indians, very unlike any of

[31]The Acoma Pueblo, built on a rock or mesa 357 feet in height, was first visited by Coronado in 1540. It is today credited with being the oldest inhabited settlement in the United States. The Taos Pueblo was also visited as early as 1540 by members of Coronado's army. Evidently both settlements were of much earlier origin.

the other tribes found on the American Continent. They have always done considerable farming, and have never, so far as I have known anything about them, done any hunting of consequence. The only time they have ever shown any hostility to the Whites was when they were stirred up to do so by the Mexicans in 1847. I shall have something to say about that, however, some other time.

Chapter VIII

Indian Customs and Superstitions

I HAVE made mention of the fact that one of the customs of the Utes in connection with the obsequies of a dead chieftain gave me considerable uneasiness at one time when I was trading among them. This was their custom of killing the first stranger found in their camp after the chief's death. That, however, was not the only sacrifice necessary to give the spirit of the defunct brave a good start in the other world. It was a Ute custom to burn the bodies of their great men, and their horses, bows and arrows, and sometimes one or more of their wives were burned with them. Ute Indians, other than the chiefs and principal men, were generally buried, but in a peculiar way. They did not dig graves for these common Indians, but would usually find a depression in some hillside or a hole under the rocks, and in this they laid the body and then covered it up with stones.

The Arapahoes, Cheyennes, Sioux, and some other Indians used to leave their dead in trees. The dead warrior was wrapped in his blanket and then in a buffalo robe, with his weapons and ornaments, along with food and tobacco, at his side. Then the body was fastened in the branches of some large cottonwood or other tree, and remained there until it fell to the earth to be devoured by the wolves and coyotes.

The Comanches left their dead in caves, and as a sign of grief, in addition to the wailings and lamentations common among all Indians, they cut off the manes and tails of their horses.

All the Indians I have ever known, with the exception of the Pueblos, were polygamous, and there was but one thing stood in the way of an Indian having as many wives as he wanted, and that was a lack of the wherewithal to buy them. Among nearly all the tribes marriage was a matter of barter and sale, and in fact that was about all there was of the marriage.

Among the Navahoes, for instance, an Indian who has taken a fancy to a particular young squaw goes to her father and offers him so many ponies for the girl. If the bargain is closed the ponies are delivered, the Indian maiden is carried away to the lodge of her purchaser, and that's all there is in the way of a wedding, as a rule. Sometimes a marriage of this kind is celebrated by a feast on horse-flesh, and I have heard, too, that they have a kind of marriage ceremony at times, although I have never seen anything of the sort. In this ceremony the prospective bride and groom take seats on opposite sides of a wicker basket, which is made so tight that it will hold water. This basket is filled with some kind of food, and when the bride and groom have eaten out of it, dipping in at the same time, they are married. The Indian who marries the first of a family of daughters can have all the others, in preference to other suitors, if he can bargain satisfactorily with the father, and as a rule he prefers to marry sisters for the reason that he thinks they will get along better together.

Among the Apaches, when a girl reaches a marriageable age her parents advertise the fact by getting up a feast at which they always have a great deal of singing and dancing. After this is over they cut off the girl's eyebrows, and a month later pull out her eye-lashes. What the object of this is I don't know, unless it is to distinguish her from other squaws who are not in the matrimonial market. Having thus made her debut, as I suppose it would be called in fashionable society, the Apache maiden is given a somewhat better opportunity of choosing her own husband than her Navaho sister. Her suitor comes at night and stakes his horse in front of her father's lodge. This may be called the Apache style of popping the question. If the proposal is satisfactory to the young squaw and her father feels assured that he will be properly compensated for the loss of this particular member of his family she takes the horse at some time within four days from the time it is left in front of her tent, feeds and waters it, and then returns it to the owner's lodge.

This signifies her acceptance of the offer of marriage, and the details are arranged later between her father and her lover, or rather the Indian whose slave she is to become, because the women of this tribe are very badly treated. When an Apache Indian has more than one wife the one last married is mistress of the harem.

The Comanches, Utes, Arapahoes, and Cheyennes conducted their courtships and marriages on strictly business principles, and horses, robes, or other Indian property always had to be given in exchange for a wife. For this reason the rich Indian always had more and better-looking wives than the poor Indian, who had to put up with the old and ugly women of the tribe. The wives of the Comanches were miserable drudges, and were not allowed to participate in any of the pleasures of the males. Even when they danced, they had to dance by themselves and out of sight of their brute masters.

The courtship of the Shoshones was a novel one. For some reason or other the Indian maidens of this tribe always seemed to be more fleet-footed than the young braves. This gave them an advantage when they were being courted after the Shoshone fashion, and made the success of a suitor dependent upon the feeling which the squaw of his choice entertained toward him. She was given a reasonable start on him in a foot race, and then if he succeeded in catching her and throwing a lasso over her head the fact that she was to be tied to him for life was settled. If she thought well of her infatuated pursuer, of course, she was easily caught, but if she was not inclined to favor his suit, she could generally distance him in the race.

The Pah-Ute lovers were of a more sentimental character, and their custom was to seat themselves on a log outside the village and wait for the likely young squaws to take seats by their sides, when the courtship was considered ended and married life began.

The Pueblo Indians had a kind of perpetual leap-year arrangement. These Indians mated after the fashion of respectable white people. That is, one man had one wife at a time and it was the Indian girl who picked out her lover. She never had to wait for some timid young buck to come a courting, but when she took a fancy to one all she had to do was to inform her father that she wanted to marry him. The father then visited the parents of the Indian upon whom his daughter had bestowed her affections and proposed a matrimonial alliance between the young people. The parents of the groom were expected, of course, to make suitable presents to the father of the bride, but there was much less of the barter and sale idea about the business than there was about marriage among the roving tribes.

The divorce system in vogue among these Indians was one which I think would be popular among the crowned heads of Europe, and possibly among some classes of people in this country. Whenever they tired of living together they could separate, and both were free to marry again. If they had any children the grand-parents were under obligation to take care of them. This was a very different arrangement from that in force among the Comanches, where divorced women had their ears and noses cut off and became perpetual outcasts.

These Indians, I mean the Comanches, differed from most other Indians in having a very vague idea of a Supreme Being. They worshipped the sun and the earth, but so far as I could ever see these objects did not represent any kind of deity. Their idea of the future state was that it was a happy hunting ground where there would be plenty of buffaloes and nobody but Comanches to kill them.

They believed in evil spirits of various grades and kinds, and always attributed a lack of rain or sunshine to the influence of some of these evil spirits. To propitiate the spirits and cause the rain to fall, or the sun to shine, their custom was to whip or flay alive one of their slaves or a captive whose life had been spared.

The Navahoes always believed in the existence of a God, to whom they gave a name so long that no white man ever remembered it. They had, when I used to be among them, and I suppose they still have, hundreds of superstitions about the existence of spirits, good and bad, who had a great deal to do with Indian affairs. A few of these Indians believed that the soul of man passes at death into some one of the lower animals, but the idea most generally prevalent among them was that when an Indian died his soul passed into the center of the earth and then by some means or other found its way into a place where there was nothing to mar the happiness of the good Indian's spirit. Those Navahoes who believed in the transmigration of souls, as I suppose you would call it, thought that every rattlesnake contained the spirit of a bad Indian, and that there were spirits of bad men in the coyotes also; women, they thought, became fishes after death.[32]

The Apaches were all strong believers in the transmigration doctrine, and they had more definite ideas about the form which the spirit was to assume after it passed out of the body of an Indian, or rather what kind of body it would inhabit next, than the few Navahoes who entertained similar notions. That the spirit of a very

[32]Because of this belief, the Navahoes abhorred the idea of eating fish. Britton Davis noted the same abstinence on the part of the White Mountain and other Apaches near Fort Apache in the mid-eighties. See *The Truth About Geronimo*, the Lakeside Classics volume for 1951, p. 69.

mean Indian would find lodgment in a rattle-snake, they all believed, but other spirits would, it was thought, assume the form of the owl, the eagle, or the bear, or that of some pure white bird, the particular form to be assumed being dependent upon the kind of life the Indian whose soul was to take up its abode in some other animal had lived. They had a superstitious reverence for all the animals which it was thought might contain a good spirit, and I never knew an Apache Indian to kill a bear, an owl, an eagle, or any kind of a white bird.

The Nez Percés and Flathead Indians had a queer belief, which might be called a cross between the Roman Catholic and the Apache idea of the future state. They thought that the spirits of all good Indians found their way at once to the Indian Heaven, while bad spirits had to go through a sort of purgatory to atone for their sins. While going through this state the spirits inhabited the bodies of animals which were hunted and persecuted, and all beavers were looked upon as Indians who were doing penance for their bad deeds.

Montezuma, as everybody knows who has heard or read anything about the Pueblo Indians, was their principal deity, or properly speaking the representation of the Supreme Being. They prayed to him for rain, and in fact for almost all the favors that they had occasion to ask from the ruler of the universe. They had a sacred snake to which they sometimes prayed also. I believe this snake was looked upon as the animal which Montezuma regarded with greatest favor—on account, perhaps, of its wisdom—and the stories which they used to tell of its appearance in various places rivaled some of the sea serpent stories which we hear now-a-days.

The sun dance of the Sioux was one of the most peculiar outgrowths of Indian superstition. The object of the dance was to gain the favor of the Great Spirit, and commencing always at sundown it lasted three days. I have seen the Mexican *penitentes* torture themselves in various ways, but I have never known them to devise any kind of self torture quite as sickening as that which accompanied the sun dance of the Sioux.

They made preparations for the dance by attaching strong rawhide ropes to good-sized saplings, which were bent over until the tops came within eight or ten feet of the ground. When the time came for the dance to commence, an Indian took his place under each of the ropes dangling from the tops of the saplings, his body entirely naked above the waist. With a keen edged knife, two deep gashes a couple of inches apart were cut in the back of the savage and the rawhide rope was passed under the skin and flesh from one gash to the other. The rope was securely fastened and the Indian *penitente*, sometimes lifted clear off the ground as the sapling swayed back and forth, kept up a sort of rhythmic motion until the rawhide cut its way through the flesh and allowed him to drop to the ground.

Most of the Indians believed that sickness was due to the influence of evil spirits, and their medicine men usually cured, or pretended to cure, rather by incantations and charms than by giving medicines, although, of course, they understood how to use a good many roots and herbs. When they went on the war path the medicine men always went along, more for the purpose of keeping off evil spirits and propitiating the Indian deities than to care for the wounded.

Their superstitions were carried to the extent of puffing the smoke in a certain direction or toward a certain object when they lighted their pipes, to bring rain or fair weather or cause the wind to blow from a certain way; and when starting out on a trip, all their plans might be changed by the appearance of a snake in the pathway or the flight of a bird overhead.

I have never known any Indians, at least none of the roving tribes, who were not inveterate gamblers. This certainly is not a vice they have contracted from the Whites. Of late years they have learned to use cards, but long before that they had gambling devices of their own and took to this vice as naturally as they took to the hunt. I have seen them lay an arrow on the ground and then one after another bounce other arrows off their bow strings, bets being made as to which arrow would fall closest to the one on the ground. Sometimes they would take three sticks and shift them from one hand to the other after the style of three-card-monte, or change a bullet rapidly from one hand to the other in the same way, and all the time they were betting buffalo robes or buckskins or something else on some feature of the shuffle, although I confess I could never understand the games myself. On the result of a horse race—and they were very fond of racing—I have seen them stake great piles of robes and furs, and not infrequently a lot of mules or ponies in addition. They were very shrewd, too, about their racing, and I have seen them get the best of white horsemen in many a match. I remember not many years ago, a band of Utes came over to Trinidad and made a big winning off of some of the Americans who haven't been in the country as long as I have, but long enough to be called old-timers. They always had a lot of horses with them, and they knew just to a second how much faster one of these horses could run than another. They would use the slower horses to test the speed of the horses brought out against them, and finally, when they thought they had a sure thing, would bring out the fast ones. In the Trinidad race the Americans had a blooded horse which had been brought out from Kansas City and thought they were very sure of winning the race, but the Indians had sized him up correctly and won, a little Indian boy, who had to be tied on the horse, riding the winning pony.

Drunkenness was quite as much a besetting sin of the Indian as gambling. I never saw one who wouldn't drink rum, and some of them had liquors of their own before any were brought into the country by the Whites.

The Navahoes, as long ago as I can remember, had a way of making whiskey out of corn, of which they have always raised more or less, and they as well as other Indians of the Mexican territory manufactured mescal. This is a fiery and very intoxicating liquor made out of the cactus.[33] Some tribes of Indians drank much more than others, and I think there was more drunkenness among the Arapahoes, Cheyennes, Kiowas, and Comanches than among any other bands of western Indians.

[33]For a more detailed account of the method employed in brewing mescal, as also of its potency, see Britton Davis, *The Truth About Geronimo*, the Lakeside Classics volume for 1951, pp. 224–26.

You have heard, of course, that some of the savages poison their arrows before going to war, but I reckon you never knew how these arrows were poisoned. I have never known of many Indians who did this, but I have known some, and I know how it was done; and when I tell you about it you will understand the deadly nature of the wound inflicted by one of these arrows.

They used to take the liver of a deer, buffalo, or some other animal and inoculate it with the venom of the rattlesnake. There were thousands of these snakes in the country in summer and it was always easy to find one, and not at all difficult to stir him up to the fighting point. The liver which was to be poisoned would be placed on a stick and held before him in such a way that he would strike it frequently. Then it would be laid aside where it would decompose and in a short time become a mass of the most fatal poison. The points of the arrows would then be stuck into this deadly preparation and allowed to remain until they became thoroughly coated with it. The Pah-Utes, the Mescalero Apaches, and the Digger Indians were the only savages among those of the Far West, so far as I have known, who used these poisoned weapons of warfare.

The Navahoes used to be charged by the Mexicans, and possibly by some of the mountain men, with poisoning their arrows before going to war, and they have figured in some of the story books as a band of Indians to be dreaded on that account. I have never seen anything, however, to indicate that these Indians went into battle with any such advantage over their enemies. They were none too good to use a weapon of that kind, nor were any of the other Indians for that matter, but the poisoned arrow was by no means a safe thing to handle. In adjusting it to the bow or drawing it from the quiver the Indian might inflict upon himself the death wound which it was designed to inflict upon an enemy. To be pricked or scratched by its envenomed point was quite sufficient to bring about a fatal result, and the risk of using poisoned arrows was considered too great by all the Indians I have ever known, with the exception of those above mentioned. Even these Indians did not use them to any great extent, and outside of the Wild West novels they have never figured prominently in Indian warfare.

Chapter IX

Perils of the Pioneers

NOW and then, when I get to thinking over the old times and the dangers the mountain men were exposed to on every hand, I wonder that any of us have lived to tell of our adventures. Even when we thought ourselves on good terms with the Indians something which we couldn't foresee or provide against might occur at any time which would change our relations in a twinkling, and the peace was at an end.

One time I had started out to trade with the Utes and had along with me, among others, a Shawnee Indian. We were twelve or fourteen miles below where Trinidad is now, on the Purgatoire River, when the Shawnee happened one day to meet a Ute Indian alone. Not long before that one of the Shawnees had been wounded, or perhaps killed, by a Ute, and when my Shawnee companion saw an opportunity for revenge the Indian instinct in him was too strong to be resisted. Notwithstanding the fact that we were within a short distance of their village the Shawnee shot and killed the Ute. As soon as I heard of it I knew that we would have the whole band of Utes after us, and that nothing I could say to them would appease their anger.

I changed my plans very suddenly and instead of trying to do any trading with the Utes undertook to get out of their country as quickly as possible. As I had expected, they followed us and overtook us in an open country where there was no chance for us to secrete ourselves or take any advantage in fighting them. I think we had eight men in our party, and with a big band of Utes against us it looked as though our time had come. We determined, however, to make a brave stand and be killed fighting, if we had to be killed.

Our pack animals, of which we had quite a number, were gotten together and arranged in a circle so that they might protect us to some extent from the fire of the Indians. We stationed ourselves inside this improvised fort and awaited the attack, which the Indians were not long in making. Circling around us, they commenced shooting and we returned the fire. There was not a man among us, not excepting the Indian, who was not able to make almost every one of his shots count, while but few of the arrows which the Utes discharged at us reached us. They had some guns, but of a very inferior kind, and at that time they had not learned to use firearms to as good advantage as they can now. We suffered comparatively little while the fight was kept up, and were picking off so many of their horses, besides killing a few Indians, that they abandoned the contest and gave us an unexpected opportunity to make our escape.

On another trip into this same country, when I was accompanied by Bill Williams—who was afterward a guide for General Fremont, and a noted scout—and a trapper by the name of Walters, we were one afternoon making our way along through a rocky and rather thickly-wooded cañon, not knowing that there were any Indians near us, when I heard the crack of a rifle and saw Walters, who was a few feet ahead of me, throw up his hands.

He cried out that he was shot, and would have fallen from the mule which he was riding had I not sprung to his assistance. He recovered himself in a few minutes, and realizing that we were ambushed and could only save ourselves by a rapid flight he clung to his mule and we started at full speed down the Cañon, with the bullets from a score of guns whistling about us.

When we emerged into an open space where, if we were compelled to fight, we should not have an unseen enemy to contend with, we stopped long enough to ascertain the condition of our wounded companion. The shot had been fired at such close range that his clothes were almost powder burned, and my first impression was that the ball had passed entirely through his body. A closer examination developed the fact that the wound was less serious than that, but still bad enough. The ball had entered the left side just above the hip, but strangely enough, its course had in some way been deflected, so that it passed just under the skin half way round the body and came out on the right side nearly opposite where it entered. We dressed the wound as best we could and made our way back to Fort Bent, where Walters finally recovered, although he was never much inclined to venture into any portion of the Indian country where he did not know that he would be perfectly safe, after that.

My own good fortune during all this time possibly had the effect of making me somewhat more adventurous than I would otherwise have been. I had had so many close calls and, as the saying goes, had escaped with a whole skin, that I began to think I led a sort of charmed life. I had heard of the old Scotch maxim to the effect that the child that's born to be hung will ne'er be drowned, and had about made up my mind that whatever the future had in store for me I was not to be killed by the Indians.

For that reason these hair-breadth escapes did not have the effect of frightening me out of the country as it did a great many, or even inducing me to follow some less hazardous vocation than that of trapping, hunting, and trading with the

Indians. There was no adventure which promised good results in a business way that I was not ready to undertake, and I was rather disappointed than pleased when I returned from one of these trips without some thrilling experiences.

It's strange how we get used to all sorts of dangers, isn't it? I remember one incident of my life—and it occurred about the time I have been speaking of too—which, while it hardly seemed to me more than commonplace at the time, sends a cold chill over me when I think of it now.

A party of five of us were trapping northern Colorado near the present site of Fort Collins. There were a lot of what we called half-breeds in that country, and they were as great a lot of cutthroat Indians as ever infested any part of the United States. I do not mean by half-breeds that they had any admixture of white blood, but that the Arapahoes, Shawnees, and Blackfeet had become mixed up, so that the Indians in this neighborhood were not pure bloods of either tribe. They were always at war among themselves, and ready at almost any time to make war on anybody else where there was a chance of getting possession of a band of horses or mules or securing any other kind of plunder. Several years later, when the half-breed Blackfoot Indians undertook to leave the country and join the Blackfoot tribe farther north, they were followed by the Arapahoes, who had against them a grievance of some kind, and the whole band, including women and children, were killed.

We had quite a number of ponies and mules along with us and I suppose the Indians thought, as our party was a small one, they could easily take our animals and our scalps at the same time. A band of them attacked us about four o'clock one afternoon and as we had nothing like a fighting force of men in our company the only thing we could do was to find the most secure hiding place which was available. We crept in among some large rocks at the foot of a steep hill, where it was almost impossible for either their bullets or their arrows to reach us. They soon discovered our hiding place and commenced trying to dislodge us. Arrows and bullets seemed to fall around us almost as thick as hail, and kept up a patter on the rocks that made us feel anything but comfortable. Whenever we caught sight of an Indian or a horse we would shoot, and with such good effect that they suffered considerable loss.

In this way the balance of the afternoon wore away. Just before night they drew off, and for a time we heard nothing of them. We were not by any means certain that they had abandoned the fight, but we were beginning to feel a trifle easier, when just as the sun was going down the crashing of rocks down the mountain side advised us of a new mode of attack. Having discovered that we were not being harmed by the fusillade which they had kept up during the afternoon, they had climbed the mountain and now sought to drive us out of our place of concealment by rolling rocks down on us. If you have ever seen a huge boulder started down the side of a steep mountain and noticed the fearful velocity which it acquires before it reaches the foot of the hill, you can understand with what terrible force these rocks struck those behind which we were sheltering ourselves from the savages. Some of them would burst into fragments, which were scattered all about us, while others struck our rock fortifications like cannon balls or battering rams, bounded to one side or the other, and passed down into the cañon below us.[34]

It seemed to us, sometimes, that if we were not crushed by the falling stones our stronghold must finally be broken to pieces, and then we should have been left at the mercy of our bloodthirsty enemies. The huge masses of rocks by which we were surrounded stood as firm, however, as the rock of ages, although the bombard-

[34]This method of waging battle was resorted to on occasion by the Apaches and other mountain tribes. See, for example, Britton Davis, *The Truth about Geronimo*, the Lakeside Classics volume for 1951, pp. 130–31, where Geronimo states that he did not waste cartridges on Mexicans, but fought them with rocks.

ment, with now and then an intermission, was kept up nearly all night. It was a moonlight night and we could see the Indians moving about from time to time, and we lost no opportunity of letting them know that we were still alive, had plenty of ammunition, and could shoot as well as ever.

The hostilities came to an end about daylight, when the Indians seemed to reach the conclusion that they had wasted ammunition enough on us. They knew that we had the most of our pack animals with us, with provisions and ammunition enough to enable us to withstand a long seige. We had killed some of their men and a good many horses and they knew we would kill more of them if the fight was kept up. There may have been other considerations which influenced them in giving up the battle, but at any rate as soon as it began to get light we could see them getting ready to leave. By and by they started off and we watched them until they were out of sight. Then we crawled out of our fort and took an inventory of damages.

We found that none of our party had been injured, although one man had been so completely changed in appearance that we scarcely knew him. That was Major Kilpatrick, who up to that time had not had much experience in Indian fighting. He was a brave fellow, but it happened that he had been placed in a more trying position than any of us and must have been worse scared. He was not with the rest of us when the fight commenced, but had sought the same kind of shelter in the rocks. While the fight was going on he had no means of knowing how many of us were alive, and as his hiding place had been stormed in the same manner as ours he imagined he was to be made the last victim of the slaughter. When he made his way to where the rest of us were, his hair, which had been black the day before, had turned as white as a man's hair can get.[35] I expect there are a good many Colorado people living yet who will remember the Major, as he afterward spent some years in the Territory as an Indian agent, but not many of them I reckon ever heard the story of his lightning change from a young into an old man.

While I am telling you about the dangers we had to contend with back in the forties in getting a foothold in this country, where it is so easy for anybody to get a foothold now, I am going to say something about another experience of mine, just to show you that it was not from Indians alone that our lives were in danger.

[35] A competent physician, consulted by the Editor, stated that such a sudden change in color of the hair is a physical impossibility. He added that belief in the myth is so deep-seated that it is useless to deny it.

Among all the wild animals with which we came in contact there were none that we dreaded so much as the mad wolf. There were thousands of these animals in the country, I mean thousands of wolves, and you know the wolf is peculiarly liable to attacks of hydrophobia at certain seasons of the year. Whenever a wolf runs mad he attacks, or rather bites, whatever comes in his way, the same as a rabid dog, and I have had a good many animals bitten by them at one time and another.

One evening when I was in camp with several other trappers I saw a big, gaunt-looking grey wolf trotting along, not very far from where we were. I had a couple of fine hunting dogs with me who could hold their own well in a struggle with a wolf and I started them after him, thinking I should see an interesting fight. Before the dogs reached the wolf they stopped and seemed to hesitate about taking hold of him. Without noticing anything peculiar about the animal I went up pretty close to him to encourage the dogs. They attacked him then, but he broke loose and paying no attention to the dogs came toward me. I had picked up a club two or three feet long, and as he came toward me I struck him with it, but the stick was rotten and the blow only stopped him for a moment. I saw then what was the matter with the wolf, and that I was in a dangerous place. I urged the dogs to come to my rescue, but some peculiar instinct seemed to warn them of the dangerous character of their adversary and they stood back, leaving me to make my own fight.

The wolf had been crippled slightly in his first struggle with the dogs, and was not as active as he would have been if uninjured. I had my hunting knife with me and just as he was about to make a spring at my throat I managed to drive it into his side, catching him at the same time by the back of the neck with the other hand and flinging him away from me. The knife-thrust killed him, and I escaped without being bitten or scratched, although it was just by the skin of my teeth. The adventure cost me two fine hunting dogs, as they both had to be killed, but it taught me to exercise greater care thereafter about coming into too close contact with wild animals in general, and mad wolves in particular.

CHAPTER X

A Convention of Grizzlies

SPEAKING of my adventure with the mad wolf reminds me of some other adventures with the original inhabitants of the mountains and Plains who were only less savage than those other wild animals, the Indians, and who would now and then resent an invasion of their domain.

There was one native of the Rocky Mountain region which the hunters and trappers always made a point of dealing with very cautiously and circumspectly, and that was the grizzly bear. The grizzly, cinnamon, and black bears were all natives of this region, but the grizzly was the big chief of the bear family. There used to be a great many of them in the mountains, but we rarely hear of one now. They have a strong aversion to civilization, and have gotten as far away from the settlements as they could get.

I have had a long and intimate acquaintance with the grizzly, and what I tell you about him may correct some erroneous notions which are prevalent as to the kind of animal he is. In the first place, let me tell you that he is not a professional man-killer, and never goes about seeking whom he may devour, as some writers of bear stories would make us believe. That he has been guilty now and then of staining his chops with human gore is true, but it was usually under circumstances which would have made justifiable homicide a proper verdict if the affair had been between man and man. It was where he met an open enemy in fair fight and got the best of it.

My experience has been that the bear will always sacrifice his reputation for courage to avoid a conflict with the hunter, provided the hunter makes no hostile demonstration when they come in contact with each other. An experience which I had one time just about forty years ago, when hunting in the Cimarron Mountains, will illustrate to what extent the bear is a peace-loving animal.

Early one morning I left my two companions in camp and started out to get some bear meat. I had not gone more than a hundred yards when I struck the trail of a grizzly, and after following it about a hundred yards farther, through a thick growth of shrub oak which was about as high as my head, I stepped into a little open space and found my bear. I found him in company with four other bears, all full grown. I was looking for bears, but I hadn't been appointed a delegate to a convention of grizzlies and I felt at once as though I was an intruder. If I had not attracted their attention I should have retired without making my presence known or interrupting their deliberations, but they had seen me as soon as I saw them.

I knew that to open hostilities would be suicidal, because while I might have killed one or two of the bears I should have been torn to pieces before the row was over, if it had once commenced. It was unsafe to retreat because a bear has no respect for a cowardly enemy, and so I concluded to stand still and give the grizzlies to understand that I didn't propose to commence a fuss. They eyed me closely for about half a minute and then commenced growling savagely, first taking a few steps toward me and then walking back to where they started from, as though they were daring me to make any hostile demonstration or even to come half way.

I didn't much like being bullied in that way, but I didn't allow my temper to get the better of my judgment. I stood perfectly still for about five minutes, when the bears seemed to reach the conclusion that they had no quarrel with me, and bringing the proceedings of their convention to an abrupt close they started off on a run in different directions. I let them go without firing a shot. Their conduct had been much more genteel than I had expected it to be and I wasn't going to break the peace under the circumstances.

I think they were even more pleased at getting away from me than I was at getting rid of them.

One of them, at least, must have been panic stricken, because he galloped away toward our camp and when he reached it was so much excited that he ran through the camp fire, scattering the sparks all over one of my companions who happened to be roasting a piece of venison at the time.

There is one thing which a grizzly resents very promptly and emphatically, and that is being shot at or threatened with a gun. He understands as well as anybody that the gun is a death-dealing weapon, and the snapping of the cap or the click of the hammer enrages him almost if not quite as much as being wounded. Under such circumstances he fights viciously and ferociously, without any further provocation.

One of the most desperate encounters I ever had personal knowledge of between the trappers and a grizzly was one in which Dick Owens, who afterward became somewhat noted as a guide and scout,[36] and John Burris, who, when I last saw him, was a California ranchman, were the par-

[36]Dick Owens was a long time associate of Kit Carson in his trapping, scouting, and ranching activities. With Carson he accompanied Fremont to California on his third exploring expedition of 1845–46. Fremont characterized him as "cool, brave, and of good judgement; a good hunter and good shot; experienced in mountain life; he ... proved valuable throughout the campaign." Owens, Carson, and Godey were succinctly denominated "three kingly men." Fremont, *Memoirs*. 427.

ticipants. They were out hunting one day and came upon an enormous grizzly very unexpectedly. Both the hunters shot at him and both missed. Before the smoke of their rifles cleared away the bear charged on them and they made for a small bushy cedar tree, hardly more than a shrub, which was the only tree in sight. Owens was ahead and got into the tree, but Burris had hardly gotten off the ground when the bear caught him by one foot and dragged him back. He was a man of rare presence of mind, however, and as soon as the bear caught hold of him he dropped to the ground, and notwithstanding the fact that his body was being scratched and torn in a score of places he lay perfectly still.

The enraged bear, thinking he had disposed of one of his enemies, left Burris and climbed into the bush after Owens, who had thrown away his gun and could do nothing but engage in a hand-to-hand fight with old Bruin. He struck at the bear with his hunting knife, but the brute caught him by the hand, and then a terrific struggle commenced in the branches of the tree, ten or twelve feet from the ground. Burris, although he was badly wounded, had by this time gotten hold of and reloaded his gun, but it was some little time, an age it seemed to Owens, before he could get in a position to shoot at the bear without taking great chances on killing his companion, who was having a wrestling match with the animal in the tree top.

Finally he managed to send a bullet through the bear's body and the big brute dropped to the ground, almost tearing Owens' hand off before loosening its hold. This shot was not fatal, but the bear left the two hunters and charged down through our camp, which was not far distant from the scene of the encounter. Several more shots were fired at him and we finally killed him, but both Owens and Burris were left badly crippled, and never entirely recovered.

The hunter who took any unnecessary chances in dealing with a grizzly always regretted it. He always discovered that to trifle with the monarch of the mountains under any circumstances was a mistake. Old Jim Baker, who next to Kit Carson was General Fremont's most noted scout, and who has been my companion on many a trapping expedition, used to tell me how he learned this lesson very early in his experience as a mountaineer, and he would always wind up by remarking, "I haint forgot that lesson yet."

Baker came to the mountains about the same time I did, and soon became known as one of the most daring fellows among the mountain men.[37] Two or three years after he came to the

[37] James Baker, another notable Mountain man, was born at Belleville, Illinois, Dec. 19, 1818. In his nineteenth

JIM BAKER

country he and a companion ran across a couple of young grizzlies one morning, when they only happened to have with them the butcher knives sticking in their belts. It was not more than a hundred yards to the camp where their guns had been left, but, as Baker said afterwards, "I lowed we could get away with the varmints with our knives, and we sailed into the fight." Baker had a hard tussle with the bear which he attacked, but finally managed to kill him.

year he started for the West and at St. Louis joined the party which James Bridger was recruiting to trap for the American Fur Company. Thenceforward the Rocky Mountains claimed him. Although Wootton characterizes him as Fremont's second-best scout, William J. Ghent, in his sketch of Baker's career in the *Dictionary of American Biography*, states that but little is known of his movements from 1844 to 1855, when he emerged as chief of scouts for General W. S. Harney at Fort Laramie. In 1857 he guided to Fort Bridger part of the Federal army dispatched against the Mormons. Passing his further activities, about 1858 he built a cabin near the site of present-day Denver, where he remained for several years. In 1873 he located permanently in the valley of Little Snake River, close to the scene of a desperate battle a third of a century earlier between a force of thirty-five trappers (of whom Baker was one) and a much larger number of Indian assailants. He died, May 15, 1898. In 1917 the Wyoming Legislature appropriated money for the removal of his cabin to Frontier Park in Cheyenne, where it was dedicated on July 23. Baker's burial place is near Savery, Wyoming. Data condensed from sketch in *Dictionary of American Biography*. For interesting additional information see General Randolph B. Marcy, *Thirty Years of Army Life on the Border* (New York, 1874), 404–11.

Just about the time this contest ended he noticed that his companion had abandoned the fight, and the second bear charged him without stopping to give him a breathing spell or waiting for time to be called. The struggle which followed between the exhausted hunter and his second antagonist was a desperate one, and poor Baker was more dead than alive when he again found himself a victor. He could barely drag himself away from the two ferocious animals that he had slain in close combat, and he never again allowed himself to be inveigled into a rough and tumble fight with a grizzly.

The closest call I ever had myself when hunting bears was not many years ago, and right here in the Raton Mountains. Bears were beginning to get scarce in the country then, and I hadn't seen one for a long time. I had boys growing up and a good many men about me who were doing different kinds of work, and every now and then some of them would come in and report that they had seen a bear. I always laughed at them and teased them more or less about their reports, because I thought if there had been any bears in the neighborhood I should have caught a glimpse of one sometime myself.

One morning I walked out with my gun on my shoulder, thinking I might see something to shoot at, and had not gone more than three or four hundred yards from my house when I came on to an old bear with two good-sized cubs. I thought to myself, "well, the boys were right, after all, and now I'll just teach them that the proper thing to do when you see a bear is to kill it." I calculated to kill the old bear and then capture the two cubs to raise as pets, just to show the travelers through the country what a live Rocky Mountain bear looked like. As I didn't often miss anything I shot at, I had every confidence in my ability to kill the bear at the first shot. For once, however, my confidence in the old rifle, which had served me so many good turns, was misplaced. A long period of idleness seemed to have impaired its usefulness. It missed fire, and the snapping of the cap made just noise enough to attract the attention of the bear. I had gotten so close that when the bear started for me I could only get out of the way by making for the nearest tree.

I reached the tree with the bear in close pursuit, and commenced to climb. It was a small pine tree, and I had grown so stout that I weighed about two hundred and forty pounds, so you can understand that I couldn't climb like a squirrel, even under favorable circumstances. The dry pine limbs that I caught hold of broke under my weight, and when I got about four or five feet from the ground, not high enough to be out of reach of the bear by any means, there I stuck. I couldn't get up, and I needn't tell you that I didn't want to come down. I expected every minute that the bear would take a mouthful of me, but I commenced hunting for a pistol that I had about me and made up my mind to kill her if she bit a leg off.

Just when I thought the biting and clawing was about to commence something frightened one of the cubs which the old bear had left behind when she started out to pay her compliments to me, and it set up that peculiar cry, which always makes one think of a child in distress. The old bear left me and ran to the cub, and then they made off together in the bushes. I didn't follow them, because I had seen enough to satisfy me that the bear had an ugly temper.

I really wanted those two cubs, but I didn't want them bad enough to try to get them that morning at the risk of another encounter with the old lady bear. I let myself down out of the tree, picked up my gun, and walked home. When they asked me what I had found that morning in the way of game, I told them nothing of consequence. I never said a word about my adventure with the bear, but some way or other the boys found out about it and for a while I had a hard time to live with them. Every once in a while they would want to know if I had seen any bears lately, and what I thought about there being any in the country.

The thieving propensities of the bears used to get them into trouble with the trappers very frequently. They would come about our camp at night and sometimes carry off meat or sugar which they found within two feet of a sleeping trapper. If the trapper happened to wake up while the burglary was being perpetrated the safest thing for him to do was to lie perfectly still and let the burglar have what he wanted, because like most other burglars the bear was ready to do some killing if it was necessary to enable him to get away with what he was after. It takes a good deal of nerve to enable a man to keep quiet when lying in camp at night with a great ugly brute snuffing about within a few feet of him, but I have done it many a time and never lost my head but once or twice.

Once I was trapping on Indian Creek, a small stream of southern Colorado, when our camp was visited one night by a grizzly. A companion named Kincaid slept under the same blanket with me that night, and about the middle of the night he awakened me out of a sound sleep by giving me a nudge in the ribs. He said something which I thought meant Indians, and pointed toward the foot of our bunk. Not two yards from our feet I saw a black object which looked to me as tall as a telegraph pole. It was a bear, sitting upon his haunches, as they do sometimes, but I took it to be an Indian and the next thing I expected was to have a tomahawk hurled at my head.

We always slept with our loaded guns at our side, in such a position that we could grab them instantly and in case of emergency shoot without getting on our feet. Without ever thinking of the thing being a bear, I raised my gun and fired. As it happened, he fell backward over a little bank and then started off through the brush in an opposite direction from our camp. I had, however, given him his death wound, and he only went a short distance before he fell over a log, and we found him there dead in the morning. If my gun had happened to miss fire or if I had wounded instead of shooting the bear fatally I should probably have had as ugly a fight as a man ever had with a mad bear, and I doubt very much whether I should be here now telling stories about my hunting adventures.

I killed another bear under similar circumstances one night with my hunting knife. I was sleeping soundly when I felt the bear's cold nose rubbed against my face. My hunting knife was in my belt and when I awakened and found the bear standing alongside of me I drew the knife and plunged it into his side up to the hilt, springing away from him so quickly that I received but a slight scratch. The knife entered his heart and he fell dead on the spot where I had been sleeping a moment before.

To train our horses to carry game, and particularly bears, into camp was a difficult thing to do. There is nothing on earth that a horse has a greater instinctive fear of than bears and you can understand how he would feel about having one of the dreaded animals thrown across his back and being compelled to carry it. Even the best broke riding horse would cut more antics than the trick pony at a circus until he got rid of a load of bear meat, if he had not been put through a previous course of training.

When we wanted to train a horse to carry this kind of a load the first thing we did was to strip off the skin of a bear and wrap the green skin about the horse's head. Of course he didn't take kindly to this performance, and made a good bit of fuss about it, but by and by he would quiet down and then he would carry any kind of a load of game we put on him.

I saw, one time when I was hunting in the mountains along Grand River, a bear which seemed to belong to a different species from those usually seen in this country. I have never seen or heard of any other animal in the mountains that looked like this one, and I have always been at a loss to know what family he belonged to. I suppose it is hardly possible that a polar bear should be found in this latitude, and yet the animal that I speak of had every appearance of a polar bear. He was of a dirty white color; would have weighed perhaps five or six hundred pounds, and was certainly the queerest looking bear I have ever seen in these parts. I shot at him and wounded him in the shoulder, but did not succeed in capturing him. It may have been that he was a grizzly who had turned pale from some cause or other, but if such a thing as finding a polar bear anywhere outside of the region of which he is a native is possible, I shall insist that I have seen one in Colorado, and he wasn't in a cage either.

The bear is the only animal I have found in the Rocky Mountain region which is at all inclined to attack a man, if there is any way of avoiding a conflict. The mountain lions, wolves, and other animals which have the reputation of being more or less fierce and bloodthirsty will only show fight when they are wounded, so that escape from the hunter is impossible, or when they are driven into a corner and compelled to defend themselves. They made the early settlers a good deal of trouble by killing their stock, but they were cowardly brutes and the hunters, trappers, and explorers had no fear of them.

Children were not so safe, and the settler never allowed his little ones to get far away from his cabin alone. I once shot a mountain lion when he was about to spring on a little child which had wandered two or three hundred yards away from home. The child was a five-year-old boy, who was playing, boy fashion, in a little stream of water, entirely unconscious of the danger he was in. I caught sight of the lion, slipping along like a cat watching a bird, on the bank of the stream. He got within ten feet of the child and was preparing to spring when I sent a bullet through him and he rolled down into the water almost at the feet of the little prattler, who would have been torn to pieces a moment later had not my shot prevented the lion from carrying out his intentions.

I never could understand why this animal should be called the mountain lion. If there is anything about him which entitles him to such distinction, I have failed to observe what it is. He doesn't look much more like the native of the African jungles, after whom he is named, than he does like a rhinoceros, nor is he like the king of beasts in any other way. He belongs to the panther family and is neither more nor less dangerous than the common run of those overgrown cats.

So many big stories have been told, however, about the ferocity of the Rocky Mountain lion that a great many people have been led to believe that he makes a business of eating people, and that to meet him in the mountains is to meet an enemy hardly less to be dreaded than the fierce inhabitant of the tropical jungles. Old hunters and mountain men know that this is all nonsense, and if they have been responsible for putting any of these wild stories into circulation they must have told the stories just to see some tenderfoot's hair stand on end.

Chapter XI

The Taos Massacre

IN the fall of 1846 and in the early part of the winter of 1847 I was in and out of the old town of Fernandez de Taos very frequently, but was fortunate in not being there at one particular time. That was when the Mexicans stirred up the rebellion which culminated in what has always been known as the Taos Massacre.[38]

In August of the year 1846 General Kearny had gone into Santa Fe with the body of troops which he had marched across the Plains from Fort Leavenworth, and had taken possession of the capital of New Mexico as well as other towns through which he had passed on his way to that point without opposition.

The Mexicans had taken the oath of allegiance to the government of the United States, and New Mexico was looked upon as a conquered and sub-

[38]For modern accounts of the insurrection see R. E. Twitchell, *The Military Occupation of New Mexico*, 1846–1851, Chap. IV; and E. Bennett Burton, "The Taos Rebellion," in *Old Santa Fe Magazine*, I,176–209 (October, 1913). The latter reference reprints Col. Sterling Price's official report of his suppression of the rebellion, dated at Santa Fe Feb. 15, 1847. An account by a participant of the trial and execution of the prisoners is contained in Lewis H. Garrard, *Wah-to-yah and the Taos Trail*, (Cincinnati, 1850).

jugated province. General Kearny then proceeded on his way to California, leaving Colonel Sterling Price with a few companies of troops at Santa Fe. Colonel A. W. Doniphan came through from Fort Leavenworth with another body of troops later, and also stopped at Santa Fe. Aside from the small force of soldiers stationed at Santa Fe and possibly small detachments at Albuquerque and one or two other places, I do not think there were any troops left in New Mexico when Kearny pushed on to the Pacific Coast.

For a time both the Mexicans and Indians professed to be very friendly, and the Americans got along well in New Mexico. By and by, however, it was noticed that a considerable number of the Mexicans were for some reason becoming dissatisfied with the condition of affairs and Colonel Price, who was in command at Santa Fe, found it necessary to keep a close watch on their movements. It was not long before he discovered that Tomas Ortiz and Diego Archuleta, two prominent Mexicans, had set on foot a plan to bring about a general uprising of the Mexicans and Pueblo Indians. They were to act in concert and at a certain time were to fall upon all the Americans and other foreigners in the Territory and either kill or drive them out of the country. The Mexicans didn't seem to have much of an idea of the size of the contract they were undertaking, and the Indians, of course, were led on entirely by the Mexicans, who promised them an easy victory and plenty of plunder.

This scheme was discovered in time to be nipped in the bud, and Archuleta and Ortiz left the country to escape punishment. There was nothing like a general uprising at that time or even after that, but a Mexican named Pablo Montoya and Tomacito, an Indian, concluded some time afterward, to go ahead with the proposed rebellion on their own account. They gathered together a considerable force of natives and marched to Taos on the night of the 18th of January, 1847.

As I have already told you, Fernandez de Taos, or Taos, as we always called it for short, was a Mexican town having a population of five or six thousand people.[39] The Pueblo de Taos was an Indian village about two miles from the town. It consisted of one large pueblo building, six or seven stories high,[40] and a church, which stood

[39]Probably this is an over-estimate. A. D. Richardson, an experienced reporter, who visited Taos in 1859, says that it was then the third city in New Mexico with a population of 2500. *Beyond the Mississippi*. . . . (Hartford, 1873), 259.

[40]There were two large pueblos, one on either side of the little stream which runs through the area. Both remain, and are occupied at the present day. They are

some little distance away, both built of adobe. I suppose there were something like a thousand Indians in the Pueblo. It was at this point that the Indians and Mexicans met to commence their march to Taos and the slaughter of the foreigners, of whom they proposed to rid the country.

There were not more than fifteen white persons, or perhaps, properly speaking, persons who had no admixture of Spanish or Indian blood in their veins, living in the town of Taos, and several of these happened to be absent from their homes on the memorable 19th of January, 1847. Those who were at home, when they got up in the morning found the town surrounded by as merciless a band of savages as ever went on the war path, and they quickly caused it to be understood that their intention was to kill every white man, woman, and child in the place.

Charles Bent, who had been appointed military governor of New Mexico by General Kearny, lived at Taos, and had come up from Santa Fe, which was, of course, his official headquarters, only a day or two before. His residence was one of the first places attacked, and he was butchered in his own doorway. James Blair, a young attorney from Missouri, who was a brother of General

clearly shown on Colonel Price's sketch map of the battle, reprinted in E. Bennett Burton's "The Taos Rebellion," in *Old Santa Fe* Magazine, I,193.

Frank P. Blair, was visiting Governor Bent at the time, and he was also killed before the murderers left the house.[41] Stephen Lee, who was acting as sheriff of the county, Pablo Armijo, prefect, and Cornelio Vigil, district attorney, were killed at about the same time by different bands of the

[41]Francis P. Blair, one of Missouri's most distinguished sons, came to St. Louis from Kentucky in 1842 to begin the practice of law with his elder brother, Montgomery. Three years of study and practice impaired his health, and he was recuperating in the Rocky Mountains when the Mexican War began. He joined a volunteer company commanded by George Bent, and upon the conquest of New Mexico by General Kearny was appointed Attorney General of the newly-organized government. In 1847, however, he returned to Missouri, where he married and remained. He served actively in public life, played a stellar role in preventing the secession of Missouri, and during the war attained the rank of Major General. From 1871 to 1873 he represented Missouri in the U.S. Senate. Present-day Blair House, opposite the White House, was successively long the home of his father, Francis P. Blair Sr., and of his brother, Montgomery.

James Blair, brother of Montgomery and Francis Preston Jr., served in the U.S. Navy and accompanied the notable Wilkes Exploring Expedition of 1838-1842 to the Antarctic and the Pacific Ocean. He was in California in the spring of 1848 and during the ensuing gold excitement profited by serving as harbor pilot for the large number of vessels arriving at San Francisco. By fortunate investments he accumulated a fortune. He died in California, December 15, 1852.

It seems evident that Wootton's narrative doubly confuses Francis P. Blair Jr. and James Blair with J. W. Leal, district attorney in the newly-organized New Mexican government, who was one of the victims in the Taos masallied conspirators.[42] The two men last named were both Mexicans, but they were loyal to the oaths which they had taken to support the laws and government of the United States and for this reason they were among the first victims of the massacre.

Several other Americans were killed, whose names I do not now remember, and the savages then turned their attention to the women and

sacre. James Blair was not an attorney, and so far as known to the Editor was never in New Mexico. Francis P. Blair Jr. was an attorney and a visitor to New Mexico but he was not killed there. Instead he lived to achieve national renown and to die, presumably in his bed, in July, 1875. Data chiefly condensed from sketches of the Blairs in the *Dictionary of American Biography*, and from information supplied by Dr. Floyd C. Shoemaker, Secretary of the State Historical Society of Missouri, in letter of Feb. 3, 1956. For a comprehensive account of the distinguished Blair family see William E. Smith, *The Francis Preston Blair Family in Politics* (New York, 1933).

[42]Those killed in the massacre at Taos on February 19, 1847 were: Governor Bent, Sheriff Stephen Lee, Circuit Attorney James W. Leal, Prefect Cornelio Vigil, Narcissa Beaubien, son of Judge Charles Beaubien, and Pablo Jaramillo, brother-in-law of Governor Bent and of Kit Carson. Wootton's list errs in naming Pablo Armijo as Prefect, and James Blair. Mrs. Bent and Mrs. Carson, sisters, were in the house along with Governor Bent but were spared by the assassins. Beaubien and Jaramillo sought refuge by hiding in a straw pile, but were discovered and were lanced to death. Lists of the victims both at Taos and elsewhere are given by H. H. Bancroft, *History of Arizona and New Mexico* (San Francisco, 1889) 432–33. See also, Edwin L. Sabin, *Kit Carson Days*, II, 558–62.

children. I do not think there was a white woman of foreign birth living in the Mexican town at the time, nor is it probable that there were any full-blood American children there. The half-breed children were, however, marked for the slaughter, and as the Mexicans and Indians all had dark complexions the color of the hair and eyes was made the test of blood.

Spanish women who were married to Americans had to disguise their children who had light hair and blue eyes, and some of those children still have a vivid recollection of having their faces and hair colored to make them look as much as possible like the natives. Those who escaped in this way were the fortunate ones, and there were comparatively few of them. A majority of the half-breeds were dispatched as summarily as Governor Bent and his friends had been. Among them, I recollect, was Narcissa Beaubien, a son of Judge Beaubien, who had lived among the Mexicans for years and befriended both them and the Indians in a thousand ways. Beaubien was a bright young fellow who had just graduated from an eastern college and proposed to make his home in the country, of which he was a native. His sympathies, however, were with the Americans, and he was not allowed to escape the fate of all those who were supposed to lean that way.

The bodies of some of those killed were horribly mutilated. All of the victims were scalped, and Governor Bent's head was cut off and carried about the town to terrify women and children and those Mexicans whom it was thought were not in full sympathy with the rebellion.

When they had made an end of the massacre at Taos these bloody butchers proceeded to Arroyo Hondo, twelve miles from Taos, where there was another American settlement, and killed everybody they could find there.[43]

Two men made their escape from that place, and one of them started for Santa Fe and the

[43]Simeon Turley had a mill and a distillery at the Arroyo Hondo, where he employed numerous Mexican workmen. With him at the time of the massacre were seven other Americans. Following a desperate defense, all of them were killed save John Albert, who, as Wootton relates, escaped to carry the news to the Americans at Pueblo. Reports are conflicting concerning the way the news of the massacres at Taos and Arroyo Hondo was carried to Colonel Price at Santa Fe. Twitchell states that it was brought by a brother of Sheriff Lee. *Military Conquest of New Mexico*, 128. H. H. Bancroft states that Price obtained news of the uprising from some captured letters sent out by leaders of the revolt appealing for assistance. *History of Arizona and New Mexico*, 443. George F. Ruxton visited the Turley Mill settlement only three days before the massacre there, and was at Pueblo when Albert brought the news of it to that place. His *Adventures in Mexico and the Rocky Mountains* (New York, 1855), 203 and 226–30 contains an account of the massacre at Arroyo Hondo substantially as it was reported by Albert upon his arrival at Pueblo.

other for Pueblo to carry the news of the slaughter to those places. The distance from Taos to Pueblo was about one hundred and sixty-five miles. Pueblo was not a town at that time, you understand. What we called "the Pueblo," stood on the site of the present town. It was an adobe fort built by the trappers which had become headquarters for a considerable number of the mountain men, and was something of a trading post. I was there at the time of the Taos massacre, and about five days later John Albert, who had managed some way or other to make his escape from Arroyo Hondo, came into the Pueblo, bringing the news of the Mexican uprising and its bloody sequel. He had traveled the whole distance on foot and was almost exhausted when he reached us.

When Albert had laid before us all the details of the tragedy our little band of trappers held a council of war to determine what we should do. The situation was as perplexing as it was distressing. The friendships of the Mountain men were warm friendships. We had never seen the time when we were not ready to attempt the rescue of a friend whose life was in danger, and it was seldom indeed that the killing or wounding of one of our number had gone unavenged. Among those who had been so brutally murdered at Taos and Arroyo Hondo were men who had been my warmest and best friends ever since I came to the country, and I felt that I should, if possible, do something toward securing punishment of their murderers and protecting the property which they had left, for the use of those who were entitled to it.

What to do, however, was the question. We should not have hesitated much about attacking an ordinary band of roving Indians, but to undertake to put down what seemed to be a formidable rebellion was, of course, out of our line. We did not know what might be going on at Santa Fe, or how long it would be before we could expect any help from the government forces, and without such assistance the small party of volunteers that we should have been able to muster could have accomplished nothing.

We parleyed over the matter awhile and reached the conclusion that there were soldiers enough at Santa Fe to put down the rebellion, and having agreed upon this point we reached the further conclusion that it was our duty to render them all the assistance possible. This determined our action, and five of us mounted our horses and started across the country toward Taos. It took us several days to make the trip, and we approached the place very carefully. We made our way into the high mountains east of Taos, and from there we could look down on the town and see pretty well what was going on without being discovered ourselves. As we could discover no sign of the arrival of the soldiers, we knew that it was not safe for us to venture farther.

In the meantime Thomas Tobin,[44] the messenger who had left Arroyo Hondo, with the news of the massacre at that place and at Taos, had reached Santa Fe, and Colonel Price had lost no time in marching against the rebels.[45] He met the first force of Mexicans and Indians at La Cañada, some distance out on the Taos road from Santa Fe, and soon had them on the run. He then sent Captain Burgwin with two companies of troops on toward Taos. Colonel Cerain St. Vrain, Gover-

[44]Save for Wootton's narrative, information that Thomas Tobin was present at the Arroyo Hondo Massacre, or that he escaped to carry the news of it to General Price, has not been found.

[45]Sterling Price was a native of Virginia who in early manhood came with his parents to Missouri, which remained his permanent home. His role in suppressing the Taos rebellion is perhaps adequately related by Wootton. For his own official report and accompanying documents see E. Bennett Burton, "The Taos Rebellion," in *Old Santa Fe* Magazine, 176–209. Upon the outbreak of the Civil War Price adhered to the Confederacy, becoming perhaps the most notable leader of the Lost Cause in the area west of the Mississippi. Upon the collapse of the Confederacy he became a voluntary exile in Mexico, but after the collapse of Maximillian's ill-starred empire he returned to Missouri, "a broken man," in 1866. He died Sept. 27, 1867. Data condensed from sketch in *Dictionary of American Biography*.

nor Bent's partner, accompanied Captain Burgwin, with about sixty volunteers, picked up in Santa Fe. At Embudo they had another skirmish with the insurgents, and did not reach Taos until the third of February.

We were watching for them, and saw them when they marched into the town. The hostiles had all gathered at the Pueblo de Taos and fortified themselves in and about the old church. The soldiers marched to the Pueblo and fired a few shots, but as night was coming on they returned to Fernandez de Taos and went into camp for the night.

The Americans were by no means certain that the entire force of the enemy had gathered at the Pueblo, but half suspected that a force was secreted in the town of Taos. Before going into camp they made a careful reconnaissance, inspecting every building in the town, to find out who was inside. Where the doors were closed they were broken down and a thorough search made of the buildings, but where they stood open it was taken as a guarantee of a friendly feeling on the part of the occupants and their residences were not disturbed.

While the soldiers were in camp that night I made my way down to where they were, along with my four companions, and joining the Santa Fe volunteers was ready for the storming of the

Pueblo, and the fight which was to commence in the morning. It commenced early, and the battle which followed was a bloody one considering the number of men engaged in it. It lasted until sundown, and I think we were resisted as stoutly as were the American soldiers upon any battle field of the Mexican War.

We soon drove our enemies out of the pueblo building proper, but their position in La Iglesia de Taos—the old church—was a strong one, and we found it difficult to dislodge them. We had three small howitzers and one six-pound cannon, but the walls of the church were so thick that the shells from the howitzers would not go through them and the solid shot from the cannon only made a round hole. As we were short of ammunition we could not afford to waste any and for that reason volunteers were called for to breach the walls with axes. This was a hazardous business, as the work had to be done while a hot fire was being kept up from the inside of the building.

Thirty-five of us, however, volunteered to make the attempt, and we gained the cover of the walls with a loss of only three or four men. It took us but a short time to accomplish what we had started out to do, and when a few shells were thrown through the holes we had made and exploded in the building they created a fearful havoc. We lighted the fuses and threw some of these shells into the church with our hands in order that they might be sure to explode at the proper time and place.

This made it altogether too hot for the besieged party, and bursting open the doors and windows they undertook to make their escape to the mountains. James Q. Quinn of Illinois, a cousin of Stephen A. Douglas, planted the American flag on the old church, but as the Mexicans were retreating they stopped long enough to shoot it down. The last stand made by the insurgents was at the old church. When they were driven out of there they fled in every direction. Of course we pursued them, and not much quarter was asked or given.[46] There was considerable hand-to-hand fighting, Colonel St. Vrain himself, I remember, engaging in a contest which in spite of the peril of the situation was amusing. The Colonel was riding along with myself and two or three others who were about to join in a pursuit of one party of fugitives when he observed an Indian whom he had seen a great many times and knew very well, lying stretched out on the ground, apparently dead. Knowing that this Indian had taken a prominent part in the massacre, Colonel St. Vrain dismounted and walked a few

[46]Colonel Price reported that 51 of these fugitives were killed, only two or three of them escaping.

feet from where we were, to see whether the red-skin was really dead or only shamming. That the latter, and not the former, was the proper diagnosis of the Indian's case, the Colonel was soon very thoroughly convinced. He had scarcely reached the side of the apparently dead Indian when the latter sprang up and, grappling with him, undertook to thrust into his body a long, steel-pointed arrow.

Both the Indian and the Colonel were large, powerful men and as each managed to keep the other from using a weapon, a wrestling-match followed the Indian's attack, which, it seemed to me, lasted several minutes before outside help terminated it in the Colonel's favor. I sprang to his assistance as soon as I saw the struggle commence, but the Indian managed to keep the Colonel between him and me, and was so active in his movements that I found it difficult to strike a lick which would be sure to hit the right head. I managed after a little, however, to deal him a blow with my tomahawk which had the effect of causing him to relax his hold upon the Colonel, and when he stretched out on the ground again there was no doubt about his being a dead Indian.[47]

[47]A widely variant account of a hand-to-hand combat between St. Vrain and an Indian in this battle is given by Twitchell in *The History of the Military Occupation of New*

We lost thirty-five men out of the comparatively small number we had engaged in this battle and among them was Captain Burgwin, who was as brave a soldier as I have ever seen on the frontier.[48] We buried him at Taos in a grave by himself, while the other thirty-four men who were killed were buried side by side in a long trench near where they fell. We never knew exactly what the Mexican and Indian loss was, but it must have been in the neighborhood of two hundred.

This battle ended the Taos rebellion, as it is generally called, although the conspirators had their plans laid to bring about a general uprising

Mexico, 300–301. According to it the man who intervened to save St. Vrain's life was Manuel Chaves, a prominent citizen of Santa Fe, who was one of the volunteers in St. Vrain's company. Whether St. Vrain engaged in two successive hand-to-hand combats, or whether both narratives relate to the same incident, it is perhaps impossible to determine.

[48]Captain John Burgwin entered West Point at the age of fifteen in 1826 and graduated with his class of 1830 five years later. For many years thereafter he served in frontier garrisons and military operations. Wounded on February 4 while "gallantly leading and skillfully directing" the desperate assault upon the church, he died three days later. Colonel Price's official report of the battle, dated at Santa Fe, February 15, stated his loss as 7 killed and 45 wounded, adding that many of the latter had since died. He estimated the Indian force at between 600 and 700, of whom about 150 were killed and an unknown number wounded.

of Mexicans and Indians in New Mexico, and they evidently thought that with this combination of forces they would be able to drive the Americans out of the territory and keep them out.

A detachment of soldiers remained at Taos after that, and the work of hunting down and punishing those who had stirred up, and been prominently connected with the insurrection commenced. Pablo Montoya and Tomacito were both captured. Tomacito, the Indian leader, was placed under guard and we proposed to give him, along with the rest, a formal trial, but a dragoon by the name of Fitzgerald saved us the trouble. Fitzgerald was allowed to go into the room where the Indian was confined, along with others who wanted to take a look at him. The soldier looked at the savage a few minutes and then quick as a flash drew a pistol and shot him in the head, killing him instantly. Fitzgerald then made his escape from the building and succeeded in getting away out of the country. If he had been caught he would, of course, have been punished. The Indian deserved to be killed and would have been hanged anyhow, but we objected to the informal manner of his taking off. Pablo Montoya was tried and hanged, and twelve others were disposed of in the same way.[49] They were all

[49]According to John T. Hughes, fourteen other rebels were executed along with Montoya. *Doniphan's Expedition,*

tried by drum-head court-martial and there was no unnecessary delay about reaching the climax of the proceedings. The twelve that I have spoken of above were hanged at the same time and dangled from the same pole. I acted as marshal in making arrests under the military authority, and was kept very busy for some days. The only law we had was military law, but that was just what we wanted, and it was not long before order was restored and the rebellion experiment has never been tried there since.

The traders who had been absent from Taos when the massacre occurred, that is, those who lived there, found, upon their return, that their stores had been sacked and burned and the most of their property destroyed, but they congratulated themselves upon having escaped with their lives and after the fashion of the pioneers set about building up other fortunes to take the place of those they had lost.

141. H. H. Bancroft states that of the prisoners conveyed by Colonel Price to Santa Fe some 15 or 20, "perhaps more," were tried by court-martial, sentenced to death, and executed. Many others were said to have been flogged and set at liberty. Apparently the culprits executed at Santa Fe were taken prisoners elsewhere than at Taos.

Chapter XII
A Trip to Old Mexico

SOON after the battle at Taos I received a letter from Colonel A. W. Doniphan, who had left Santa Fe for old Mexico with about four hundred troops, requesting me to join his command to act as guide and scout on the expedition which he was about to undertake.

I had met Colonel Doniphan at Santa Fe some time before this, and agreed to go with him into Mexico should he desire me to do so, and when I received this letter I was under obligation to obey the summons promptly. I left Taos at once on horseback, and after four days of as hard riding as a man ever did I reached his command and was assigned to duty.[50]

Doniphan had been reinforced by a detachment of troops forwarded from Santa Fe, and when I reached him he had a force of about eight

[50]It is difficult to reconcile some of Wootton's statements concerning his movements at this time. The battle of Taos occurred Feb. 3–4, 1847. Wootton's account of his role in the subsequent punishment of the rebels as described in the preceding chapter must have occupied him at Taos for several days. Yet Colonel Doniphan occupied El Paso on December 27, 1847 and after a stay of 42 days awaiting the arrival of his artillery began his farther advance from that point to Chihuahua on February 8, 1847, but four days after the battle of Taos. It is dif-

hundred men. With this force he was to march to Chihuahua to meet General Wool, who was marching toward the same point from some place lower down on the Rio Grande. We had a rough country to travel through and the position of guide was a responsible one. It was my duty to keep the commanding officer informed as to whether or not there were any enemies in front of him, to pick out the easiest and most practicable route to travel over, to find water, and select camping grounds.

Finding a sufficient supply of water for eight hundred men and the large number of horses we had with us was not always an easy matter in as dry a country as Chihuahua, but the men who followed my guidance on that march never had cause for serious complaint. Something which I can't explain, and which I think must be an instinct, has always enabled me to find water in any country where there was any water to be found.

Every night when we went into camp I was able to give Colonel Doniphan correct information as to the character of the country over which we were to pass next day, and in the morn-

ficult to see how Wootton could have joined the army at El Paso, even if he had left Taos the day after the battle. Since he remained with the command until the battle of Sacramento on February 28, his nine-day return ride to Albuquerque, as described *post* 176–79, must have occupied the period of March 1 to March 9.

ing I again went ahead to learn the lay of the land beyond the place which was to be our next camping ground. I always had with me a detail of ten or fifteen men, so that if we should have come upon any hostiles I would not have been entirely without support and assistance.

We had rather a limited supply of provisions to start out with and before we had gone very far we had to draw on the resources of the country. The wild game which we found, particularly wild turkeys, helped out a little, but there wasn't enough of it and ammunition was too scarce to be wasted getting it anyhow. There were large bands of wild cattle roaming over the hills and mesas, however, and whenever we wanted a supply of meat we rounded up a lot of these cattle and butchered them.

When we first commenced killing the cattle it was thought advisable to lasso, instead of shooting them, as some amunition would be saved thereby. The experiment was tried by the soldiers with varying degrees of success and upon the whole was by no means satisfactory. Lassoing wild cattle was a new business to most of them, and they had some very amusing experiences. That is, it was amusing to those who looked on, although there was nothing funny about it for the participants. They had practiced throwing the lariat more or less and did not, as a rule, have much difficulty in catching a steer when they started after him. It was right there, however, that the trouble began. At first the soldier always thought he had the steer, but before much time had elapsed he usually learned that the steer had him.

Being able to lasso an animal of that kind is one thing, and knowing how to land him on his back, instead of being landed on your own back and perhaps seriously hurt, is quite another. The soldier cowboys made this discovery, and soon abandoned the plan of catching the beef cattle for the more practical scheme of riding into a herd and shooting as many as it was necessary to kill to supply the demand for fresh meat.

Colonel Doniphan's march toward Chihuahua was unobstructed by the appearance of an enemy until we reached the Rio Sacramento. The road to Chihuahua crossed the Sacramento River at the Rancho Sacramento, a fine old Mexican hacienda, which belonged to Angel Trias, the governor of Chihuahua. This house and the adjoining corrals had been converted into a fortress, and was occupied by General Heredia with a force of about four thousand Mexican soldiers.

A strong body of horsemen was sent out to meet Colonel Doniphan, but two or three volleys fired by our artillery sent them scurrying back to the rancho, where they soon got under cover of their fortifications. Their position was one which gave them a great advantage, but after about three hours fighting they were driven out of the fortress and Colonel Doniphan and his troops entered the rancho, having gained their first victory on the soil of old Mexico.[51]

Colonel Doniphan remained here some days before pushing on towards Chihuahua, the capital then, as it is now, of the state of the same name, which he captured a little later.[52] Just before he

[51]For a contemporary account of Doniphan's campaign to Chihuahua see John T. Hughes, *Doniphan's Expedition. Containing an Account of the Conquest of New Mexico*, (Cincinnati, 1848). For modern accounts see Ralph E. Twitchell, *Leading Facts of New Mexican History*, Vol. II (Cedar Rapids, 1912), pp. 215–28; and the same author's *The History of the Military Occupation of the Territory of New Mexico 1846 to 1851* (Denver, 1909), Chap. III. Although the battle of Sacramento, fought February 28, 1848, was Doniphan's major encounter, it was not the only one. On Christmas Day, 1847, at the Brazito River, a short distance below Las Cruces, New Mexico he defeated a force of over 1,000 Mexicans. Their army in the battle of Sacramento numbered some 4,000, carefully posted in a chosen position. Accounts of the losses in these two battles seem almost incredible. At the Brazito the American loss was 8 wounded, none killed: the Mexican loss was 71 killed and "not less" than 150 wounded. At the battle of Sacramento the Mexican loss was 304 killed and "perhaps not less than 500" wounded: the American loss was 1 killed and 11 wounded (at least 3 of whom subsequently died of their wounds).

[52]This is an error. The battle of Sacramento was fought on February 28, 1847, and on the following day, March 1, Chihuahua was occupied.

started for Chihuahua, which was only eighteen miles distant, he sent for me and wanted to know if I was willing to undertake to carry some dispatches back to Santa Fe.

I told him I should like to see the famous city of Chihuahua, but if he wished me to return to Santa Fe I would make the attempt. He asked me how many men I wanted to accompany me and I told him I thought I could take care of myself, but wasn't sure that I could take care of anybody else. For that reason I thought I had best go alone. If I met any enemies fighting them would be out of the question, and it would be easier for one man to get through the country unobserved than it would be for a party of men to do the same thing. I was allowed to have my own way about the matter and I made the trip to Albuquerque, where some of the government troops were stationed, in nine days.

I had to carry horse feed and a supply of provisions for myself, and that made it necessary for me to have two horses. My stock of provisions consisted of some hard-tack and dried meat and I had to lay in enough of it to last me until I reached Albuquerque, as there was no prospect of my meeting any friends on the way.

What I wanted was to get through without seeing anybody, or rather without having anybody see me. To do this I knew that I should not only have to keep in the mountains as much as possible, but travel by a different route from that over which I had led Colonel Doniphan's regiment. The hostiles—and all the natives were supposed to be more or less hostile—had discovered, of course, after we passed over the ground, what our line of march had been, and they would very naturally be on the lookout for other parties coming the same way, or messengers returning with news from the front.

Loading my traps and provisions on one of the horses and pocketing my dispatches, which, of course, were in sealed packages, so that I don't know to this day the nature of the information I carried, I mounted the other horse and set out. I think I managed to keep out of sight of everything in the shape of a human being during the entire trip. Now and then when I looked down into the valleys from the mountains I would see either Mexicans or Indians, but I never allowed them to catch sight of me. I never once kindled a fire or even lighted my pipe. I refrained entirely from shooting at game or making any noise which would attract attention. Whenever I saw an open space ahead of me I spent a good deal of time looking over the ground from some secure place before I ventured out from under cover. I traveled much of the time after dark and had no such thing as a night's sleep on the trip. Now and then, at very irregular intervals, when I reached what seemed to be a very safe place I lay down and took a few hours rest, and I slept a little as I rode along. I was almost worn out when I came within sight of Albuquerque, which was along towards sun down of the ninth day that I had been riding.

There I encountered a difficulty entirely unlooked for and unexpected. The Rio Grande had risen and was flooding the country, so that when I reached it, it looked to me as wide as the Mississippi when it reaches high water mark. This stream is noted for its treacherous quicksands, and fording it at that point is always more or less dangerous. I had to cross it someway, however, and I prepared to wade and swim until I reached the opposite bank on which the troops were encamped.

I don't think I ever had a more trying experience than I had, in my exhausted condition, getting across that stream. Several times I sank in the quicksands, but floundered about until some way or other, I don't know just how, I made my way out. Then the sentinel on the bank challenged me, for it was dark by this time, and wanted me to give the countersign. I was down under the bank so that he couldn't see me, and of course he wouldn't have known anything about who I was if he had seen me.

It was his business to demand the countersign, but I had no means of knowing what it was, and being cold, wet, hungry, and exhausted I didn't want to be kept waiting for any red tape proceedings.

The sentry's peremptory "Halt!" and his demand for the countersign while I was still knee-deep in the ice-cold river water put me out of humor, and I yelled back, "Countersign be damned. I am an American, with dispatches from Colonel Doniphan, and I want to get out of this water." This appeal did not have the desired effect. He kept me where I was until the officer-of-the-day came out and admitted me inside the lines in due form. That night I ate the first square meal and got the first night's rest I had had in almost a fortnight.

The next day I went on to Santa Fe, delivered my package, and ended my mission as a bearer of military dispatches. I was anxious then to get on to Taos which I had decided to make my headquarters, as I had established a business there and it had begun to seem more like home to me than any other place. I learned at Santa Fe that both the Ute and Apache Indians had gone on the war-path in my absence, and that bands of the hostiles were somewhere between Santa Fe and Taos.

This was no very pleasant news and I hesitated about trying to get home, but finally concluded to make the attempt. I knew the country so well that there was no necessity for my following the established trail in order to avoid getting lost. I was careful to keep away from it when I got a few miles out of Santa Fe and it was to this precaution that I probably owed my safe arrival in Taos, as a party which attempted to follow the trail across, the next day, fell into the hands of the Apaches and several persons were killed. I did not see one of the hostile Indians on the way, although I passed close to a large band of Utes when I crossed the Rio Grande twelve miles below Taos. I had to swim the river at that point, and the Indians must have been in hiding very near there at the time. Three companies of soldiers were sent out against them only a day or two later from Taos and at about the point where I crossed the river they were ambushed by the Indians and badly defeated, thirty-five or forty men being killed.[53] The officer who commanded this expedition had requested me to go with him as guide, and had I not been so much in need of rest I would have done so.

[53]Here also Wootton's chronology is confused. He reached Santa Fe on or about March 10. The ride from there to Taos can hardly have consumed more than two or three days. The defeat of the three companies of soldiers near Taos can hardly have escaped reporting. The only affair which it seems possible to identify with Wootton's account was an attack by some 200 Mexicans and Pueblo

I remained at Taos the greater part of the time for several years after my trip to old Mexico, and was there when General, then Colonel, Fremont made his way into the town after he and his little band of explorers had come so near freezing to death in the Uncompahgre Mountains in the winter of 1848–49.

Fremont, who was then on an exploring expedition, was on his way to California and had with him as guide Old Bill Williams, one of the best-known of the mountain men, who had been famous for years as a hunter and trapper.

Williams knew every pass in the mountains and almost every foot of the Rocky Mountain country, and if General Fremont had taken his advice he would never have run into the death-trap which cost him the lives of three men, and in which he lost all his valuable papers, his instruments, and the animals which he and his men were riding.[54]

They had followed the Arkansas River to its source, and General Fremont had picked out the

Indians on July 9, 1847 upon a detachment of 31 Americans on the Cienaga about eighteen miles from Taos. Five of the little detachment were killed and nine wounded, yet the survivors defended themselves until they were rescued by Captain Shepherd's company. See John T. Hughes, *Doniphan's Expedition*, 143.

[54]An understatement. Fremont "entered the mountains with 33 men, Old Bill, the guide, and over 100 mules, in the last of November; in the middle of December he was

route which he wanted to travel over in crossing the mountains. Williams told him that it was not practicable to cross the range by the route which he had selected, in the winter season, but the great "Pathfinder" listened to an inexperienced member of the party who volunteered to pilot him over.

Before they had fairly gotten started they were caught in a terrific snow storm in which all their horses and mules were frozen to death. Then they turned back and undertook to make their way down the mountain, leaving all their accoutrements behind and carrying with them but a small stock of provisions. The snow storm continued, and even Old Bill Williams could not keep them from getting lost. They wandered about for several days before they finally found their way into Taos, in great distress from hunger and fatigue.

Three of the eighteen men who composed the party that started into the mountains had frozen to death on their way down, and the others were little better than dead men when I happened to run across them, and brought them into town. I took Fremont to the home of Kit Carson, who

stalled by the snow, 12,000 feet up in the divide. He was forced back, with casualties of eleven men frozen to death and starved to death, others crippled, the loss of all his animals and practically all his baggage." E. L. Sabin, *Kit Carson Days*, II, 614.

then lived at Taos, and the other members of the party were at once fed and cared for at other places.

After resting for some days General Fremont decided to again push on toward California, but not until three of the most noted mountain men in the country at that time had consented to accompany him as guides. These were, Kit Carson, Lucien B. Maxwell, who afterward became owner of the famous Maxwell land grant, and Dick Owens.[55] Five members of his original party concluded they had had enough of the exploring expedition and declined to start out with the General, when he got ready to leave Taos, but he had no difficulty in finding others to take their places.

Before starting, he arranged with me to go into the mountains, when the spring opened, and bring down his instruments, papers, and such other things as he had left behind when caught in the fatal snow-storm. After he had gone away, however, the five former members of the party who had remained behind laid claim to all the

[55]Carson did not accompany Fremont on this journey. See Sabin, *Kit Carson Days*, Vol. II, 615–16. Fremont himself says, in his notes of the journey from Taos to California: "engage a New Mexican for guide." Allan Nevins, *Fremont, Pathfinder of the West* (New York, 1955), p. 370. It is plain that he would not have alluded to Carson in this manner.

valuables which I had been promised as compensation for making the trip, and I came to the conclusion that they might go after the stuff themselves. They started out, and again took Bill Williams as guide. They found their way into the mountains all right, found the saddles, instruments, and accoutrements of all kinds where they had left them, and commenced the return trip, but they never reached Taos.

Coming back, they passed a Ute village and not knowing that this particular band of Indians was on the war-path and had just been soundly whipped by a party of soldiers they went into camp within half a mile of the savages. At daybreak on the following morning the Indians attacked them, and every member of the party was killed. Not even poor Old Bill Williams, who had been among the Utes for years, could speak their language, and knew a great many of them personally, escaped.

That was the last trip made by the old mountaineer, who was known to everybody in the country fifty years ago and who figured more or less in nearly all the old-time stories written and told of the mountain men and their adventures. He was a queer character. I never knew where he came from or how long he had been in the country, although I have sat by the same camp-fire with him a hundred times. All I ever knew was that he had been a circuit preacher in early life in Missouri and had been in the mountains longer than any of the other trappers. He had been so much among the Indians that he used to look and talk like an Indian, and had imbibed a great many of their superstitions and peculiar notions.

Among other things he had picked up from them was a belief in the transmigration of souls. He had pondered over this matter and dreamed over it until he had reached a conclusion as to the kind of animal he was to become when he ceased to be a man.

One night when there were a dozen or more of us together in camp—that was when he was growing quite old—he told us, with as great an air of solemnity as though he had been preaching his own funeral, that when he ceased to be Bill Williams he was to become a buck elk and would make his home in the very neighborhood where we were then encamped. He had pictured out, in his own mind, what kind of a looking elk he would be, and he described to us certain peculiarities which he would have, which would enable us to distinguish him from other elks, and cautioned us not to shoot an elk of that description, should we ever run across one after his death. Poor old fellow! He was a warm-hearted, brave, and generous man, and in whatever state he continues his existence I hope he is happy.[56]

[56]Bill Williams (Old Bill, William S. Williams) was perhaps the most picturesque character of his era. Both the place of his birth and the manner of his death are uncertain, along with much else that concerned him between these terminal events. He himself claimed to have been an itinerant Methodist preacher in Missouri before resorting to trapping, so well known that upon his approach to a farm house even the chickens would cackle "that is Preacher Williams; one of us must prepare to die." Although he was shrewd and capable in many ways, his eccentricities were extraordinary. For details of his mountain career see *Dictionary of American Biography* and Edwin L. Sabin, *Kit Carson Days, 1809–1868* (New York, 1935), I, 200–202. Concerning the manner of his death in the spring of 1849 see the variant accounts summarized by Sabin, *ibid*, II, 924–25. His name is commemorated in Bill Williams Mountain, Bill Williams Fork of the Colorado, Williams River and Williams Mountains in Colorado's Middle Park, and Williams Station, Arizona.

CHAPTER XIII

A Stage Coach Massacre

IN 1847 the Utes fell out with the Mexicans and from that time on for several years they were at war more or less of the time with everybody. They robbed and murdered the Mexicans, killed a trapper or hunter every now and then, fought with the other Indian tribes, and kept up a general commotion in northern New Mexico and southern Colorado.

I made peace with them at different times and traded with them more or less, but they robbed me just the same as anybody else when they got a good chance, and some of their robberies were very extensive. I had taken a contract to furnish beef for the troops stationed at Taos, and had to go a long distance away from there sometimes to get cattle. On every one of these trips I ran the risk of having my stock captured and driven off by the hostiles. I had cattle of my own in the Arkansas Valley and one time when my men were driving a hundred head of fine beef steers from the Arkansas over to Taos the Utes met them at Clifton, now a station on the Santa Fe Railroad in northern New Mexico. The Indians wanted the cattle and they took them without asking anybody's permission, leaving me to

187

pocket a loss of not less than five thousand dollars.

It was not long after this that a horrible massacre in the same section of country, and not very far distant, attracted general attention and compelled the military authorities to take some action which would look like an effort to suppress the savages.

The Santa Fe stage was on its way from Independence, Missouri, to Santa Fe, loaded as usual with passengers. Among the passengers was a Mr. White, a wealthy farmer of Jackson County, Missouri, who was accompanied by his wife, a small child, and a colored nurse. They were on their way to Santa Fe to visit friends, as were also two prominent citizens and business men of western Missouri by the name of McCoy.

I do not now remember the names of the other stage passengers, but including the stage driver and conductor and the two men with the baggage-wagon, which followed the stage, there were fifteen persons in the party. When the stage reached Whetstone Springs in northeastern New Mexico, the head of the little stream called Whetstone River, it had to pass for some distance through a narrow defile, on either side of which were high, overhanging rocks.

The Utes, knowing it was about time for the stage to come along, hid themselves on these rocks and the first knowledge the travelers had of the ambuscade was when they heard the crack of rifles and saw the mules behind which they were riding fall dead in the harness. That, of course, brought the stage and baggage-wagon to a stop, and the massacre of the entire party was an easy matter. Not one of them escaped from the merciless savages, and it was not until the failure of the stage to arrive on time at the next station occasioned alarm and a party was sent out to learn the cause of the delay that anybody knew what had happened.

Inquiry at the last station which had been passed by the stage furnished full information as to the number of persons in the party when it left that place, and at the scene of the massacre the bodies of all of them, with the exception of Mrs. White, the child, and its colored nurse, were found.

The horribly mutilated remains of the victims were gathered up and buried in one grave on a bluff overlooking the place where their lives had been so suddenly and unexpectedly cut short. Then the news of the killing and as much as could be learned of the circumstances in connection with it were sent to Taos, where several companies of troops were stationed under the command of Major Grier.

As the bodies of Mrs. White, the child, and its nurse were not found among the others it was evident that these three persons had been carried away by the Indians, and Major Grier was appealed to, to undertake to rescue them and punish the red murderers at the same time. It was more than two weeks after the massacre, which occurred early in January, before the news reached Taos, and two or three days later before the soldiers got ready to go in pursuit of the Indians.[57]

As was always the case when an expedition of this kind was planned, the services of the mountain men were in demand. Kit Carson, Antoine Leroux, Tom Tobin, and myself, along with several others who had been in the country a long time and who had had a good deal of experience in Indian fighting, volunteered to go with Major Grier.

It was midwinter, the snow being a foot deep or more on the ground, and it was intensely cold. We knew that the trip would be a hard one, but that was not to be taken into consideration when women and children were to be saved from the miserable fate which we knew always awaited them when they had been carried away by these savages.

[57]News of the massacre reached Taos on October 29, 1849. Since the site, Point of Rocks, was some 160 miles distant, the outrage must have been perpetrated at least several days earlier. Several days elapsed before Major Grier's rescue party set out from Taos. See E. L. Sabin, *Kit Carson Days*, II, 618–19.

KIT CARSON

We started out with five companies of cavalry and went direct to Whetstone Springs, because we had no knowledge of the whereabouts of the Indians at that time, and could only gain that information by striking and following their trail. That we should have expected to be able to follow a trail nearly three weeks old will seem somewhat strange to persons who have never had any experience in that kind of business, but that was one of the things which a mountain man had to learn. When we struck a trail and had followed it for a little distance we could always tell about how much time had elapsed since it was made.

Where we could discover the footprints, of course, it was easy to tell what kind of track it was, and in which way the person or animal making it was traveling. We could tell the difference between the track of an Indian and that of a white hunter because, although both always wore moccasins, the moccasins differed in shape. In the same way we could pretty generally distinguish the tracks made by Indians of one tribe from those made by Indians of another tribe. Here and there, too, they would always drop an arrow—because only a small proportion of them had guns—and we could tell from the marks on these arrows what tribe the Indian belonged to who lost it. No two tribes made and marked their arrows exactly alike, and I used to hear the Indians say that each individual Indian could identify his own arrows, among those picked up on a battlefield.

In following a trail where there were no well defined footprints, by looking ahead of us we could discover now and then a stone rolled out of place, a bush or twig broken off, or the grass bent over, and this indicated to us the direction taken by whatever we were following.

The fact that considerable snow had fallen after the Utes left Whetstone Springs made following their trail unusually difficult. It happened, however, that there was no snow of consequence about the Springs and this enabled us to see which way the Indians had started out. It was evident that they had gone down the cañon of the Canadian River, or Red River as it is sometimes called at this point, and we followed them in that direction. Striking the Canadian River proper, farther down, we traced them down the stream until we had traveled nearly four hundred miles.

I began to think then that we were getting close to the redskins. There was nothing about the trail to indicate this, and I suspect nobody but mountain men, or those who had had similar experiences, would have reached that conclusion.

It was the flight of the ravens which led me to believe that we were nearing the hostiles, of whom we were in pursuit. The direction of their flight indicated the location of a camp where they could find the carcasses of dead animals to feed on, and the time of their flight in the afternoon indicated the distance of the camp from us. When they passed over us we calculated about how far they would fly before nightfall, and my conclusions were that the Utes were not more than a day's march distant from where we had gone into camp for the night.

We did not reach them the next day, but early on the morning following we came in sight of two Indians driving up a band of horses. Then we knew that we must be very near their village, and soon located it in a grove of large cottonwood trees, on the banks of the river. The Indians had not seen us, and we prepared to give them a surprise. We dismounted, and stripping off our overcoats tied them behind our saddles and put everything in readiness for a fight.

The plan of attack which Major Grier had decided upon was to charge into the village, giving the Indians no time either to mount their horses and escape or to obtain any vantage ground from which to fight.

The order to advance was given, and we started on a double quick toward the village. When we had gotten within two hundred yards of it and could see the startled and surprised Indians dodging about among their lodges one of the strangest ideas that ever entered the head of a commanding officer who was about to engage an Indian or any other enemy suggested itself to Major Grier.[58]

What occurred to him was that there should be a parley before there was a fight, and he ordered a halt for that purpose. A storm of protests, coming not only from the little band of mountain men, who saw before them an opportunity to practically annihilate the murderous band of Utes, but from the subordinate officers of the command, as well, greeted this remarkable order. Kit Carson swore and Antoine Leroux, whose French blood was up, railed at the Major in broken English and for a moment it looked as though the battle would open with mutiny in our own ranks.[59]

[58]Major William N. Grier of the First U. S. Dragoons, a West Point graduate in the Class of 1835. He retired from the army in 1870 with the rank of colonel, having been brevetted brigadier general for faithful and meritorious service during the Civil War. It is interesting to note that Governor William Henry Harrison of Indiana Territory, who in November, 1811 led an army against the force of Tecumseh, culminating in the battle of Tippecanoe, made the same mistake as Major Grier, in halting his army for a parley. Thereby he afforded the Indians the initiative of making a surprise assault upon his camp at dawn the following morning.

[59]Antoine Leroux was a veteran mountain man, whose skill and experience as guide and scout rivalled the attainments of Kit Carson in these respects. In 1846–47 he

A delay of ten or fifteen minutes followed, and while the soft-hearted Major was trying to convince his subordinates that his course was a proper one a bullet struck him in the breast, but, as it happened, a suspender buckle changed its course and he was not seriously wounded.

When the Indians opened fire on us, without waiting for any further orders and disregarding the one which had been issued, the troops dashed forward to complete the charge which had been so unexpectedly checked. That little delay had, however, been fatal to our plan of capturing or annihilating the band of Indians, and also to the prime object of our expedition, the rescue of Mrs. White.

served as guide to Colonel Philip St. George Cooke, who led the storied Mormon Battalion from Santa Fe to California. In April, 1852 John Russell Bartlett, then engaged as U. S. Commissioner conducting the survey to fix the boundary between the United States and Mexico, encountered Leroux at San Diego and engaged him to guide his party back to New Mexico. See Bartlett's *Personal Narrative*, II, 85–86. Sabin affirms that Leroux had chief command of the scouts accompanying Major Grier's expedition, and that it was by his advice that Grier delayed the assault upon the Indians, thereby affording them time to kill Mrs. White. *Kit Carson Days*, II, 619–20. Wootton's recital impliedly negatives this statement. Carson's subsequent *Autobiography*, the Lakeside Classics volume for 1935, states that he was afterwards informed that Leroux had advised the halt for a parley, and comments bitterly upon the failure to rescue Mrs. White and her child. See pp. 133–34.

It had given the Indians time to hide their women and children, to mount their horses and gallop down the cañon or up the steep hill-sides into retreats to which we could not follow them, and worst of all it had given them time to murder poor Mrs. White when those who sought to rescue her were within hailing distance.

When we rode into the village, which was almost deserted, we found her body still warm and drew from her breast three arrows which had pierced her heart. Had the charge been made as originally contemplated the savages would have had no time for this last act of fiendishness and we should have saved the life of an estimable woman. Some of us would most likely have been killed, to be sure, but we were there to fight and to take the chances on losing our lives.[60]

[60]James M. White was a merchant of Independence and Santa Fe who for some years had been engaged in the Santa Fe trade. In October, 1849 he undertook a journey to Santa Fe, accompanied by his wife and ten-year-old daughter, and traveling with the caravan of Francis X. Aubrey, a well-known Santa Fe trader, until a point supposed to be beyond danger of Indian attack had been reached. Here White hurried on in advance of the train, accompanied by only a few men, and the slaughter described by Wootton followed. For another first-hand account of the affair and the death of Mrs. White see *Kit Carson's Autobiography*, the Lakeside Classics volume for 1935, pp. 131–34. Carson agrees fully with Wootton that but for the unfortunate decision of Major Grier to hold a parley, Mrs. White might have been rescued. He adds,

What became of the child and its nurse we never knew. We could find no trace of them in the Indian village, nor did we discover anything to indicate that they had been killed while on the road to this point, or carried away by the Indians in their hasty flight. While the mistake which we had made, or rather which our commanding officer had made, proved so serious a blunder, it did not enable all the Indians to escape. Some of them undertook to cross the Canadian River on the ice and these were nearly all killed. Other small parties and stragglers met the same fate, so that altogether eighty or eighty-five

however, the reflection that because of the terrible mistreatment to which she had been subjected her death was a mercy to her.

Chief Lobo Blanco, or White Wolf, leader of the marauding Apaches, himself met a fitting end. In March, 1854, Lieutenant David Bell's dragoon company of 30 men, while conducting a scout from Fort Union, came upon about an equal number of Apaches led by White Wolf. A parley between the two leaders followed, both Bell and White Wolf advancing to a point midway between the two hostile lines. At length the two leaders engaged in an impromptu duel from which Bell escaped unscathed. The dragoons immediately charged, riding over the Indian line, and for good measure turning and again riding over the Indians, many of whom had thrown themselves upon the ground. Those who survived fled to a near-by deep ravine. As for White Wolf, he had been shot several times; his existence was finally terminated by a soldier who crushed his head with a great rock. E. L. Sabin, *Kit Carson Days*, II, 622; Inman, *The Old Santa Fe Trail*, 166–68.

Indians were killed in the fight. A pursuit of the scattered survivors of the band would have been unavailing and after the fight was over we turned back, and returned by way of old Fort Union to Taos.[61]

Not long after I returned from this expedition I was called upon to act as guide to a company of soldiers sent out from Taos to rescue a party, of which L. B. Maxwell was the most prominent member.[62]

Maxwell had left Taos two or three weeks earlier, going up the Rio Grande to gather up a band of horses for government service. He had succeeded in getting something like a hundred horses and was on his way back to Taos when he

[61]Kit Carson (*Autobiography*, 135) states that the Indians were pursued for six miles on a level prairie. All of their baggage was captured, along with some of their horses, and two or three children. One Indian was killed. In the camps, also, was found a book, "the first of the kind I had ever seen, in which I was represented as a great hero, slaying Indians by the hundreds. I have often thought Mrs. White must have read it, and knowing that I lived near-by, must have prayed for my appearance in order that she might be saved." Thus dramatically the real Carson encountered the popular hero of the paperbacks.

[62]Wootton's old-age memory here confuses the sequence of events. The rescue of Maxwell's party, related in the following pages, occurred in March, 1848. The slaughter of the White party took place in October, 1849.

Lucien B. Maxwell was a native of Kaskaskia, Illinois and a grandson of Pierre Menard, a notable citizen of early nineteenth-century Illinois. In early manhood he struck the trail of a large band of Utes. To avoid this band, he turned down the Arkansas River and went one hundred and fifty miles out of his way, intending to go over the mountains and come into Taos from the east. Whether the same band of Utes that he had seen turned back and followed him or whether it was another band which attacked him is uncertain, but when he was within two or three days' ride of Taos he had one of the bloodiest battles with these Indians that any of the mountain men ever had.

There were twelve men in the party, including Maxwell himself, and they had with them two children, whom he was taking from one of the upper Rio Grande settlements to their friends in Taos. While they were taking their breakfast in camp one morning, the Indians suddenly made their appearance and in less time than it takes to tell it had stampeded and driven off their horses.

followed the Santa Fe Trail to Taos and became a permanent resident of New Mexico. He was a hunter for Fremont on the latter's first western expedition (1842), which Kit Carson served as guide. He also was a member of Fremont's third expedition to California in 1845–46. In 1842 he had married a daughter of Charles Beaubien, co-owner of the vast Beaubien-Miranda land grant, and most of his remaining career was devoted to the affairs of this estate. In 1864 Beaubien died and Maxwell, by purchasing the interests of the other heirs, became sole owner of the huge Maxwell Grant. He sold it in 1871 and died in 1875, his later years clouded by financial adversity. See *Dictionary of American Biography.*

While a portion of the band was stealing the horses, thirty or forty mounted warriors rode up and fired on Maxwell and his party, killing one and mortally wounding another of his men. It happened that there was a small grove of trees not far from their camp, and hurriedly getting under cover of these trees they determined to fight as long as there was a man of them left.

In that position they defended themselves against the whole band of redskins until the latter tired of the fight and withdrew. Then they found themselves in a sorry plight. All but two of them had been wounded, some very seriously. They had no horses, and were a long way, not only from home, but from any white settlement. They could not stay where they were, however, and that night they set out under cover of the darkness to walk to Taos. Traveling in this way by night and hiding in daylight, without food and suffering at the same time from hunger and numerous festering wounds, they reached the point where we met them about thirty miles east of Taos.

We had heard through a friendly Arapahoe Indian of their fight with the Utes and knew that they were making their way toward home under great difficulties, but we had not expected to find them in so pitiable a condition as they were. Some had lost nearly all their clothing in crawling through the thick growths of underbrush, all had been so much weakened by starvation that they could scarcely stand on their feet, and their undressed wounds were in a fearful condition.

They had almost given up the struggle to reach home when we found them, and several of those who were most seriously wounded were begging their more fortunate comrades to leave them to die where they were, and take care of themselves. I shall never forget how the tears ran down the cheeks of those poor fellows when they caught sight of us and realized that they were saved, just when they were about to give up all hope. We dressed their wounds as well as we could and carried them into Taos, where with careful nursing they all recovered in time.

The two children fell into the hands of the Utes and were carried away. We got track of them, however, not long afterward and the Indians made a proposition to return them for a certain consideration. This was their usual custom when they made a raid on the early settlers. Small children, if there were not too many of them, were usually taken prisoners. If the friends of the children could not be persuaded to ransom them the little ones would sometimes grow up with the savages, and soon forgetting all about their early associations they became as wild as the Indian children themselves.

The two children of whom I have spoken were promptly returned, however, when we counted out and paid to the Ute chief by whom they were held two hundred and fifty Mexican dollars.[63]

[63]Several material errors in Wootton's account of the White family massacre should be noted. Instead of the Utes, a band of Jicarilla Apaches perpetrated the massacre. Instead of traveling west by stage coach, White had accompanied in his own conveyance the overland caravan of Francis X. Aubrey. See *ante,* 196. Escorted by only a few men he had hurried on in advance of the caravan, to be waylaid and the party slaughtered (save for Mrs. White and the little girl) much as Wootton has described. A report of the massacre was received at Taos, 160 miles distant, on Oct. 29. Instead of midwinter, therefore, it occurred in late October, perhaps a week or so before the 29th. The rescuing expedition was conducted in early November, the attack upon the Indians being made on November 17. However, there had been some snowfall prior to this date, and upon the return march to Taos the soldiers were overtaken by the worst storm Kit Carson ever experienced. See E. L. Sabin, *Kit Carson Days,* II, 618–22, and Carson's account in his *Autobiography,* 131–36.

Chapter XIV

A Campaign Against the Navahoes

THE Utes were not the only Indians to give us trouble at that time. We had hardly gotten back from our campaign against them when there was a demand for the services of the soldiers in another quarter.

The Navahoes, as I have said, were the most industrious of all the Indian tribes. At the same time, I suppose I should have said that they were the greatest lot of thieves among the Indians. They had gotten an idea of stock-raising and as their flocks and herds did not grow fast enough to suit them they added to the number of their horses, cattle, and sheep by stealing what they wanted from the Mexicans. Like almost every other band of robbers, they committed other depredations and outrages in addition to stealing. They had not only taken a great many horses and sheep from the Mexicans, but had been guilty of some very atrocious murders and had carried away several Mexican women and children as prisoners.

General Kearny had promised the Mexicans, in the name of the government of the United States, that they should be protected against the hostile Indians, and when an appeal for that protection came from those who were loyal it had to be given the same attention that would have been given to the same request coming from Americans.

Colonel Newby was then at Santa Fe with a small force of soldiers and he left there in March of 1848 with six companies to whip the Navahoes into better behavior, three of the companies, under command of Major Runnells,[64] having been sent from Taos to join the expedition. I joined that expedition as a guide, and put in about four months more in the service of the government.[65]

[64]No officer bearing the name of Runnells is listed in Heitman's *Register and Dictionary of the United States Army*. John T. Hughes, *Doniphan's Expedition*, 144, names a Major Reynolds as one among a number of Missouri Volunteer officers who left Leavenworth for Santa Fe in August, 1847. Apparently he was the officer to whom Wootton ascribes the name of "Runnells."

[65]Efforts to elucidate the facts concerning this campaign have proved largely futile. Colonel Edward W. B. Newby of the First Illinois Regiment relieved Colonel Sterling Price in the command of Santa Fe in mid-summer 1847. The campaign against the Navahoes in which Wootton says he participated as guide was waged the following year. It is disposed of by Twitchell in a single sentence. *Leading Facts of New Mexican History*, II, 263. Farish (*History of Arizona*, I, 306–307) likewise devotes a single sentence to the campaign. Twitchell's *History of the Military Conquest of New Mexico from 1846 to 1851* does not mention it. Wootton states that the expedition started from Santa Fe in March, 1848. Yet *ante*, pp. 200–202 he relates his role in rescuing the Maxwell party, which occurred in March, 1848. Heitman's *Dictionary of the Officers of the U. S. Army* lists Newby as colonel of the Regiment

We crossed the Rio Grande at San Felipe and from there marched to Jemez. Then we proceeded in a southwesterly direction, striking the Rio Puerco and crossing over into Arizona. It was while we were going down the Rio Puerco, which by the way means dirty river, and it is well named, that I saw for the second time those famous old ruins of stone buildings which I think are marked on the map as Ruins Leroux.

Leroux was the Frenchman of whom I have spoken in connection with our campaign against the Utes. He accompanied us on this expedition and I suppose must have gotten credit for having discovered these remarkable ruins and had them named after him, although they had been seen by hundreds of white men long before that time.[66]

June 8, 1847 and mustered out of service Oct. 16, 1848. Obviously the Navahoe campaign must have been conducted earlier this year, as Wootton states. Professor Frank D. Reeve of the University of New Mexico, Editor of the *New Mexico Historial Review*, states, in answer to a letter of inquiry, that "that particular military action has never been investigated to my knowledge . . . the general story of government relations with the Navahoes for the period 1846 and following has been worked out by myself, but I never ran across any material on the Newby campaign." Apparently, then, Wootton remains its only historian. On page 218 *post*, he says that he arrived back at Taos on July 4 to hear the news of the Treaty of Guadalupe Hidalgo, concluded the preceding February 2.

[66]In the opinion of Professor Frank D. Reeve of the University of New Mexico, Editor of the *New Mexico His-*

I have never yet heard of any tradition or read anything which gave a very satisfactory explanation of the origin of these buildings. The Navahoes, who have claimed and lived in the country for I don't know how long, certainly know nothing about the people who built them or the purpose for which they were built. When asked about the ruins the Indians say they have always been there, and seem to think they were built at the same time the world was made.

One thing is certain, and that is they were built by people who thoroughly understood stone cutting and masonry. Both granite and sandstone were used in the construction, and some of the blocks of stone which have been placed in the

torical Review, Wootton's "Ruins Leroux" were the pueblo stone structures in Chaco Cañon. Instead of being in the Puerco Valley, Chaco Cañon drains from the westward side of the Continental Divide near the headwaters of the Puerco, which drains southward into the Gulf of Mexico by way of the Rio Grande. No other ruin in this general area would meet Wootton's description. Statements in letter to the present Editor. February 10, 1956. In August and September, 1849 Col. John M. Washington led an armed force against the Navahoes, in the course of which the Chaco Cañon was visited. The ruins there are adequately described, with excellent illustrations, in Lieutenant James H. Simpson's Journal of the expedition, published in Senate Exec. Doc. No. 64, 31st. Cong., 1st. Sess (U. S. serial 562) pp. 56–139. Simpson's report was also separately published at Philadelphia in 1852, titled *Journal of a Military Reconnaissance from Santa Fe, New Mexico, to the Navajo . . . in 1849.*

walls would weigh, I should think, a dozen tons. The buildings are several stories high and very large, the style of architecture being similar to that of the adobe buildings put up by the Pueblo Indians, although in no other respect are they at all alike. A small party of us ventured into the old ruins and found rooms which had apparently been as well finished as those of the average modern residence.

I leave you to hunt up the history of these ruins, if they have any, or to build up your own theory of their origin if you can find nothing authentic about them in history, because, like the Indians, I can only tell you that they are there and how they look. Anyhow I didn't start out to talk about ruins, but about a war with the Navahoes.

We didn't see any of the hostiles until we had gotten some distance away from the Rio Puerco. I was riding along one afternoon, a mile or two ahead of the soldiers, when all at once I caught sight of four Indians. They did not see me and I rode back a little distance and waited until Colonel Newby came up. I told the Colonel what I had seen, and assured him that the four Indians belonged to a large band not far away. I pointed out to him the place where I thought we should find them and advised him to halt his command and remain where he was until dark, when we could make a quick march and take the Indians so much by surprise that they would have no time to get away with their horses and other stock. If we captured their stock it would be easy to compel them to make restitution to the Mexicans who had been robbed, and this was one of the objects of the expedition.

It seemed to be a custom of some of the military officers we had in the country in those days, however, to employ guides, when they started out on an expedition, and pay no attention to their suggestions after they got started. When we were employed to find Indians we always found them, and then, knowing the character and habits of the savages as we did, we did not think it impertinent, now and then, to volunteer a little advice as to the best method of effecting their capture or encompassing their defeat, and I can tell you that we always knew pretty near what we were talking about. Colonel Newby was one of those officers who didn't think that a mountain man's experience as an Indian fighter was worth anything, and when I suggested that we should wait until night before marching against the Navahoes he very promptly squelched me as a military adviser by ordering a forward movement at once. Before we had gone half a mile we passed into an open space on high ground and the four Indians I had seen caught sight of us.

Away they galloped, and a few minutes later a slender column of smoke shot up from a brush-covered elevation to warn the band, which we had not yet seen, of the approach of danger. That was just what I had expected, and it was not long before a cloud of dust in the valley below told us that the signal had been observed and that our enemy was on the move. This was one of the things which always made it difficult to follow Indians in the mountains, I mean their system of signaling to each other. They knew the country so well that they had scores of what you might call signal stations. These stations were elevated points, from which a column of smoke in the day time or a fire at night could be seen over a large area of country. They had a way of sending the smoke up in puffs and making their fires blaze up at intervals, which communicated any information they desired to communicate to each other as satisfactorily as any code of signals ever devised.

It took us some time to get down to where the Navahoes had been encamped and when we got there not an Indian or anything belonging to an Indian, which he cared to carry away, was in sight. Of course we could see which way they had gone, but with jaded and worn-out government horses, as I looked at the thing, we stood about as good a chance of overtaking them as a bull pup would stand of catching a greyhound in a race in which the greyhound had two or three hours the start.

Nevertheless Major Runnells was ordered to push forward with a detachment of troops in pursuit of the Indians and I was directed to go with him. Colonel Newby was to march to a point where I had informed him there was a spring, to go into camp for the night, and Major Runnells was ordered to return to that point to rejoin the balance of the command in case he did not overtake the Navahoes before nightfall.

Well, of course, we didn't overtake them, but it was eleven o'clock at night when we got into camp. The camping ground was in a small valley which was surrounded by high bluffs. Before we reached there we heard firing and I knew the Indians had gotten up on the bluffs and were shooting into the camp. We didn't much like the idea of riding in under fire and so we moved along cautiously until we were within a short distance of camp and then commenced shooting off our guns. At the same time we raised a yell and went in on a run, the Indians scattering as we approached, without firing at us.

They returned in a little while, however, and again commenced shooting into camp. No particular harm was being done, as we were well protected by over-hanging rocks, but the fire was annoying and Colonel Newby, after a time, got exceedingly nervous and ordered out a company or two of soldiers and the fire was returned. The Indians fell back and retreated in the direction in which the main band had gone and the troops followed them.

Early the next morning a courier came in to inform us that they had fourteen Indians in their camp, a few miles distant. The Indians, it was said, wanted to hold a pow-wow and were ready to make peace. What seemed to me a very suspicious circumstance, however, was the fact reported by the messenger that the Indians had come into camp with their guns and still had possession of them.

We started for the front, but before we got there the rattle of musketry informed us that a battle, and not a peace pow-wow, was going on. Colonel Newby, who had ridden on ahead of us, had made a mistake which precipitated hostilities. Instead of coming to an understanding with the Indians and inducing them to lay down their arms voluntarily at the same time that the soldiers laid down theirs, which was always a preliminary to a peace conference, he ordered his soldiers to disarm them. This caused the Indians to believe that they were to be taken prisoners, or perhaps killed, and the fight commenced.

All but two of them got away. One of these was killed and the other taken prisoner. The other twelve retreated and we followed them, but as they had splendid horses all but two soon left us a good ways in the rear. I could see those two Indians some distance behind the others. One appeared to be badly wounded and the other was trying to aid him in making his escape. Finally, the wounded Indian was left alone and disappeared.

I knew about where he was and by and by caught sight of him. He had the appearance of being dead, but when I looked at him closely I noticed that he had a bunch of arrows and his bow in his hand. Major Runnells had seen him also, and at the head of a party of six men, I being one of them, rode toward him. I called out to the Major to be on his guard, but thinking the Indian dead he paid no attention to my warning. We were riding single file and as I was satisfied the Indian was alive and would not be taken prisoner I threw my foot out of the stirrup so that I could instantly dismount if he made a hostile movement. He lay perfectly quiet until we were within a few yards of him and then, scarcely changing his position, I saw him bend his bow.

I threw myself off my horse on the opposite side from him and the others followed my example. As I was the first man on the ground the Indian very naturally expected me to be the first to shoot and directed his arrow toward me. My horse got frightened and as I had to hold on to him, before I could raise my gun to shoot fourteen arrows whistled past my head, and I tell you some of them came awful close to it. Some of the other members of the party shot at the Indian, but missed him, and it was not until I sent a bullet through his head that he dropped his bow and arrows. I have often wondered how all those arrows happened to miss me and I still credit it to my good luck, which in those days never failed me.

On the day after that, I think it was, I saw two Indians not far ahead of us and Colonel Newby expressed a desire to have them come into camp for a conference. I told him if he would stop his command and allow me to go ahead, remaining where he was until I should signal him to advance, I thought I could get to talk with them. He agreed to this and called a halt. I rode forward three or four hundred yards where the Indians could see me plainly and dismounted. Then I held up my gun and other arms and dropped them on the ground.

This signified that I wanted a peace pow-wow, and the Indians understood it. They both had guns, which they laid aside and advanced to meet me. We came together at a point about midway between those from which we had started and sat down together.

I smoked the pipe of peace with them and then explained to them that the representative of the Great Father at Washington had come out to punish them for their stealing and other depredations, but that he was willing to make peace with them if they would promise to behave better in the future.

They were very distrustful of Colonel Newby, but finally consented to talk with him. I signaled him then and he came up to where we were. A long pow-wow followed, of which the result was that they promised to bring their band into camp and to turn over to us three thousand sheep, in lieu of those which had been stolen, and all Mexican captives. Having completed this arrangement we turned back and camped at Cow Springs to wait for the Indians to come in.

We remained there twenty-seven days and got so short of supplies that each man's ration was two ounces of pork and three ounces of flour per day. It was in a barren country, where there was no game, and as the only thing we found to add to our rations was a few wild potatoes we had mighty slim living. Some of the Indians would come in every day or two to report that they could not get together as many sheep as the Great Father demanded of them, and ask for more time and a modification of terms. Finally, on the twenty-seventh day they all came in with something less than a hundred old rams which they turned over to us, and that was all the sheep we got. They also brought in five Mexican children and the treaty of peace was signed.

The next day we broke camp and started for Taos, Major Runnells with a portion of the command going ahead under my guidance. We made our way to the San Juan River and then followed it up to where the Rio Chueco and the San Juan come together. There we crossed the river, passed by the present site of Fort Lowell, and proceeded toward Abiquiu.

About half of the sheep which we had taken from the Indians had been allotted to our party and it was not long before they had been butchered and not long after they were butchered before they had been eaten up. Then we were out of meat again, and in fact had very little of anything to eat. The day after we left the San Juan River I rode ahead of the soldiers to see if I could find some game. I killed a couple of deer without much trouble and was about to ride on after another one when I heard a growl behind me and looking around saw a big grizzly about to take possession of my first deer.

It was no part of my business to kill deer for grizzlies, and I wanted some bear meat anyhow, so I just laid the grizzly out alongside of the deer. The next morning I killed another bear, and this supply of meat had to last us a couple of days.

Major Runnells then directed me to go on to Abiquiu and make arrangements to give the men a good feed there. Abiquiu is about forty miles from Taos, on the opposite side of the Rio Grande, near Ojo Caliente Springs. I knew if we reached so small a place without making some preparations for securing provisions in advance, it would be impossible for us to get anything like the amount of supplies required to feed our men and horses.

I reached Abiquiu a day in advance of the troops, and soon found a man who agreed to have a supply of bread ready by the time they came up. In addition to this I wanted meat for the men, and some kind of grain for the horses. The only man in the village who had any stock or grain was a Mexican padre who had half a dozen hogs and a big granary full of corn. This old fellow was an unreconstructed native who cordially hated *Los Americanos,* and when I approached him on the subject he refused to furnish the desired supplies, either for love or money. I did not press the matter, because I knew very well that we should get what we wanted when the troops came up, although I should have preferred an amicable arrangement to force of arms proceedings.

When Major Runnells came up next day I showed him my stock of bread and then told him I had corn and hogs, but it would require a detail of soldiers to get possession of the meat and horse feed. He gave me thirty men, and it didn't take us long to convince the old padre that he had made a mistake in refusing to do business with me.

From Abiquiu we made the march to the Cienega, where we had to swim the Rio Grande. The men who couldn't swim tied knots in their horses' tails and holding onto them were taken across in that way. We had expected to reach our destination before nightfall, but crossing the river delayed us and we had to go into camp some miles out from Taos.

The soldiers had breakfasted at Abiquiu early in the morning and when they got through with that meal they had cleaned up about everything in the way of eatables in the town. Nothing was left to carry away, and the prospect was when we started out that we should get nothing to eat until we reached Taos.

After marching all day without anything to eat it was a hungry lot of men who began making preparations to go into camp for the night, with the prospect before them of another twelve-hour fast, but before much grumbling had been done I succeeded in providing a sumptuous repast compared with what we had been living on most of the time since we started out on this campaign.

I saw a flock of goats coming down the mountain side, and suggested to Major Runnells that we appropriate to our use as many as were necessary to supply the soldiers with a meal. He at once acted on the suggestion and about eighty of the goats were killed to appease the hunger of his half-starved command.

In a little time an aged Mexican presented himself before the Major and after going through innumerable salaams and prostrations informed us that he was the owner of the goats, and that as they were the only property he had, we had taken away his only means of supporting his family. The Major informed him that he had only to present a claim in proper form and he would receive pay for his property. This the old fellow did a day or two later, and when he left the camp with the money to which he was entitled in his pocket he had no ill feeling toward *Los Americanos.*

We reached Taos on the morning of the fourth of July, where we learned that the treaty of Guadalupe Hidalgo had been signed and a peace concluded with Mexico. News traveled slowly in those days and although this treaty had been signed early in February we had not heard of it when our expedition started out in March. We celebrated the event that day in old-fashioned style, and the soldiers wound up their long campaign by taking a day off, along with all the other Americans in the country.

CHAPTER XV

Dull Times on the Frontier

WE had dull times on the frontier for two or three years after the Mexican War and we felt it particularly at Taos. The soldiers were all moved away from there with the exception of one or two companies. Money began to get scarce; that is, it was scarce in comparison with the amount which had been in circulation for several years prior to that time.

I don't suppose there ever was a place outside of a bonanza mining camp where a lot of frontiersmen got hold of more money or spent it more recklessly than at this old town of Fernandez de Taos from 1840 to 1848. I have seen men stand in the door of one of the old time resorts there with their hands full of silver coin and throw hundreds of dollars into the streets, just to see the Mexican urchins scramble after them.

About that time we heard of the gold discoveries in California and quite a number of those who had gotten as far west as New Mexico concluded to go on to the Pacific Coast. I was married then and had settled down at Taos, or I expect I should have started out with the rest of the gold hunters, because it promised to be just such a life of adventure as I had learned to like. As it was, however, I only had a mild attack of the gold fever and instead of going to California I concluded to make a search for some of the famous old Spanish mines we were always hearing so much about in New Mexico and Colorado.[67]

Both the Mexicans and the Indians used to talk about marvelously rich mines in certain localities, but as a rule they did not claim to know the real location of such mines. The same stories that were told to us forty years ago of lost mines which were fabulously rich have been handed down to the present time, and every once in a while we hear of a party of adventurous miners going in search of one of these mines. They are always disappointed, just as we used to be, and I reached the conclusion long ago that the traditionary "rich diggins" of the Mexicans and Pueblo Indians would be considered very poor paying properties now-a-days.

In the Sandia Mountains of New Mexico, for

[67]Lieutenant Britton Davis, whose book, *The Truth About Geronimo*, was republished as the Lakeside Classics volume for 1951, came as close as any one to discovering the secret of the lost Tayopa mine, "probably the most widely-talked-of lost mine in North America." See his narrative, 244-45. Two books which may be commended to all who seek, or merely enjoy reading about, buried treasure and lost mines are J. Frank Dobie's *Coronado's Children. Tales of Lost Mines and Buried Treasures of the Southwest* (New York, 1931); and the same author's *Apache Gold and Yaqui Silver* (Boston, 1939).

instance, I heard of a rich, abandoned mine which the natives called the Devil's Palace, believing it to be haunted. The stories that I heard of this mine raised my expectations to the highest pitch. It seemed to me that if what I heard was true there must be a vast amount of treasure hidden away in the dark recesses of the Devil's Palace.

I was shown the entrance to the mine, but at the same time was cautioned by the Mexicans who acted as my guides not to venture into it. I had never had any fear of spooks, however, and notwithstanding their protests I went into the mine with one or two companions and explored it thoroughly.

What I found was a cave, or pocket, from which a considerable amount of lead ore had at some time been taken, and the bones of three or four miners, who had probably been crushed to death by falling rock. That was all there was in the haunted palace, which the natives supposed contained more hidden wealth than King Solomon's mines. At the time this lead ore was taken out it brought a good price and was probably looked upon as a rich find, but at the time I was there it would not have paid the cost of mining and transportation.

Hunting these old mines has always been about as unprofitable as chasing a rainbow, and every time we entered the abandoned treasure houses we were a good deal more likely to find a den of wild animals than gold or silver. I never saw enough of the precious metals to make my eyes sparkle, but in one of the mines of the Sandias I caught sight of the fiery eye-balls and heard enough of the growling of some kind of an ugly wild beast to make my hair stand on end.

One of the old Spanish mines from which, according to Indian tradition, a fabulous amount of gold had been taken was said to be somewhere in the neighborhood of the Pueblo de Taos. The Indians claimed they knew the exact location of this mine and one of them finally agreed, for a consideration of three hundred dollars, to show some of us where it was. The night before the party to receive the much desired information was to start out for the Eldorado the Indian was murdered. We never knew who killed him. All we could ever learn was that he was found dead and his secret, if he really knew anything about the gold mine, died with him. Our supposition was that the Indians killed him to prevent him from telling the white men what he knew.

After that, those Indians who professed to know anything about the mine refused to talk about it and its location is still a secret. I fitted out one or two parties after that to look for old diggings of this kind, but never made any discoveries which paid me for the outlay of time and money.

At one time when coming through the Sangre de Christo Pass with a small party of prospectors I came near running into an Apache ambuscade, where my career as a gold hunter would have been very suddenly cut short had I not discovered the presence of the Indians in the nick of time. I always made it a point never to ride into any place which looked like a good hiding place for the savages without taking a careful survey of the situation in advance.

That was what I did when we were about to enter a narrow defile in the Sangre de Christo and a quick sharp eye, which has, no doubt, saved my scalp a good many times, enabled me to discover an Apache lying flat on the rocks above us, so close to the road we should have taken in going through the pass that we should have been powder-burned when they fired on us. I could see only the one Indian—although I knew there were more of them—and he had covered himself with dust and looked so much like a rock that I think nine out of ten of the mountain men even, would have passed along without noticing him.

I didn't know how many Indians a shot would scare out, but I knew that the one I saw would be a dead one and so I raised my gun and fired. At the crack of my rifle he sprang up, but only to tumble over, as dead as Julius Caesar, a second later. At the same instant the very rocks seemed to turn into Indians, and they jumped out of a score of places where we could see no sign of them before. My party commenced firing on them then and the Indians ran. They did not stop until they got out of reach of our guns and we passed along in safety.

At another time we were prospecting along the Rio Grande del Norte in the mountains bordering on San Luis Valley. One day we saw what looked to us like a band of elk down in the valley on the opposite side of the river from where we were.

I suggested to a companion that we should ride down to where they were and kill a couple of them, as we were in need of meat.

We started and had ridden perhaps half the distance to where the elk were moving about when they began to look rather queer to me. Just about this time we had to cross a deep ravine and there we saw a band of Indian ponies without their riders. We looked at the band of elk again and made up our minds that there were Indians under the elk skins, and that we had gotten altogether too close to them.

We turned back, and had barely gotten started towards our own camp when, just as we had surmised, the harmless-looking elk turned out to be Ute Indians. They threw off their disguises and running to their horses started in pursuit of us. We had a pretty good start of them and crossed the river before they reached it.

When we got up on the high ground we were in a good position for a fight, if that was what the Indians wanted. We had only thirteen men, but the Utes knew, although they had a large band, that we would kill a considerable number of them while they were crossing the river. They stopped on the opposite bank and watched us some time, but finally turned back and left us to make our way out of the country without molestation. We only waited until nightfall, however, to abandon prospecting in that section.

In the winter of 1849–50 I did the only trading I ever did with the Comanches. I got enough of it, too, and if I had kept on trading with Indians all my life I should never have had anything to do with these treacherous scoundrels again as the risk was entirely too great, even for a man who liked adventure as well as I did.

The Comanches never had even that small sense of honor which characterized the average western Indian. They never made a pledge or promise of any kind for which they had any regard whatever. When they made peace it was always for a purpose. It was either to save their lives when whipped and cornered or to obtain something which they stood in need of, and every such peace was made to be broken at the very first opportunity which presented itself.

It was at their request that we started out on the trip I am going to tell you about. Two or three of them came into Bent's Fort and told us that they had a lot of buffalo robes and buck skins and wanted us to come out and trade with them. They agreed to make peace and we were to meet them down on the Canadian River some time later.

I took twelve or fifteen men and two wagon loads of goods and went down to the old adobe fort, the walls of which are still standing on the Canadian River. Few people know, however, how it happened to be built. It was put up for the firm of Bent & St. Vrain, who at one time contemplated establishing a trading post there.[68]

---

[68]The old adobe fort, better known by its subsequent name of Adobe Walls, was built by Bent and St. Vrain on the South Canadian, probably about 1840, to serve as a trading center for the Kiowa, Comanche, Apache, and other tribes. Abandoned prior to 1850, the place afforded a shelter for traders and others. In the immediate vicinity of Adobe Walls Kit Carson with several hundred troops in 1864 fought a desperate battle with hostile tribesmen, in which he was fortunate in escaping complete destruction. Ten years later, in June, 1874, a party of buffalo hunters encamped here were furiously attacked by a large force of Indians who wished to prevent their further destruction of the buffaloes. This action has become celebrated as the battle of Adobe Walls. See George B. Grinnell, "Old Bent's Fort," in *Kansas Hist. Colls.*, XV, 42–44.

It was some time after we reached the fort that the Indians came in, and we were kept down there pretty much all winter getting through with our trading. The first thing, of course, was to make peace. This was arranged at a pow-wow at which we went through the usual ceremonies, and then made the Indians an unusually large number of presents. As I remember it now we had to give them something like seven or eight hundred dollars worth of trinkets of various kinds and some things which were not exactly trinkets, before they appeared to be satisfied that we would deal with them fairly and generously.

Among other things that they insisted on having were some of our guns and a considerable amount of ammunition. Of course we expected to trade these things, but would very much have preferred to deliver the goods just on the eve of our departure, because we did not feel by any means sure that we were not furnishing them weapons with which to take our own lives.

The bulk of the presents which changed hands came from us, the Comanches giving us in return a few ponies of perhaps one-twentieth the value of the goods which they received from us. We would not agree to go to their village, as we were in the habit of doing with other Indians, but stipulated that they should bring their peltry

BENT'S FORT

Colorado's most famous trading post. After a sketch by Lt. J. W. Abert, 1845

to the fort and that the trading should be done there.

They went away after their robes and buckskins, and after awhile a big band of them came back. They were naturally so quarrelsome, ill-tempered, and treacherous that we anticipated trouble if we allowed any considerable number of them to stay about where the trading was carried on.

To make the business as safe as possible we shut ourselves up in the fort, laid out our goods, and then admitted two or three Indians at a time. When these had gotten through with their trading others were admitted and disposed of in the same way.

Some of these goods we passed out through a hole in the wall about as big as the ticket window in a railway station and took in the robes and deer skins the same way. The Indians who had to remain outside were not pleased with being kept at a distance, and in order to impress upon us that fact they would get off some distance and shoot at our general delivery window. Then we would have to suspend operations until the old chief and others who were responsible for the good behavior of their band would go out and put a stop to the hostilities.

The tendency of such little episodes as this was to make one feel nervous, and I assure you there was no one in the party who wanted to make a steady business of trading with the Comanches. We all liked excitement, but we didn't like it in quite that form.

From a business standpoint we got along well enough, because when we got through trading and started home we loaded twelve old-fashioned Pennsylvania wagons with robes and buckskins which we had received in exchange for the goods we took out with us. We got away safely and reached home without having to do any fighting, although I have often wondered since how we happened to have such good luck. There were very few frontiersmen who ever went among the Comanches for any purpose other than to fight, and all things considered that was the most hazardous trading expedition I ever had anything to do with.[69]

While I had been away from Taos a great deal of the time in 1848–49 I had built up quite a business in the merchandising line at that point, and after I got back from the Comanche country I devoted myself mainly to this business and to looking after my herd of cattle, which had grown to

[69]Wootton's experience in trading with the Comanches parallels the experience thirty years earlier of General Thomas James, whose narrative was published as the Lakeside Classics volume for 1953. The similarity of conduct existing between the Comanches and the Communists of present-day Russia will not escape the reader.

such proportions, that in those days I was something of a cattle king.

A year later I determined to take a trip back to St. Louis to lay in a stock of merchandise. That was in 1851, and I had not seen the Mound City or been east of Independence, Missouri, since 1835. I had to go to Kansas City either by wagon or on horseback, and from there I could go by river steamer to St. Louis. I determined to go through on horseback, and set out with a small party, of which Major Grier, whose name I have mentioned in connection with a campaign against the Utes, was a member.

Going through from here to Kansas City now, on horseback, would be considered a pretty big ride, but I made the trip in a little over seven days on a wager which I made with Major Grier that I would beat him into St. Louis. I did beat him very badly, because, although he was an old army officer and used to hard riding, his power of endurance was not so great as mine. He got laid up on the way, and I reached the end of our journey nearly two weeks ahead of him.[70]

[70]Francis X. Aubrey, a well-known citizen of New Mexico, is reputed to have ridden from Santa Fe to Kansas City, a distance of perhaps 800 miles (varying somewhat according to the precise route taken) in eight days. Wootton's ride from Taos to Kansas City was in the neighborhood of 700 miles. Both riders, apparently, traveled approximately 100 miles per day. Note that on another occasion

When I got through purchasing goods in St. Louis it was a month or two before I could get them shipped, on account of low water in the Missouri River. I finally got started, however, and got up to Westport. I had left my horses there, and had intended to stop several days to look after unloading my goods from the boat and loading them on the freight wagons which were to carry them across the Plains.

I changed my mind though, when I got there, and only stopped long enough to settle my bills and make contracts to have my goods forwarded after me to Taos. My exit from Westport was very unexpectedly expedited and I will tell you how it happened, just to show you that while I was a pretty good Indian fighter and didn't run from anything we found in the mountains, I could be as big a coward as anybody sometimes.

The cholera broke out in the town just about the time we arrived there, and as soon as I found out about it I began to feel sick. There was no business important enough to keep me there long after that. After escaping all the dangers of fifteen

Wootton rode from Pueblo to Taos, 165 miles, in less than twenty-four hours. See *post*, 280.

Aubrey was subsequently stabbed to death in the bar room of the Exchange Hotel in Santa Fe by Colonel Richard H. Weightman, who in turn perished in the battle of Wilson's Creek, Missouri, during the Civil War. See Twitchell, *Military Conquest of New Mexico*, 381–94.

years spent among the savages I didn't want to be carried off by an epidemic disease the first time I crossed the border line of civilization. So I just ordered out my horses and put about a hundred and fifty miles between me and Westport within the next forty hours. What I wanted was to get to the Rocky Mountains. I knew there wouldn't be any cholera there.

Chapter XVI

Overland to California

REPORTS which reached us from California in 1852 induced me to make a trip to the Pacific Coast. I did not go as a gold-hunter, or at least not for the purpose of digging gold out of the ground, but planned a trading trip which I thought was certain to be profitable provided I succeeded in getting through with it.

Thousands of people had flocked to California, and hundreds of thousands of dollars were being taken out of the mines. There was plenty of money in the country, or rather plenty of gold dust and nuggets, but there was a great scarcity of provisions of all kinds. Beef and mutton were particularly in demand and cattle and sheep commanded prices which were almost fabulously high.

In New Mexico, where the Mexicans had large flocks, fine sheep could be bought at about one-tenth of the price per head they were reported to be selling for in California and it looked to me as though a handsome fortune might be realized as profit on a large band of sheep driven through and disposed of at Sacramento or some other point on the coast. Up to that time nothing of the kind had been attempted, but I thought the

234

scheme a practicable one and determined to try it.[71] I knew it meant sixteen hundred miles of travel over mountain ranges, across barren plains and still more barren deserts, and in addition to this I knew that there was scarcely a mile of the road which was not beset by savages who were making it their principal business to rob and murder a white man or band of white men whenever opportunity offered. I did not think the undertaking more hazardous, however, than others in which I had engaged, and I began making my arrangements to set out on the trip.

In the neighborhood of Watrous, New Mexico, I gathered together nine thousand head of sheep. They were driven through to Taos for me, where I supplied myself with everything that I thought would be necessary for the trip, got together the men who were to accompany me, said good bye to my family, and started out.

[71]Unknown, probably, to Wootton, another American, named Coons, conducted a much larger flock of sheep to California this same season, apparently going by the southern (Gila River) route. See John Russell Bartlett, U. S. Boundary Commissioner's *Personal Narrative*. . . . II, 213, report of meeting Coons' party of 60 men and 14,000 sheep at Tucson. The following year (1853) Kit Carson conducted several thousand sheep to California going by the northern route. See his *Autobiography*, the Lakeside Classics volume for 1935, pp. 146–47. Returning to Santa Fe by the southern route in the closing months of 1853, Carson reported meeting enroute over 100,000 sheep bound for the California market.

I carried with me about one thousand dollars worth of supplies which consisted mainly of flour, coffee, dried meat, and ammunition. My equipment was pretty much the same that it would have been if I had been going out on a long trapping expedition. All our supplies were loaded on pack mules. We took no horses with us, believing that mules would serve our purpose better.

I had with me when I started out twenty-two men in all, fourteen of them being Mexican sheep herders and the others Americans. I did not find it an easy matter to secure the kind of men I should have liked to have accompany me on this trip. It was a different lot of men entirely from those I had usually had with me on hunting and trapping trips. On those trips my associates had almost always been men who had demonstrated in many an Indian fight that they did not lack either nerve or judgment, who never lost their heads in the presence of danger, feared nothing so much as being looked upon as cowards, knew what their guns were made for, and never failed to use them to the best advantage when there was occasion for it. The eight Americans who started for California with me were discharged soldiers and teamsters whom I had found at Taos and I knew nothing of their fighting qualities and very little about their general trustworthiness. I had to pick up such men as I could find, however, and take the chances of their failing me at a critical moment, or perhaps planning murder and robbery on their own account.

I relied mainly upon the Americans to protect my property as well as our lives, and expected the Mexicans to look after and drive the sheep. I armed each of the men, Americans and Mexicans alike, with a first-class rifle, a pistol, and knife, and thus equipped we started on our long drive on the 24th of June, 1852. I had been over the greater part of the route I expected to take, before, and although there was no such thing as a road or trail even, in some places, I did not expect to have much difficulty in finding the shortest and most available path to the Pacific Coast.

Starting up the Rio Grande del Norte from Taos, we followed it nearly to its source and then turning westward crossed the Divide. We had much difficulty in traveling the next two or three hundred miles and made slow progress, on account of high water in the streams. Every river, creek, and it seemed to me every arroyo was bankfull of water, the result of snow melting in the mountains. We had to swim the sheep across all the larger streams, and then swim across ourselves. In crossing a few of them, such as Grand River, the Uncompahgre, Gunnison River, and Green River we had to construct rafts on which to carry our provisions across.

It was just before we reached the Uncompahgre River that we had our first trouble with the Indians. I knew that the Utes claimed all the territory through which we were passing and I intended to embrace the first opportunity to make peace, after the usual style, and obtain formal permission to go through their country. Instead, however, of coming to me they made their presence known by attempting to steal my sheep when we were in camp at night. My custom was to keep four men on guard all the time when in camp, each night being divided into four watches. We first kindled our camp fire and then gathered the stock around us, so that the four men who stood guard did not have to patrol a very large area. The Indians crept up on us and made an effort to stampede our pack animals as well as the sheep, but fortunately for us they failed in the attempt, the guards discovering and frightening them away.

The next day they showed themselves and demanded that we should compensate them for driving our stock through their country before going any farther. Uncotash, the chief who acted as spokesman for the band and made the demand, was very insolent in his manner of approaching me, but I paid no attention to this and told him that when we reached the river we would go into camp for the night, and that we should then have time to hold a pow-wow and make everything satisfactory to him.

I sent two or three of my men on ahead with him to the camping place, but before they reached it they began to get afraid of the Indians and made an excuse to leave them and come back where I was. This led the Indians to believe that it was not our intention to carry out the agreement I had made with them, and the first thing I knew, Uncotash and a hundred or more of his followers came galloping back acting in a very warlike manner. At the same time that the old Chief with several other Indians rode up beside me I noticed that his band divided into small squads and each of these squads stopped beside one of my men.

I divined in a moment that their object was to kill or capture my entire party and then drive away the stock. We were separated so that we could not have fought them to any purpose, and as a matter of fact, I had made up my mind by this time that I had very few fighting men in my company. I tell you it was a critical situation, and just at that time I think an old-fashioned Mexican dollar would have bought my entire outfit.

Uncotash was more insolent than he had been at first, and accused me of acting in bad faith. I had never been so badly scared in my life before, but I had sense enough not to let him know it. I tried to pacify and explain to the old heathen, but he wouldn't listen and kept railing at me until I got mad. I forgot for a moment all about the danger of the situation and jumped off my horse with the intention of making his body serve as a shield, or breast-work, while I convinced the Indians that I wouldn't be bullied, if I was in their power. The chief jumped from his horse at the same time and as it happened we both fell, coming down close together. I dropped my gun in falling and knew well enough that I had no time to pick it up.

As I attempted to rise I locked arms with the Chief, and being a much more powerful man than he I held him down, at the same instant drawing my knife and threatening to kill him if he did not at once put a stop to the hostilities. Our position was such that it would have been impossible for any of the Indians to come to his rescue in time to save his life, although of course there would have been no chance of saving my own. Life is very sweet to an Indian and old Uncotash, seeing there was but one way for him to preserve his, agreed to make peace. The Indians had commenced shooting my sheep and I made him put a stop to this and also call his band together, leaving my men to drive the sheep.

We then walked along together about two miles, down to the banks of the Uncompahgre, where I picked out a camping ground in a place that would afford us a fair show of successful resistance in case we were attacked during the night. I arranged the camp as usual, and then we sat down for a peace pow-wow.

It didn't take us long to come to an understanding. I was so much pleased over my own deliverance from the danger which had threatened me only two or three hours earlier in the day that I was disposed to be liberal. I gave them several hundred dollars' worth of flour, ammunition, and other things I had with me that they happened to take a fancy to, as a consideration for their "love and affection" during the brief space of time that I expected to remain in what they were pleased to call their country.

As a guarantee of their good faith they left one of their number with me during the night as a hostage, the understanding being that his life was to be forfeited if any attack was made on us. I stood guard over him myself, because I wanted him to understand that there was no chance for him to escape in case hostilities were commenced, but they made us no trouble. In the morning we crossed the river and saw no more of that band of Utes, nor had we any further serious trouble with other bands.

Crossing the Grand River a little later was a dangerous business and it took me nearly two days to accomplish it. I have not told you yet about some of the help I had on this trip. I had eight trained goats and a shepherd dog, which were worth more to me than four times the number of men would have been. The goats led the flock and the dog brought up the stragglers. Two of the goats were picked out every day to act as leaders and they could be guided as easily as a well-trained yoke of oxen. When we had a stream to cross the two goats were driven into the water just as you would drive a team of horses and they always took the sheep across safely.

At Eagle Tail River I found a little band of Utes who had large, fine horses, accustomed to crossing the river at all stages, and I called on them to assist me in getting my provisions, clothing, blankets, etc., across. I made a bargain with them, stipulating that they were to take my men and the packs across for so much, and gave them the goods which they were to have.

They took everything over according to agreement, while I remained behind to see that nothing was left. All the men were on the opposite side of the stream and I was left alone with the Indians. I told them I was ready to go, but they hesitated about starting, and finally told me that I hadn't paid my own fare, but had only compensated them for carrying over my men and goods, and would have to make a new bargain if I wanted to get across myself.

I didn't think much of that way of doing business, but they had the advantage of me and I commenced looking about among the few articles I still had with me for something with which to pay my passage across the stream. I laid out a cotton shirt, half a plug of tobacco, five charges of powder, five bullets, and five gun caps and this paid my way across the river on one of their big horses.

I anticipated a quarrel with another band of Utes that I fell in with just before reaching Salt Creek in southeastern Utah, and I expect I should have had difficulty with them had I not taken the precaution to hold one of them as a hostage for their good behavior. It was very evident to me that all the Indians looked with longing eyes upon the large band of sheep I was driving through the country. We had had fine pasture for them pretty much all the time, and they had been driven slowly, so that they had done as much grazing as if they had been running at large. As a result they were in prime condition and every time an Indian looked at one of those fat sheep I thought I could see his mouth begin to water.

The band which met us as we were driving toward Salt Creek appeared to be very friendly when they first came to us. They rode along with us nearly the whole of one day and insisted that we should go to their village to camp that night.

I understood the purpose of this apparent hospitality. I knew well enough that their object was to get us into a place where they would have an opportunity of stampeding and stealing some of my sheep during the night, if they did not contemplate a more extensive raid, and I declined to go with them.

One of the Indians was rather an old man, who appeared to have a great deal of influence with the band. He spoke good Spanish, and as I understood that language well I had no difficulty in carrying on a conversation with him.

Their village was a short distance from the trail which we were following and when we reached the point nearest to it the Indians reined up their horses and arbitrarily demanded that I should turn aside and go with them. Although I had not manifested any impatience I had been very much annoyed by them all day, and this was the straw that broke the camel's back.

I informed them in very forcible and possibly somewhat profane language that I would not go to their village and that I would camp where I pleased. Then I wound up by telling them that if they didn't like what I had said and were not suited with what I proposed to do I would fight them if that was what they wanted.

The Spanish-speaking old Indian interpreted what I had said and it created a commotion.

They had no arms with them, but without any further parleying they started towards the village and I supposed that meant fight. My interpreter was about to follow the other Indians when I caught his horse by the bridle and gave him to understand that I proposed to take him into camp with me and that his life would depend upon the good behavior of his band during the night. His comrades noted the fact of his detention and stopped long enough to learn the purpose for which he was held and the conditions upon which depended his safe return to them.

They gave neither my prisoner nor myself any intimation of what they proposed to do and I think he was left in a much more unpleasant frame of mind than I was. He knew his band was anxious to attack us and felt very certain, as I intended he should, that the moment hostilities were commenced he would be a dead Indian. He knew that his friends understood the situation and were fully aware of his peril, but he was by no means certain that regard for his safety would outweigh their longing for white men's scalps and the large amount of plunder in sight. His anxiety deepened as he looked from time to time toward the village, which could be plainly seen from where we went into camp. The Indians seemed to be gathering up their arms and sending the women and children to a place of safety.

I was watching these proceedings with no small uneasiness myself, but I could hardly help pitying the poor old savage who sat in my camp, showing on his countenance the alternations of hope and fear as he contemplated the situation. He sat down to supper along with the rest of us, but his appetite failed him and he ate but a few mouthfuls and that under compulsion.

Before it became quite dark I could see that the Indians had quieted down, but whether this meant that they had completed their preparations for a fight or had decided not to attack us, I was uncertain. I doubled the guard, and then after examining my rifle and pistols carefully to see that they were all properly loaded and primed, in the presence of the old Indian, I ordered him to lie down, taking a seat a few feet away from him on a sack of flour, with my rifle across my knees.

Of course I didn't sleep, and if my prisoner slept any that night it was very little. Every few minutes he would raise up and look about, anxiously peering into the darkness to see if he could discover any signs of Indians about the camp. The night passed away however, without anything happening to disturb or alarm us and in the morning my old Indian ate his breakfast with a good deal better relish than he had eaten supper. Then I told him that as his people had behaved well during the night and had shown that they were good Indians I would not keep him any longer. I gave him the last cotton shirt I had, a little powder, some bullets, and a few gun caps and he left me feeling about as happy as any Indian I ever saw.

Chapter XVII

Hobnobbing With Brigham Young

AFTER getting across Green River with a great deal of difficulty, but without any serious mishap, we turned to the north and crossing the Wasatch Mountains at the head of Spanish Fork followed it down into the Great Salt Lake Valley. There we saw the first evidence of civilization we had seen since leaving Taos, and struck the first well defined trail we had had to travel over. This was five years after the Mormons had located in the valley, and Salt Lake City had become a place of some consequence.

I camped outside the city after a hard day's travel and rode in alone to look after supplies for the balance of the trip, because the Ute Indians had drawn so heavily on my stock of provisions that I had very little left. When I got into the town I met Ben. Holladay, the famous old freighter and stage owner, for the first time. He was the man who started the noted Pony Express, which got over the road almost as fast as a railway train, and also a stage line from Sacramento to Omaha. He was a partner in a large general store at Salt Lake City and happened to be there at the time. I purchased what I needed from him, and remained in the town

248

three days getting ready for the last half of my journey.[72]

The day following my arrival in the flourishing City of the Saints, as they called it then and still call it, I very unexpectedly met and formed the acquaintance of Brigham Young. I was riding along at the head of my flock of sheep when a stoutly built, florid faced, genteel-looking man, whose hair was just turning gray, walked down to the street from one of the most pretentious residences in the place and inquired whose sheep I had charge of.

I told him they belonged to me and that my name was Dick Wootton.

He wanted to know then where I came from and where I was going.

[72]Although Ben Holladay was not the creator of the Pony Express (this honor belongs to William H. Russell of the freighting firm of Russell, Majors, and Waddell) his career was sufficiently notable. A native of Kentucky, Holladay removed with his parents to western Missouri in early boyhood. At the outbreak of the Mexican War he furnished supplies to General Kearny's Army of the West and at its close purchased wagons and other equipment from the Government at bargain prices. He now launched a trading enterprise to Salt Lake City, where the favor of Brigham Young insured his success. He subsequently became a large-scale promoter of stage, steamship, and railway enterprises until the panic of 1873 dealt his career a staggering blow. He died at the age of sixty-seven in July, 1887. Data condensed from *Dictionary of American History* and *Dictionary of American Biography*.

I informed him that I lived in New Mexico, that I had been in the mountains a good many years, and was on my way to California.

He said then that he had heard of me and after telling me who he was he invited me into his house.

I hesitated a little about accepting the invitation because I didn't know how many of the Mrs. Youngs I might be presented to and I wasn't looking as handsome as I always liked to when going into the company of ladies.

I had on a buckskin suit when I left home, and I was still wearing that same suit. It had changed wonderfully in appearance, however, and it wasn't for the better either. Swimming a dozen or more Rocky Mountain streams had spoiled the fit of my buckskin garments and had been particularly disastrous to my trousers. Every time they got wet the legs stretched out a few inches, and every time this happened I had made it a point to cut them off at the bottom. When I entered the Salt Lake Valley and got into a hot, dry climate I learned that I had made a mistake in cutting off those trousers. They commenced to shrink, and when I got into Salt Lake I should have been in just the fashion if knee breeches had been the style.

It was a good enough suit for the Plains and mountains, but I hardly liked to appear in it when paying my respects to the Chief of the Deseret Hierarchy. Still, I had a curiosity to see the inside of the Mormon apostle's residence, and as he insisted on my coming in I got down off my mule and followed him into the house.

We sat down together and chatted for perhaps half an hour while we drank a bottle of wine which the hospitable head of the church brought out and set before me. It was good wine, too, and when I left him, I felt that I could commend his wine if I couldn't his religion. I left him with a promise to call again in the evening, which I did, and received as courteous treatment as I have ever received before or since that time.

Two days later I left Salt Lake and started across the desert plains of Nevada. Several of the men who had travelled with me as far as Salt Lake stopped at that point, and although I had employed others I only had eighteen men besides myself when I left there.

I heard of several parties of emigrants on their way through to California having been massacred by the Indians along the road we were to traverse, and was not sure that I should be able to defend myself successfully if attacked, but decided to take the risk. What was known as the Emigrant Trail had by that time become well established, and I followed it, or rather kept close to it, all the way through. It was necessary for me to leave the Trail every few miles to find sufficient feed for my stock, and this made the trip longer than it would otherwise have been.

A few of my sheep were shot and killed by the Digger Indians as we were passing through their country, but aside from this we were not molested by Indians after we left the Ute country, and the only serious trouble I had after leaving Salt Lake was with my own men. That was while we were crossing Nevada and some little time before we reached Humboldt Lake.

I had observed that several of my men were slack about doing the work which they had been hired to do. They were sullen and ill natured, and every now and then when we were in camp I would hear them grumbling about something among themselves. I didn't know what their grievance was or what they intended to do, but I became suspicious of them and watched all their movements very closely.

One day I rode ahead some distance and lay down to sleep a little way off the Trail, leaving orders with one of the men to wake me when they came up to where I was. I was very much fatigued and soon fell into a sound sleep. When I awoke neither men nor sheep were in sight, and I discovered that they had passed by me.

They were several miles ahead, and it was some time before I overtook them. The man who should have called me, to move along with the train at the proper time, made some plausible excuse for not doing so, but I was satisfied that when they left me behind they had done so with the expectation that some of the Indians, who were near us all the time, would find me alone and kill me.

The next day I discovered that one of the malcontents, who was behind the sheep, was leaving small bunches of them along the road. I brought up the sheep, and then riding up to one of the men in whom I had most confidence, asked him what scheme was on foot. He told me that half a dozen of my employes who had been behaving the worst had entered into an arrangement with an emigrant train, which had been traveling alongside of us but had dropped behind, to steal enough sheep to pay their passage to California.

That night when they got into camp and had laid aside all their arms I unloaded the packs which belonged to these six fellows and ordered them to pick up their traps and march out of camp. I enforced the order by forming them into line, with the assistance of a trusty rifle and a pair of pistols, and following them some distance. I suppose they joined the emigrant train that night for I never saw them after that, and had no further difficulty of consequence with the men who remained with me.

After leaving Humboldt Lake we crossed the desert and struck Carson River. We followed this to its source, passed through Pleasant Valley and made our way over the Sierra Nevada Mountains. We got over the Sierra Nevadas just in time to escape a heavy snow fall which came on as we were going down the western slope. I followed the American River down into the Sacramento Valley and went into camp twelve miles from the city on the 9th day of October.

I had made the trip in one hundred and seven days, and had gotten through with eight thousand nine hundred of the nine thousand sheep I started with, having lost but very few outside of those I had butchered on the way. After looking about for a day or two I arranged for winter quarters at Elk Grove, twelve miles out from Sacramento on the Stockton road, where I remained until I had disposed of all my sheep and the rest of my stock.

I found Sacramento a city with a resident population of perhaps six or seven thousand, and a floating population of ten or fifteen thousand more. It was the headquarters of the miners and was a fast town in those days. Outside of the city there were very few settlers, and I did not think then that it would ever become the great farming and fruit raising country that it is to-day.

It took me all winter to get through with my business, and during that time I saw the city of Sacramento entirely wiped out by fire, and after it had been partially built up again almost submerged in water.

The great fire which had destroyed practically everything in the town occurred on the night after the presidential election of 1852, when Pierce and Scott were the candidates for President. That was just after California had been admitted as a State, and it was the first time that her citizens had voted for a President of the United States.

It had been a great day in Sacramento and at night the fire was started in a disreputable quarter of the town, and as the buildings were nearly all wooden ones they were licked up like snowflakes by a scorching sun. Scarcely a building was left standing when the sun rose next morning, but before the embers had stopped smoking hundreds of men were at work clearing away the debris and preparing to build anew.

I never saw just such a resurrection as followed that fire. Buildings seemed to go up almost as rapidly as they had been burned down, and within a few weeks the place again had all the appearance of a city. Then the flood came. The entire valley was covered with water and people were driven into the second stories of their houses.

That did a vast amount of damage, and altogether it was a bad year for Sacramento.[73]

I had determined to return home by a different route from that which I had taken in going to California, not only because I thought I could save something in the distance but because I should have an opportunity of seeing some new country. After visiting San Francisco which was then a straggling town, although there were a good many people there, I went by steamer down to Los Angeles. There I purchased pack mules and mules to ride, and with three men besides myself started overland for New Mexico.

At San Bernardino we fell in with a party of six Mexicans and two Americans who were coming through to Taos and we agreed to travel together. The route that we were to take was one over

[73]The fire which destroyed Sacramento, inflicting an estimated loss of $10,000,000, occurred Nov. 2, 1852. Prior to 1845 there was no Presidential election day common to all the States. Abuses which developed by reason of the varying dates led to a popular demand for fixing upon a single day for the choosing of presidential electors, and a law enacted January 23, 1845 fixed the date as the first Tuesday after the first Monday in November. November 1, 1852 fell on Monday, hence the Presidential election was held the following day. The city had experienced a disastrous flood on March 7, 1852, when at one o'clock A.M. the American River broke through its restraining levee. A second flood which befell on January 1, 1853, subsiding rapidly and causing much less damage than the one of March 7, 1852, is the one Wootton witnessed.

which a considerable number of people had been passing, but it had always been looked upon as a dangerous road on account of the great difficulty in following any trail across the deserts, the intense heat, and the scarcity of water.

Had we traveled by the most direct route, we should have crossed Arizona and entered New Mexico, going only a little south of east from San Bernardino. I was anxious, however, to avoid the Apache Indians who, I had been informed, were then raiding southwestern Arizona and I determined to turn south and pass through Sonora.

We made good time to Fort Yuma and then, as I had intended, I turned south into Old Mexico. The party which had joined mine at San Bernardino declined to follow my lead at this point and I left them behind, but they followed along later. We turned back into Arizona again after a little time and reached Tucson after a terrible experience in crossing the desert. I shall never forget that fearful ride over the burning sands, where not a drop of water could be found.

We had started on the perilous trip with well-filled canteens, but although we drank sparingly this supply of water was exhausted long before we reached a place where the canteens could be re-filled. For nearly two days we were without water and my companions, and the animals we were riding became almost crazed from thirst. I suffered less than the others, but nothing I had ever seen before, nothing I have ever seen since, delighted me as did the sight of a large spring which we reached a few miles from Tucson.

People who live in a land of springs and streams, who have never known what it is to want water, can form no idea of the sufferings which travelers across these western deserts sometimes endured. As long as we had water we could struggle along, even if our supply of provisions ran out. We could find ugly-looking lizards and beetles, which, although they did not make very palatable food, would sustain life. There were roots and seeds which would satisfy to some extent the cravings of hunger, but there was nothing could take the place of water.

It was the failure to find water, in crossing these barren wastes, which in the early days of overland travel to the Pacific Coast set the brain of the traveler reeling and caused him to wander aimlessly over the broad seas of sand until death came to his relief. Many of the early adventurers lost their lives in this way, and years after they had been forgotten their bones were found whitening beneath the torrid sun, which, with its intense rays, had dried up the fountains of their lives.

The names of some of these deserts are significant and serve to remind one of the perilous journeys of old-time adventurers. Having in mind, perhaps, the gold-hunters and emigrants who perished when trying to make their way across it, somebody has given to one of these arid plains which lies in southern California the name of Death Valley, and that is the name by which it is generally known on the Pacific Coast.

Another stretch of desert which lies in southern New Mexico, the Mexicans have very appropriately named Jornada del Muerto. That means, in English, the journey of death, and a journey of death it has been to scores of unfortunate travelers.[74]

[74]The name JORNADA was applied throughout the Southwest to extensive waterless stretches of highway. One of the longest and best known of these was the Jornada del Muerto, or Journey of Death, on the route from Santa Fe to El Paso, reaching from Valverde to El Paso, a distance of about ninety miles. Here the Rio Grande makes a deep turn to the West and the Jornada constituted a cut-off from point to point of the river. When Zebulon M. Pike was carried captive to Mexico in the winter of 1807 his conductor chose to avoid the Jornada (commonly a two-day journey) by making the 5-day detour along the course of the Rio Grande. John T. Hughes (*Doniphan's Expedition*, 95) supplies a graphic picture of the suffering endured by Colonel Doniphan's army in passing over "this dreadful desert," enroute to Chihuahua in the winter of 1846–47. Senator Thomas H. Benton, in a speech welcoming Doniphan home to Missouri, July 2, 1847 described the Jornada as "an arid plain of ninety miles, strewed with bones of animals, perished of hunger and thirst; little hillocks of stones and the solitary cross erected by pious hands, marking the spot where some Christian had fallen

To get back where I left off telling you about my return trip from California, we camped at the spring which furnished us the only water we had found in traveling more than a hundred miles, and the next day rode into Tucson.[75] There we found a company of Mexican soldiers and secured some supplies which lasted us until we got to a Mexican settlement farther along on our way. We traveled in a northeasterly direction until we struck the Rio Grande del Norte just above the Jornada del Muerto, and from there we followed the river pretty much all the way to Taos.

On the 8th day of January, 1853, I reached home, having been thirty-three days on the road between Los Angeles, California, and Taos, New Mexico. It had been a little less than eleven months before that that I had started with my big flock of sheep for California and while I had

victim of the savage, of the robber, or of the desert itself— no water, no animal life, no sign of habitation." Quoted in Twitchell, *Military Conquest of New Mexico,* 254. For another interesting account of a passage of the Jornada in 1850 see A. D. Richardson, *Beyond the Mississippi* (Hartford, 1873), Chap. XXI.

[75]Until April, 1854, when the Gadsden Purchase was concluded, Tucson belonged to Mexico. By the Purchase the United States acquired some 45,500 square miles of territory comprising portions of present-day Arizona and New Mexico lying chiefly south of the Gila River. For it, the sum of $10,000,000 was paid. For details concerning the boundaries of the Purchase see Richard E. Coan (Ed.), *History of Arizona* (Phoenix, 1930), Chap. X.

been gone longer than I expected to be when I left home, financially and otherwise my trip had been entirely satisfactory.[76] My trip westward had not been without some thrilling adventures, in which I narrowly escaped losing not only my property but my life. The return trip had, however, been characterized by no more stirring experience than our hard ride across the desert. We were never at any time harrassed or threatened by hostile Indians.

Only twice on the way did we come in sight of the Apaches, the only Indians we had any occasion to fear at that time. Once we met a few stragglers, with whom we held a friendly conference and then proceeded on our way unmolested. At another time a large band came close to our camp one morning before we discovered them, but our pack animals were loaded and all we had to do was to mount our horses and set out. As the Indians were on foot we soon left them far behind us and escaped without firing a shot or hearing the whistle of an arrow.

[76]Since he began the journey on June 24, his arrival home must have occurred some time in May, 1853, instead of January 8. The latter date is obviously incorrect for another reason. He states earlier that he witnessed the flood of January 1 at Sacramento and that it took him all winter to dispatch his business there, and he spent thirty-three days on the journey from Los Angeles home. The eleven-month statement, rather than the date of January 8, is approximately correct.

The Yumas, Pimas and other Indians through whose country we passed treated us with the greatest consideration and kindness, the Pimas going to some trouble to direct us on our road. The Maricopas, also, seemed to take a deep interest in our welfare, and were exceedingly friendly. They were a thrifty lot of Indians, and presented the best appearance of any Indians I have ever come in contact with. The Maricopa women struck me as the handsomest lot of Indian women I had ever seen. They were fine featured, well developed, and much fairer skinned than any of the other southern and western Indians and the whole band seemed to be far above the average of the Indians in point of intelligence.

I have never visited their country since, but I have heard of them from time to time and my impression is that they have made considerable progress in civilization, and that they are now engaged quite extensively in the cultivation of the soil. If all the Indians had been as kindly disposed toward the whites as were these Indians we should not have had much trouble in settling up the western country.[77] The Navahoes and Apaches

[77]A detailed picture of these tribes shortly before Wootton's visit to them is presented in John Russell Bartlett's *Personal Narrative of Explorations and Incidents Connected with the United States and Mexican Boundary Commission in the Years 1850, '51, '52, and '53* (New York 1854), II, Chaps. XXIX-XXXII. The chronicler of General Kearny,

were the worst enemies of the peaceably inclined southern tribes, and it has been on account of the encroachments and depredations of these roving robbers that the Pimas and Maricopas have not been more successful in farming and stock raising. They have not always had the full protection that the government should have given them, but they have fared better of late years than they did before the Apaches were gotten under control.

who made the initial American contact with the Pimas in 1847, wrote: "To us it was a rare sight to be thrown in the midst of a large nation of what are termed wild Indians, surpassing many of the Christian nations in agriculture, little behind them in useful arts, and immeasurably before them in honesty and virtue." Quoted in Thomas E. Farish, *History of Arizona* (Phoenix, 1915), I, 35–36.

Chapter XVIII

Old Fashioned Justice

I CARRIED fourteen thousand dollars in gold and more than twice as much more in drafts on St. Louis back from California with me in a pair of saddle bags. Now-a-days the man who would carry that amount of money with him in going or coming through by rail would be thought very foolish, and the chances of his being robbed would be about nine out of ten.

I don't know that people were any more honest in those days than they are now, but it is certain that there was a great deal less robbing and stealing going on. Of course there was less to steal, but what money there was in the country was not protected as it is now. We had no fire and burglar-proof safes or time locks, or anything of that kind. The man who got a few hundred dollars ahead didn't carry it to a bank to deposit it, but laid it away in his house and felt less concern about it than most people do about a few dollars worth of silverware now-a-days.

I have seen men go to sleep in a room where they kept a trunk full of silver dollars, and if it wouldn't sound like bragging I might tell you that I had done so a good many times myself without ever dreaming of being robbed. The man

264

who has to keep a thousand dollars in his house over night in these times dreams about being murdered, and if any considerable number of people know that he has the money the chances are that his dream comes true. I think the way we used to administer justice in those days had a great deal to do with the remarkable security of property. There was less security for human life than there is now, perhaps, but every kind of property was certainly a great deal safer.

The fact is that stealing of any kind or character was not a safe business in the early history of this country. We had no jails filled with well-fed and well-kept criminals whose trials were postponed from time to time until all the witnesses against them died or moved out of the country. There were no delays in the trial of cases and no scoundrel ever escaped punishment on account of an error in the indictment or a technicality of the law. When a man committed a crime against property his punishment was certain and the execution of justice summary if he remained in the country or again made his appearance in the neighborhood where the crime had been committed.

What we looked upon as murder, although perhaps we didn't draw the line fine enough, was the killing of persons for the purpose of robbery or of a man not prepared to defend himself, and such killings as these we punished promptly. There was a good deal of promiscuous shooting and men were frequently killed in brawls and quarrels, but in such cases one party was usually as much to blame as the other and we allowed them to take care of themselves and settle their own difficulties in their own way.

We had just three grades of punishment for different classes of criminals. For minor offenses the punishment was thirty-nine lashes on the bare back of the offender. For the most serious offenses the punishment was death. Where the offender was a man whose criminal transactions could not be so clearly proved as to warrant the infliction of either the whipping or death penalty, but who was known to be a bad man generally, we notified him to leave the country and he always found that the only safe thing to do was to go.

I have told you that while engaged in other pursuits I had been raising a herd of cattle. These cattle I kept at the mouth of the Huerfano River, where I had picked out a fine body of land and started a stock ranch.

After my return from California, although my family remained at Taos until 1854, I spent a good portion of my time at the old fort on the Arkansas River which we called the Pueblo, and from which the city which has since grown up in the same place took its name. Some miners were coming into the country at that time and a great many emigrants were going through to California, Utah, and Oregon. Many of the miners and emigrants passed by the Pueblo and I remained there for the purpose of trading with them as they went along.

They generally had ox teams hitched to their wagons, and very frequently a party would come along with a lot of jaded and worn-out cattle which they were anxious to trade for oxen in good shape to travel. I could always trade fresh oxen for these footsore and broken-down animals to good advantage, generally getting about three or four for one. I sent the lame cattle out to my ranch and after pasturing them a few weeks in the Arkansas Valley I would have them in prime condition and ready to be traded for more disabled cattle. In this way I increased my herd very rapidly.

In 1853–54 we had a good deal of trouble with Indian and Mexican horse and cattle thieves, who would every now and then run off a few cattle or horses.

I had a neighbor on the Huerfano, who also had a large band of cattle. That was Joseph Doyle, who was for some years a man of considerable prominence in Colorado, and died while serving as a member of the territorial legislature. Doyle and I noticed that our cattle were disappearing mysteriously, and there was complaint of the same thing from the bands of emigrants passing through the country.

It took some time to find out what became of the stock, but we learned after a while that our cattle were being stolen by an organized band of thieves who ran them into New Mexico and disposed of them. The members of the band were all Mexicans and made their headquarters on the Fountain River, not far from Pueblo.

We found it necessary to organize a little party of regulators to deal with this band of robbers, as well as to punish some Cheyenne and Arapahoe thieves, and they made me captain of the party. We were not long in breaking up the gang. A close watch was kept on the stock and whenever any of it was stolen we took the trail and usually brought it back. Sometimes we brought back the robbers and sometimes we left them where we found them, but in either case they never stole any more of our stock.

Our court houses were like the primitive churches, and we could set up a temple of justice wherever it was most convenient. There used to be a cotton-wood grove near where the Union Depot stands now in the city of Pueblo, which very frequently served that purpose.

We always had a jury and a judge and counsel for the prosecution and defense when we tried a man for the violation of frontier law. The judge, who would be selected for the occasion, would take his seat on a stump or log, or more frequently on the ground. The jury box was as primitive as the judge's bench and the attorneys in the case didn't sit behind big desks with a cartload of books piled up before them. Sometimes there were three members of a jury and sometimes a dozen or half dozen.[78]

The witnesses were called and examined, and the lawyers never took up a whole day questioning and cross-questioning a single witness, or arguing to convince the judge that a confession of guilt should not be admitted as evidence.

Our trials seldom lasted more than an hour or two, and the jury always brought in a verdict promptly. Sentence was then pronounced and promptly executed, no time being given for an appeal from the decision of the court. If whipping was the penalty to be inflicted, the rawhide was brought out, the culprit was tied to a tree or post,

[78]On the organization of miners' courts and vigilance committees, see Baker and Hafen, *History of Colorado*, II, 480–85. The practical necessity for such measures was succinctly stated in an address to the citizens of the proposed State Government on the date of the first Convention, held in Denver City, May 7, 1859: "Government of some kind we must have," it stated, "and the question narrows itself down to this point: Shall it be the government of the knife and the revolver, or shall we unite in forming here [a new state government]?"

and some one of our number who was thought to have a sufficient development of muscle gave him the stipulated number of lashes.

If the judgment of the court was that capital punishment should be inflicted, two men were selected to act as executioners. Two rifles, one of which was loaded while the other contained only a blank charge, were handed to them and the affair was soon ended. It is possible that judgment in these cases may sometimes have been hasty, and now and then a mistake may have been made. I have never heard anybody claim, however, that the regularly constituted courts make no mistakes, and I doubt very much if we were in error any oftener than they are.[79]

There was one bandit who commenced operations about this time who eluded all efforts at capture and terrorized the country for ten years or more. That was the notorious robber, Espinosa. When I first knew Espinosa he was living on the Conejos River, and up to the time of the Mexican War he led a very reputable kind of a life.

[79]A.D. Richardson records a California story as typifying the frontier attitude which Wootton here expresses. A miner was called as a juror in a murder case. When asked by the judge, "Have you any conscientious scruples about capital punishment?"

"I have," he replied, "in all such cases when it is not administered by a vigilance committee." *Beyond the Mississippi,* 488.

The story runs, although I don't know how true it is, that in 1848, or perhaps a year later he formed the acquaintance of a young American adventurer who had with him a considerable amount of money. Espinosa and the American became intimate friends, and the latter became the guest of the Mexican at his home.

At the Espinosa homestead the stranger met a beautiful, dark-eyed, dark-haired, but fair-skinned senorita, sister to the man who afterward became the pirate of the mountains, with whom he fell deeply in love. As a consequence of his infatuation his intended visit of a few days lengthened into a stay of several weeks, and in the meantime he had taken Espinosa into his confidence to the extent of informing him what amount of money he had in his possession.

The cupidity of the Mexican then got the better of him and he planned to rob his friend. With this object in view he one night entered the room in which the American was sleeping and had just placed his hands upon the buckskin sack which contained the coveted wealth when the owner awoke and with pistol in hand sprang up to defend his property. A struggle ensued in the dark in the course of which Espinosa was slightly wounded by a shot from the young American's pistol and a moment later, to save his own life, he had struck his long, keen-edged Spanish knife into the heart of the man who had entered his home as a guest.

The noise of the scuffle and the report of the pistol shot aroused the household, and just as the American sank bleeding and dying upon the floor his Mexican sweetheart, followed by several other members of the family, stepped into the room with a light and Espinosa's crime, in all its hideousness, was laid bare.

The unfortunate adventurer had not been more deeply enamored of the mountain maiden than she had been of her handsome suitor. She had returned his love with all the warmth of her passionate nature and when she saw him dead at her feet her grief knew no bounds. Falling upon her knees beside the body of her murdered lover her tears rained down upon his face, while between her bursts of grief she called down curses upon the head of his murderer.

Standing, as he did, convicted of this fearful crime in the presence of perhaps half a score of witnesses, Espinosa saw that he must henceforth be an outcast and at the same moment he appears to have made up his mind to become an outlaw as well. In the confusion which followed the discovery of the murder he slipped away unobserved, carrying with him the treasure which had incited him to robbery and murder, and mounting his fleetest horse he made his way to the mountains which were afterward his home.

It was several years before he gathered around him a band of followers large enough to enable him to terrorize whole communities and defy the authorities, but for a long time he was noted as one of the most daring and desperate scoundrels that ever infested any country.

His headquarters were in the Sangre de Christo Mountains, and from there he made periodical marauding expeditions into the surrounding country. There was nothing which comes within the province of a freebooter which Espinosa did not consider a feature of his calling. He would undertake the robbery of a stage coach, burglarize a Mexican hacienda, or drive away a herd of cattle or horses just as the notion happened to strike him, and whenever murder was necessary to expedite or facilitate the carrying out of his plans he committed murder. He also committed many murders which were purely malicious and for which there was not the shadow of an excuse.

He added to his other crimes that of kidnapping, and many a handsome Mexican girl was carried away to his mountain haunts to be held for ransom or kept for the purposes of debauchery.

It was not until 1864, or possibly a little later than that, that we finally got rid of Espinosa. His raids had been so extensive and his crimes so numerous that a large reward had been offered for his capture, either dead or alive, and I think the authorities preferred that he should be turned over to them dead.

He was captured by an old compadre of mine, who had been in the mountains many years and who is still living. Tom Tobin, of whom I have spoken before, was the man who captured him, and to whom Colorado was indebted for ridding the country of the Bandit King, as he has since been called by those who have written about him.

After keeping comparatively quiet for some time, Espinosa had come down from his hiding place and raided the country about Cañon City. After paying his respects to the people there he started towards the mountains when Tobin, with four or five men who had been detailed to assist him, struck the trail of the robbers and followed them closely. I had gone over to the Sangre de Christo to look after a wagon train which had been caught there in a snow storm, and stopped over night at a sort of public house on my road.

When I walked into the bar room several men were sitting by the fire and among them I recognized Espinosa and his nephew, who was a member of his band, hardly less notorious than the robber chief himself. They took a drink or two and in a little while went out, quietly mounted their horses, and rode away.

The next morning Tobin came along with his posse and told me what his business was. I informed him that the man he was looking for had been there only a few hours earlier, and pointed out the direction which he had taken when he rode away. Tobin followed in the direction I had indicated and after a little time caught sight of a smoke curling up out of a grove of cottonwood trees. He left his men behind and crept up, very cautiously, toward the grove, until he could see Espinosa and his companion sitting by a camp fire.

Capturing the robbers alive, under the circumstances, was not to be thought of. Capturing them dead was much easier and safer. Tobin laid his rifle across a log and waited until Espinosa stood up, when the rifle cracked and the robber fell dead. A second shot killed the remaining bandit and Tobin had accomplished what he set out to do.[80]

[80] Wootton gives a more detailed account of the activities and death of Espinosa than has been found elsewhere. H. H. Bancroft (*History of Nevada, Colorado, and Wyoming*, 424–25) relates that in the summer of 1863 a small band of Mexican guerrillas led by "the bloody Espinosas" terrorized the South Park area of Colorado. The leaders were reputed to have been brothers, or cousins, from Chihuahua, who in a period of a few weeks perpetrated a series of wholesale murders. One of them was killed by a pursuing party led by Joseph Lamp. The other (the man to whom Wootton refers), along with his nephew, was slain by Tom

Before he could receive the reward to which he was entitled it was necessary that he should prove to the satisfaction of the authorities that he had killed his man, and in order that this fact might not be questioned he cut off the heads of the two brigands, tumbled them into a gunny-sack, and carried them to Fort Massachusetts, located at the base of Wet Mountain, and afterward called Fort Garland.[81] The heads were identified as those of the two robbers and in due course of time the reward which had been earned at so great a risk of life was paid; at least I understood at the time it was paid, although it has since been stated that such was not the case.[82]

Tobin. He had written a letter to Governor Evans of Colorado in which he acknowledged killing 22 men. It seems worthy of note that although Wootton knew him and was aware of his numerous crimes he made no effort to arrest or restrain him.

[81]Fort Massachusetts was established in 1852 about seven miles north of the present-day town of Fort Garland. The site is on the Denver and Rio Grande Railroad some 108 miles southwest of Pueblo. The fort was established to afford protection to the Mexican farmers of the San Luis Valley. In 1858 it was replaced by Fort Garland at the site of the town of Fort Garland. See Baker and Hafen, *History of Colorado*, II, 431 and 580.

[82]The practice of beheading wanted criminals or other enemies was widespread in frontier and border areas. Wootton here correctly states the reason for it. In *Vanished Arizona*, the Lakeside Classics volume for 1939, Mrs. Summerhayes supplies data concerning it in Arizona in the seventies. At an earlier period deserters from the

We managed to preserve pretty good order in the mountains early in the fifties and the lawlessness which disgraced the country at a later period did not commence until immigration to Colorado set in. Then the thieves and cut-throats and desperadoes flocked into the country and we had single-handed robbers, bands of robbers, vigilance committees, and lynchings by the score.

Some of these bands had to be hunted down by organized military companies, and a war of extermination was kept up until they were driven out of the country, killed, or imprisoned. Comparatively few of them, by the way, had the good fortune to escape with a term in the territorial

British garrison at Fort Drummond in Lake Huron are reported to have been pursued and beheaded by Indians eager to collect the reward for their apprehension. From this practice a legend of the headless soldiers of the area has developed. Following the massacre by white settlers and soldiers from Fort Harker, Kansas, of a band of Pawnee Indians in February, 1869, a contemporary settler related that a Negro came with an ambulance from Fort Harker, beheaded the dead Indians, and carried the heads back to the Fort, for which he was rewarded by the officers who had employed him. Although the narrator did not know why the heads were wanted, Wootton's account supplies the reason. I have been told in recent years by a participant in the Philippine War that the bringing in of heads of guerrillas or other wanted individuals was practiced there. See Martha Summerhayes, *Vanished Arizona*, 110–113; Adolph Roenick, *Pioneer History of Kansas* (n.p., 1933), 129; Joseph and Estelle Bayliss, *River of Destiny. The Saint Marys* (Detroit, 1955), 137–38 and 319.

prison. Most of them were very summarily dealt with and when their criminal careers ended they ended suddenly and permanently. When the country had become to some extent settled up the courts were organized and the men who had been in the habit of taking the law into their own hands have demonstrated that they are content to allow the law to take its course as long as there is a reasonable certainty that justice will be administered promptly.

Now and then, when some particularly atrocious crime is committed, there is a revival of the old spirit and a trial takes place in Judge Lynch's court, followed by a prompt execution of the sentence pronounced. It is very seldom, however, that we hear of a lynching, and taken all in all, the people of Colorado are to-day quite as law-abiding as the people of older states. All they want is the assurance that criminals will receive the punishment prescribed by law without unreasonable delay, and that is something which the people of any community have a right to demand at the hands of those whose business it is to administer and execute the laws. If their demands are not respected, if they receive no consideration at the hands of the authorities, I am inclined to think it is still an open question whether they have not the right to take the law into their own hands, after the fashion of the old-timers.

Chapter XIX

Penned Up by the Utes

I DIVIDED my time between Taos and the Pueblo during the closing months of 1853 and the early part of 1854. I had decided to try ranching, as we called it, stock raising it would be called now, on an extensive scale, and the first thing to be done was to build a fort which would afford protection against the Indians.

As I have already said, I had started a ranch on the Arkansas River near the mouth of the Huerfano, about twenty miles from the Pueblo. I went down there with a number of workmen and in a short time had completed a very substantial fortress. What I intended should be my dwelling house, built of logs, was protected by a high wall and stockade and at two corners of the surrounding wall, diagonally across from each other, I put up strong bullet-proof bastions. From one of these bastions I could see two sides of my fort and from the other the opposite two sides, so that in case of an attack I was prepared to receive an enemy coming from any direction.

My location was just above where the two rivers came together, and altogether the position was one which could be easily defended. I built a kind of primitive ferry boat with which to get back and forth across the river, and then I had everything in readiness for the reception of my family. It was not until July of 1854, however, that I thought it safe to attempt to bring my wife and children over the mountains, because the Indians were all the time on the war-path. While I crossed over several times myself, it was only by hard riding— sometimes without stopping an hour for sleep during the trip—and aiming to keep clear of the established trail, rather than to follow it, that I managed to get through safely. I made one of these rides from the Pueblo to Taos, a distance of one hundred and sixty-five miles, in a little less than twenty-four hours. That time I caught sight of the Indians at several points along the way and once they saw me. They fired several shots at me and some of the bullets came so close that I could hear them whistle as they passed by.

I finally arranged to have my family sent to Fort Massachusetts, or Fort Garland as it was called afterward, and from there we had an escort of soldiers to accompany us to our new home on the Arkansas. Our nearest neighbor was my old friend and partner, Doyle, of whom I have spoken before, and we lived only a hundred yards apart. Two miles up the river lived another old hunter and trapper, and eight miles farther up, at the mouth of the St. Charles River, were some traders who had located there temporarily. Then the next nearest settlement was at the Pueblo, where there were a few people at the old fort.[83]

I kept a few men with me at my place all the time, and after we had gotten fairly settled down we felt pretty safe. Nothing happened to disturb us, or at least to cause us any particular uneasiness, until the early part of the winter, when the Utes swept down through the Arkansas Valley leaving a trail of blood behind them and frightening some of the settlers, who escaped with their

[83]The settler two miles above Wootton's place was Charles Ortebees, who is identified by Wootton *post*, 288. Ortebees had been a trapper employed by Bent and St. Vrain before the building of Fort Bent. He married a Mexican wife, and following the American occupation he settled on a farm near Wootton's place. Besides his Mexican wife he had a Cheyenne woman named Picking Bones Woman. A son, John Ortebees was living in Oklahoma in the early twentieth century.

In April, 1860 the Editor of the *Rocky Mountain News* toured the valley and reported his observations in the issue of April 25: "First we pass the ruins of J. B. Doyles' trading post abandoned years since. Next is the farm of Charley Autobee and his village of retainers, Mexicans, and Indians, occupying log cabins surrounding a plaza or open square." On July 22, 1861, the *News* stated that Doyle had over 600 acres of growing corn, in appearance as "luxurious" as any in Iowa or Illinois. September 6, 1861, the *News* reported the arrival of a flour mill for Doyle and Company, to be shipped to the Huerfano for use in grinding the grain the firm raised there. Data adapted from Baker and Hafen, *History of Colorado*, II, Chap. XI, and George B. Grinnell "Bent's Old Fort," in *Kansas Hist. Colls.*, XV, 65–66.

lives, so badly that they left the country and never returned to it.

The outbreak was so sudden and unexpected that we were not entirely prepared for it. Of course we knew that the Utes might make a raid on us at any time, but we had gone along without receiving a visit from them until we began to look upon their coming as a possibility rather than a probability.

My neighbor, Doyle, had gone up among the Arapahoes on a trading trip, in which I was interested with him, and I was to look after the safety of his family as well as my own during his absence. Just before Christmas, as I could see no sign of hostile Indians being in the country, I concluded to go with a party of friends on a hunting trip up the Arkansas.

There were five of us in the party, one of the number being a brother of James A. McDougall, the first Attorney-General of California, and afterwards United States Senator from that State.[84]

[84]James A. McDougall was born in New York State in 1817. He studied law and began its practice in Chicago in 1837. From 1842 to 1846 he served as Attorney General of Illinois. He subsequently removed to the Southwest and eventually settled in San Francisco. From October, 1850 to December, 1851 he served as Attorney General of California. From March, 1861 to March, 1867 he represented California in the U.S. Senate. He died at Albany, Sept. 3, 1867. Data condensed from *Biog. Directory of the American Congress*, 1774–1849.

We found plenty of wild turkeys and other small game, but no deer. McDougall was anxious to get larger game and I had promised to kill a couple of deer for him before we returned. With this promise in mind I rode out from the camp early one morning, when we had gotten as far up the river as Coal Creek, and soon caught sight of some elk tracks.

If I had seen nothing but the elk tracks I should have been very much pleased with the discovery just at that time, but I saw something else which at once made me decidedly uneasy. There were horse tracks among the elk tracks and I could see that the game had been chased by hunters. The tracks were only a day old, apparently, and I got down off my horse and after examining them carefully came to the conclusion that the hunters were Indians.

I went back to camp and told my companions that the Utes were in the country and that I proposed to get out of it. They laughed at me and intimated that I was easily frightened. I told them it might be that I was unnecessarily alarmed, but I was scared just bad enough to make me get back down the Arkansas as soon as possible and if they didn't want to go with me I would go alone.

McDougall reminded me that I had promised him a couple of deer, and I told him I would go out and get them that day if they would start home with me in the morning. They agreed to this and I went out after the deer. I kept a sharp look-out for Indians, and once, when I rode up on a little hill where I could get a good view of the surrounding country, I caught sight of an Indian's head. I only saw it for a moment, but I knew just as well what it was as if I had looked at it all day and I knew that where there was one Indian there were more.

I turned toward the camp and on my way back ran across two deer. They happened to be standing side by side and I killed them both at one shot. I loaded them on my horse, and carrying them to camp told McDougall that my promise to him had been made good.

We remained in camp that night, but I didn't allow myself to sleep any. I thought it more than likely that the Indian whom I had seen had also seen me, and I hardly expected we should get away without a fight, if we got away at all. Luckily, however, we were not attacked, and at three o'clock the next morning we started for home. When we got to the Pueblo an old Mexican came running out to meet us and said that a big band of horses had crossed the river the night before, as they had discovered by seeing the tracks.

I told him that the Ute Indians had been riding those horses, and that they were evidently watching for a chance to attack the fort. He insisted that we should go into the fort and stop over night, but I refused to do so, telling him that I had my own family and that of a friend to protect and should not stop until I reached my own place. I warned him, however, that he and his people were in great danger, and that their safety lay in keeping the Indians out of the fort.

This was the evening before Christmas, and I cautioned the old Mexican particularly about allowing the Indians to come into the fort, knowing that the following day would be one of their feast days and that they were likely to be caught off their guard on that account.

I went on down the river, stopping again where the traders were encamped at the mouth of the St. Charles to warn them of the impending danger, and reached home late that evening. The next day I kept close to my little fort and spent a good deal of the time on the house top, looking for Indians. The traders above me on the Arkansas, whom I had warned of the danger the night before, gathered up what they could carry with them and started down the river to what they thought would be a more secure place. They wanted me to go with them, but I thought it better to stay where I was and if necessary make a fight to protect my property. I could not induce the traders to stop with me and I was left with only four men to do garrison duty.

About the middle of the afternoon I happened to be on the lookout and saw a man on horseback, riding as fast as his horse could carry him, from the direction of the Pueblo. I was satisfied then that the trouble had commenced, and the information that he brought me was of a most startling character.

The Pueblo, he said, had been captured by the Indians and every man, woman, and child in it had probably been killed. He had been riding towards the place when he saw the Indians enter the fort. He rode up on to one of the high hills overlooking the old rendezvous of the trappers, and witnessed the beginning of the conflict between the Utes and the Mexicans. He had not waited to see the finish because he knew well enough what the result would be, and his statement that every man, woman, and child in the place had been killed was justified by his knowledge of the situation and the Indian custom under such circumstances.

As they had started in to raid the valley I had no doubt they would soon reach my place, and I prepared to give them as warm a reception as possible. I stationed two men in each of my bastions, and as we had plenty of arms and ammunition I did not feel that our lives and what little property I had in the fort were in great danger, but I fully expected that my large herd of cattle, which I could see grazing down along the river, would be driven away by the redskins.

The traders whom I have mentioned as moving down the river sent a party of nine Cherokee Indian teamsters back to their old camping ground to bring away some goods which had been left behind, and early on the morning following the massacre at the Pueblo they passed my house. I had seen nothing of the Utes in the meantime, and began to think it possible that they had turned back up the river from Pueblo. The teamsters had scarcely gotten out of sight, however, when I heard shooting in the direction they had taken, and a little later saw the smoke rising from their wagons, which the Indians had captured and were burning.

None of the teamsters escaped to tell how they were attacked, or how many Indians they killed in the fight which followed. We found all the bodies and buried them later, and the position in which we found them indicated that they had made a brave fight, but they had driven into an ambuscade and had no show for making a successful resistance.

After killing the teamsters the Indians came on down the river and passed the home of my neighbor two miles above me. This neighbor was Charles Ortebees, a Frenchman, who had been in the country a long time, was a good Indian fighter, and had his place as well protected as mine. He had several men with him, all of whom were inside his fort and ready to fight, with the exception of one. This one was outside the fort digging a grave for poor old Charlefou, one of the early trappers, whom I have already mentioned once or twice. The man who was digging the grave did not see the Indians but he heard them coming, too late for him to gain the fort. He dropped down in the nearly-finished grave and the Indians passed along without seeing him. They did not stop to make an attack on Ortebee's place, but divided into two parties, evidently with the intention of rounding up and driving off a lot of our cattle.

There were about sixty Indians in the whole band, but only a small number in the party that came nearest to my place. I had been reinforced by this time by something like a dozen men who had come up the river, and they mounted their horses and dashed out of the fort toward the small band of Indians, although they were careful not to get far away.

The Indians ran, and this little sally led them to believe that we were prepared to fight outside the fort as well as from the inside. They withdrew to a considerable distance, gathered up what cattle they could without coming any nearer to us, and started back in the same direction they had come. They did not succeed in getting one of my cattle, and I escaped without any loss whatever. One thing which perhaps hurried the Utes out of the valley was the fact that they were getting dangerously near the Arapahoes, with whom they were at war. As it was, the Arapahoes followed and overtook them at Coal Creek, where they had a hard fight.

The Arapahoes gave the Utes a thorough whipping in that fight, but they were themselves the greatest sufferers in the long run. They destroyed the Ute village, tore down their lodges, and carried away their blankets and such other things as they cared for. It turned out that the small pox had broken out among the Utes and the plunder which the Arapahoes carried away being infected, many of them caught the disease and died of it. They rendered the whites a great service, however, and one which we fully appreciated at the time.

As soon as it was safe for us to do so, we went to the Pueblo to learn, if possible, whether any of the people there had had the good fortune to escape with their lives, or if we could do nothing else to give the victims decent burial. We found but one person alive in the fort; that was an old

Mexican who had been badly wounded, and who died a few days later.

We learned from him about all that was ever known about the fight. This was that the Indians came to the fort on Christmas morning, professed friendship, and asked to be allowed to come inside for the purpose of holding a peace conference. All those who had taken refuge in the old fort, or Pueblo, were Mexicans, and I had expected the Indians would undertake to outwit them in this way. That was my reason for cautioning the old fellow—of whom I have spoken as having come out to meet us as we were returning from our hunting trip—not to allow the Indians to come inside the fort under any pretext.

Notwithstanding the warning the Mexicans, thinking perhaps they might be able to do some trading with the Utes, allowed the whole band to come inside and the result was that a wholesale massacre followed. Of the seventeen persons whom the Indians found in the fort all were killed, with the exception of the wounded man whom we found there and a woman and two children who were carried away as captives. The woman, a good-looking young Mexican girl, was killed before the Indians left the valley. We could never learn what became of the children, but they probably met the same fate. Besides those killed at the Pueblo and the nine teamsters killed near my home there were some others who fell into the hands of the Indians, so that altogether they probably murdered between thirty and forty people on this raid.

So far as myself and my family were concerned, however, we found when the hostiles had been driven out of the country that we had only suffered to the extent of a good scare. I took this as another evidence that I had been born lucky, and felt more secure than ever from that time on.

That was the only time I was ever threatened by hostile Indians while I lived on the Arkansas. The Plains Indians used to visit me frequently; that is, the Cheyennes and the Arapahoes did, but I was on good terms with them always and their visits were at all times friendly ones. What trading I did during this time was with these Indians. My relations with these two tribes were always friendly and even after the Cheyennes went on the war path some years later I had no difficulty in making peace with them on my own account.

When they were plundering other wagon trains and killing scores of emigrants my wagon trains were always safe from attack so far as the Cheyennes were concerned, and I could trade with them at any time when they had anything to trade. I had to be liberal in making presents, but I thought their good will cheaply purchased as long as it only cost me a few sacks of flour, sugar, or coffee when I met them with a train load of goods.

This trading with hostile Indians had, by the way, to be carried on in a sort of clandestine manner. In the first place, the Indians themselves did not want to show their friendship for any white man openly or allow it to be understood that they had any favorites among them. In the second place, no license could be procured to trade with the hostiles because those in charge of Indian affairs sought to prevent them from procuring arms and ammunition and other supplies, and were under the impression that if they could keep the traders away from them the Indians could not get those things.

In view of the fact, however, that the authorities seemed at times to be powerless to afford us any protection from hostile Indians, I used to think I had a right to protect myself, even if I had to pursue a course which was not strictly in accordance with the rules laid down to govern us in our intercourse with the Indians.

A single visit which I made to one of the Cheyenne villages resulted in our coming to an understanding which prevented any trouble between us thereafter. The Indians kept a close watch on the trails all the time and they generally knew about when I should be passing through their country.

When they caught sight of my train one or two of the Cheyennes, or perhaps a small party, would show themselves long enough to apprise me of their presence and then I was expected to drop a few sacks of sugar, coffee, or something else which would be a sufficient token of my good will and friendship, out of the wagons so that the Indians could come along by and by and pick it up. In this way we got along without having any open dealings with each other, and at the same time kept up our friendly relations.

Chapter XX

Colorado's Oldest Farmer

I REMAINED on my ranch more than a year after the Pueblo massacre and did fairly well in a business way, trading with the emigrants and raising cattle, along with a little farming, but it seemed a very quiet life for me after almost twenty years of constant changing about and almost daily adventure. There were two things about it I didn't like. One was that it was too tame an existence, and the other was that I wasn't getting rich as fast as I wanted to.

I had had some bad luck in the two years before I commenced ranching. When I returned from California I found that several thousand dollars in silver coin which I had left at home had been loaned to a friend, who squandered it all, and misplaced confidence on my own part lost me nearly fifty thousand dollars more soon after that.

We didn't mind the loss of a fortune so much in those days as we do now, because they were more easily, or at least more quickly, made. Still, I had not entirely given up the idea of going back to my old home by and by with enough to live on, and I was anxious to make up what I had lost as rapidly as possible.

After the Ute scare, neighbor Doyle thought it unsafe to keep his family in that country any longer and moved down to Fort Barclay, seven miles from where Fort Union is now.[85] My next nearest neighbor abandoned the country, too, and I was left alone in the valley. This made it necessary for me to remain about home most of the time and interfered with my trading and hunting trips.

I made several trades with the Indians which served to break the monotony of living on a farm, and did some trapping along the Arkansas, not because there was any profit in it but because I wanted something to do.

My hunting trips were short ones and I killed just about enough buffaloes, deer, and bears to keep me supplied with meat. On one of these trips I killed the queerest specimen of a deer that anybody ever shot at in the Rocky Mountains. It had a full-grown deer's body, perfectly formed, and large antlers, but its legs were no longer than those of a six month's-old pig. That was the only

[85]Our only information concerning Fort Barclay, apart from Wootton's allusions to it, is a statement in the biographical sketch of William Kroenig that in 1856 he bought Fort Barclay with 700 acres of land. Since Fort Union had been established by the Government near-by in 1851, the usefulness of Fort Barclay had evidently ceased. See Charles F. Coan, *History of New Mexico* (Chicago, 1925), II, 53.

dwarf deer that I ever saw, and if its skin had been properly stuffed and mounted it might have attracted more attention than the skeleton of a mastodon in the Smithsonian Institution or some other museum.

The only company I had at my ranch home, outside of my own family and a few employes, was now and then an old trapper who would come out of his way to see me or a company of emigrants who would stop long enough to trade for fresh cattle and put their wagons in repair.

Those who cross the Plains to reach the mountain country or go on over the mountains to find homes farther west, nowadays, sometimes imagine that they are undergoing great hardships, but their experiences are pleasant compared with those of the early emigrants. On the long, tedious trip across the Plains they were menaced continually by Indians, suffered sometimes for food and water, were buffeted by wind and hail storms, and what was worse than all the rest, women and children and sometimes men fell sick when they were hundreds of miles away from any place where medicines or the attendance of a physician could be procured. Those who died were buried on the Plains, and to their friends this seemed almost like casting the remains of their loved ones overboard into the sea.

When these bands of emigrants reached my

home they used to tell me that it seemed to them like finding an oasis in the desert. It was the one spot which they found by the wayside, in traveling hundreds of miles, where they saw growing wheat and corn and other crops which reminded them of the farms and homes they had left behind. They would almost always stop with me a day or two to rest and trade, and at the same time to obtain such information as I could give them about the country they had to travel through before reaching the end of their journey.

I used to hear some sad stories of their sufferings on the way, and sometimes would be a witness of their misfortunes. I remember one peculiarly unfortunate family which started from Independence, Missouri, with a party of emigrants that reached my place in the summer of 1855. This family, which came originally from western Pennsylvania, had stopped for a year or two in Missouri, and then, like hundreds of others, had concluded to seek the Golden West.

When they left Independence the family consisted of George Shaw, a young man perhaps thirty years of age, his wife, and two small children, a boy and girl, and Mrs. Shaw's mother, a lady about fifty years old. Their troubles began when they reached the Indian country. First, one of the children and then the other sickened and died. Then about two weeks before they reached my house the Comanche Indians attacked the train and in the fight which followed young Shaw was fatally wounded and died two days later.

The heart-broken wife never recovered from the shock caused by the loss of her husband and children, and when the train stopped at my house she was lifted tenderly out of the wagon, in which she had been made as comfortable as possible, and carried into the house, that she might die, as she said, "surrounded by some of the evidences of civilization." She lasted only a few hours and the next day, which happened to be Sunday, an old Methodist minister who was with the party preached a funeral sermon and they buried her under a cottonwood tree on the bank of the Arkansas.

The grief of the poor old lady who was thus left alone, having been bereft of son, daughter, and grand-children, was one of the most pitiable things I have ever seen, and the tears ran like rain down the rough, bearded cheeks of a score of men who witnessed it. There was no way for her to return to her friends in the East, and the only thing she could do was to journey along with the kind-hearted emigrants, who promised to care for her to the best of their ability in the future.

This incident was unusually pathetic, but there were many similar occurrences which came under my notice at that time, and I think I am safe in saying that the Pilgrim Fathers never endured such hardships or braved such perils as did the early settlers of the Far West.

I have mentioned the fact that I engaged to some extent in farming after the eastern fashion while I lived at the mouth of Huerfano River. I constructed irrigating ditches and raised corn, wheat, and other kinds of grain and all kinds of vegetables. I think I am to-day the pioneer farmer of Colorado. What I mean by that is, that I was the first American to do any farming in the territory now embraced within the state lines. Possibly some of those who came to the country at an early day may have engaged in farming before 1854, but I did not know of any farming being done at that time.[86]

[86]Note that while the chapter head reads "Colorado's oldest farmer," Wootton himself carefully limits his claim to being the first *American* farmer. The distinction is important. Wootton's farming operations began in 1854. In 1851 some New Mexican settlers established themselves on the Culebra near present-day San Luis, where they dug irrigating ditches and began farming operations. Terrorized by the Utes, they abandoned the undertaking and returned to New Mexico. In 1852 Fort Massachusetts was established by the Government to afford protection to settlers in this area, and the farming operations were resumed, with settlements established at San Luis and other points on the Culebra and also on the Costilla and the Trinchera. They have been continuous since that time. See Baker and Hafen, *History of Colorado*, II, 431 and 580.

When I got to raising corn and wheat I had to have some way of grinding what I wanted to use for bread, and as I was a sort of jack of all trades I went to work and put up a pretty good mill for those times. The mill-stones we cut out of the rocks which we found along the banks of the Arkansas, and the water wheel didn't look much like the modern turbine wheel, but it answered the purpose for which it was designed. We poured a few bushels of grain into the hopper at night and the next morning we went around and scraped up the flour. A mill of that kind would be a little slow for these times, but we managed to get along with it very well.

I came as near losing my life once or twice while I lived at that place as I ever did anywhere, and it wasn't at the hands of Indians either.

I had had in my employ more or less of the time for several years a Frenchman by the name of Murray, who was married to a Mexican woman and lived in a cabin only a little distance from my own. He was an idle, drunken, worthless fellow and had made me a great deal of trouble, but his wife was an industrious woman who put in her time making grain sacks for me and doing house work for my family. The woman's wages were always paid to her, and when she got a few dollars ahead she would frequently leave the money at my house to prevent her vagabond husband from getting hold of and squandering it.

This made him very angry and he threatened to kill me because I would not give him the money which his wife worked hard to earn.

I paid no attention to his threats because I didn't think they amounted to anything, but one day when I was doing some odd job about the house the click of a rifle attracted my attention and looking up I saw Murray standing about ten feet away from me with his gun cocked and raised, ready to shoot. He said he intended to kill me if I didn't give him the money he wanted, and as he had the drop on me it wouldn't have been good policy for me to refuse. I commenced parleying with him, however, and while talking kept edging closer to him. When I got within five or six feet of him I made a spring and grabbed his gun, wrenching it out of his hands. Then I turned his own weapon on him and made him get down on his knees and beg me to spare his life. He promised to behave better in the future and after taking his ammunition away from him I fired off his gun and handing it back to him told him to go about his business.

I got along with him pretty well for a time after that, but one day he was with his wife when she received some money, which was left at my house for safe-keeping. He came around alone in a little while and demanded the money. When I refused to give it to him he ran out of the house in a great rage, and my former experience with him, led me to believe he meant mischief. Anyhow, I proposed to keep a close watch on him as I didn't want to take chances on again talking him out of shooting me.

I picked up my gun, which was always loaded, and walked out in front of my house, so that I could see the door of his cabin, only a hundred yards distant. A second or two later I saw the muzzle of a gun poked out of the door, and Murray followed it. He caught sight of me and was in the act of raising his gun, when he let it fall very suddenly and abruptly about the time my gun cracked.

My first impulse was to kill the miserable fellow, who seemed determined to take my life without any sort of provocation for it, but as I brought my gun up to my shoulder it occurred to me that I could get along without killing him and might feel better over it afterward. I thought shooting an arm off would answer every purpose, and aimed at his right elbow. That was the reason he dropped his gun just as he was bringing it to bear on me. What little shooting he did after that he did left handed, and never bothered me.

As I started out to tell you awhile ago, after two or three years of farming I got tired of it because it kept me too much in one place, and just at that time a proposition came to me from my former neighbor, Doyle, to go into partnership with him in the freighting business. We kept up a correspondence about the matter for some time and finally reached an agreement by which I was to take full charge of the business and run all the wagon trains, while Doyle was to furnish his share of the capital that we should have to invest.

We proposed to make one trip through to Kansas City and back, starting from Fort Union, each year, and the balance of the year we expected would be taken up freighting for the government from Fort Union to Albuquerque. There was a military post at the latter place and its supplies were received mainly from Fort Union.

About the time I completed my arrangements for going into the freighting business and was preparing to move my family to Fort Barclay, my wife died, leaving me with four small children to care for. Mrs. Wootton, was a daughter of Manuel Le Fevre, a Canadian Frenchman, who came to this country from St. Louis at an early day and was one of the best-known traders in the mountains. He lived at Taos, and after the death of my wife, my children were cared for at his home until I married again.

After completing arrangements for the care of my children, I went down to Fort Barclay in the winter of 1856 and commenced getting things ready for a trip to the States as soon as the spring opened.

Chapter XXI

Ox Teams and Prairie Schooners

NOW that I am going to tell you something about my experience as a freighter I must describe more particularly than I have yet a freighting outfit. The old-fashioned wagon trains and the stage line were contemporaries and both went out of existence at the same time. To-day they are reminiscences of ten years ago, and while it seems to me that only a few years have passed since I was whacking the ox teams across the Plains the country is full of people who never saw a wagon train or went bumping over the mountains in a stage coach.

Sometimes I sit here half dreaming, after the fashion of old men, and almost expecting to hear the crack of the stage driver's whip and the rattle of the stage wheels, when the whistle of a locomotive as it comes tearing down the mountain reminds me that the old days are gone and we have a new order of things. Then, when I look around for the old fellows who handled the reins over six or eight horses and kept a lookout for Indians at the same time and my old partners in the freighting business I don't find any of them, and that impresses upon me the fact that what I am telling about now happened a long time ago.

The freight train with which I started from Fort Union to Kansas City on the first day of March, 1856, was a typical train, and a description of it will give you a general idea of all freight trains, although some were larger and some smaller than this one. To begin with then, I had thirty-six wagons and to each of these wagons were hitched five pairs of oxen. This made ten head of cattle to each wagon, and three hundred and sixty in all. In addition to these I drove along with the train a pretty large herd of cattle upon which I could draw to fill out the teams in case any of the oxen were killed or injured in any way or, as frequently happened, got sore-footed. Altogether it took over four hundred cattle to keep up the train, and when the teams were hitched and stood ready to start we had a procession nearly a mile long.

Our wagons were what we called the prairie schooners. They were strong, heavy wagons, with long, high beds, and would carry loads three or four times as big as can be carried on the ordinary farm and road wagons in use now.[87] It took forty

[87]The prairie schooner was the descendant of the famed Pennsylvania or Conestoga wagon, a brief sketch of which is supplied by the present Editor in *Chicago Highways Old and New* (Chicago, 1923), 142–43. Josiah Gregg states that the wagons then most in use (as of 1844) on the Trail were made in Pittsburgh, and were usually drawn by eight oxen or mules. More recently, he added, larger and

men to manage the train. There was one driver to each wagon, and then the wagon-masters, who had a general oversight of the train, and the herders, who took charge of the stock when we went into camp, brought the number up to forty.

In addition to the freight wagons we always had an ambulance in which we carried some of our provisions, and had room for a teamster or any one else traveling with the train who might happen to get sick along the road. Sometimes we would carry two or three passengers in the ambulance.

The men were divided into parties of ten each, which we called a mess, and each mess was furnished with a camp outfit for cooking purposes. Then each mess selected a cook, who was also a teamster but got extra pay and was relieved of guard duty and certain kinds of work which the others had to do.

When we selected a camping place and got ready to stop for the night the wagons were driven up into two lines so as to form a pen, or as we called it, a corral. The tongues of the wagons

heavier wagons drawn by ten or twelve and with a cargo capacity of 5000 pounds had become common. Wootton, entering the trade a decade or so later than Gregg's book was written, of course employed the heavier wagons, loaded with large cargoes. See Josiah Gregg, *The Commerce of the Prairies,* the Lakeside Classics volume for 1926, Chaps. II and III.

were turned outside the corral and the fore wheel of a wagon rested against the hind wheel of the one directly in front of it. Driving them up in this way left the cattle all outside of the corral, and they were then unyoked and driven to water, after which they were watched by the herders while they fed on the prairie grass until they got ready to lie down for the night. That was what we called a camp corral. What we called a fighting corral, which we formed when we were attacked or likely to be attacked by the Indians, was made by turning the wagon tongues inside the circle of wagons. This brought the cattle all inside the corral and made it easy to protect them and keep them from stampeding.

We always started on the drive early in the morning. The cattle were driven inside the corral, yoked together, and hitched to the wagons in the order in which they were to start out, those which had been driven behind and had taken the dust of the train one day going ahead the next.

As I had charge of the train I was called the major domo, a term we borrowed from the Mexicans and always used. My two assistants were wagon-masters. My orders had to be obeyed by all my employes as promptly and strictly as would the orders of the captain of a military company by the men under his command, and we moved with about the same precision as a military organization on the march. I had so many men on guard all the time at night, and one detail was relieved by another at regular intervals. When the wagons were driven into line in the morning each man took his place alongside his wagon and then awaited the order to start. When the start was made the wagons had to be kept up within a certain distance of each other, like soldiers marching in single file.

By observing these precautions and preserving perfect discipline among the men I avoided having any stragglers to look after when we were surprised by the savages, and could always be prepared for a fight in a few minutes.

We started from camp in the morning without breakfast and drove until about ten o'clock, when we stopped to eat. Then we rested until two or sometimes three o'clock in the afternoon, while the cattle were grazing and getting water. In this way I always got over from fifteen to twenty miles a day, sixteen miles being an average day's travel. It usually took about four months to make the trip from Fort Union to Kansas City and return.

Our wagons were not more than half loaded as a rule when we were going east. About all there was to be hauled that way was the peltry taken in the mountains, and I generally aimed to buy up or trade for enough of this to enable me to make my expenses out of the profits which I could realize by selling in Kansas City. When we got ready to return from Kansas City, however, we always had big loads. To put six or eight thousand pounds on a wagon was not loading uncommonly heavy; frequently we put as high as ten thousand pounds on a wagon.

We were paid then for carrying goods through from Kansas City to Fort Union eight dollars per hundred, so that a freight bill on a train load of goods in those times amounted sometimes to many thousands of dollars. Say, for instance, that an average train load of freight for my wagons was two hundred thousand pounds. I have loaded more than that on the thirty-six wagons, but we will call two hundred thousand pounds the average. Billed at eight dollars per hundred this brought me in sixteen thousand dollars, out of which I had to pay my expenses, provided I had not succeeded in getting enough out of the trip eastward to meet the outlay.

I paid teamsters twenty dollars per month and provisions cost me perhaps a thousand dollars for the trip, so that altogether I was out perhaps four or five thousand dollars. This, you see, would leave ten thousand dollars or more as net profits of the trip and you can understand that freighting was a pretty good business. The men who were engaged in it at that time, however, took their lives in their hands every time they started out on a trip and they deserved to be well paid.

When I had made one trip to Kansas City and got back to Fort Union my wagons were unloaded and I commenced hauling military supplies from there to Albuquerque, and my contracts with the government yielded quite as handsome returns as teaming across the Plains. This business usually lasted until the snows fell in the early winter. Then I drove my cattle into the prairie country, where they shifted for themselves until I got ready to start out again the following spring.

While I was handling government freight I made the acquaintance of many of the regular army officers who were stationed out here at one time and another, some of whom afterward became known all over the country on account of their prominence in the War of the Rebellion.

Among them were General Albert Sidney Johnston, who was killed at Shiloh, General E. R. S. Canby, who was killed by Captain Jack's band of Modoc Indians in the Lava Beds, in 1873, and Colonel Henry H. Sibley, who invaded New Mexico, won a victory over General Canby at Valverde, captured Santa Fe, and was defeated at Glorieta, in 1862. After the war Sibley went to Egypt and became a general in the Khedive's army.

CAMP OF PRAIRIE FREIGHTERS

Reproduced from *Harper's Weekly* for December 23, 1871

The wagon trains had been crossing the Plains several years before regular trips were made by the stages. If my memory is not at fault the stages first commenced running in 1847 between Independence, Missouri, and Santa Fe. Then they made one trip each month; that is, a stage coach started each month from Independence, and at the same time one left Santa Fe, going east. After awhile the company started stages from each of these points once every week, and at a later date three times a week.

Six mules, or horses, were attached to each stage, and when they got to making what they called fast time they changed horses about every twenty miles while going through the mountain region. It took about two weeks to make the trip if there were no mishaps along the road, but a break-down or two or a fight with the Indians would sometimes stretch the time out several days.

Each stage coach could carry eleven passengers, nine of them going inside and two outside. The fare from Independence to Santa Fe was two hundred and fifty dollars and the passenger was allowed to carry forty pounds of baggage. If he carried more than this the extra charge was usually about fifty cents per pound.

The stage company boarded the passengers, but I don't suppose I am giving away any secret when I say that they didn't live very sumptuously.

Hardtack and pork were the principal items on the bill of fare, aside from the buffaloes and other game picked up along the way[88]. What sleep the passengers got they took sitting up in the stage as they rode along, because they traveled day and night from the time they started until their destination was reached.

When the country began to settle up to some extent along the Santa Fe Trail, stage stations were established at which hotel accommodations were provided, so that if nothing happened passengers could get square meals at regular intervals, although if they expected to have served up to them all the delicacies of the season at these frontier taverns, they were usually very much disappointed. There was one thing they always got, however, and that was plenty of buffalo meat and other kinds of splendidly cooked wild game.

There was but one way to break the monotony of a stage trip and that was to get out and walk when one got tired of riding. Sometimes walking a considerable distance was compulsory, because

[88]Hardtack was a species of cracker or biscuit, whose capacity for preservation made it a convenient food for soldiers and sailors. "Hardtack and sow belly" were the staples of diet of the Union soldiers in the Civil War. If their old-age stories, listened to by the Editor in boyhood, can be credited, the hardtack could be made edible by soaking in coffee or other liquid, or by shattering with a musket-butt.

breakdowns were frequent and horses and mules gave out every now and then between stations. It cost just the same to walk that it did to ride, and except in case of accident the passenger was allowed to choose his own mode of traveling, provided he kept along with the procession. This he always made a point of doing, because the hostile Indians made it very uncomfortable for stragglers.

After the Plains Indians went on the war path it became necessary to have the stages accompanied over a considerable portion of the trail by escorts of soldiers; but prior to that time, or when an escort could not be obtained, the safety of those who crossed the Plains by stage depended mainly upon their own courage and fighting qualities, the kind of arms they had, and the amount of ammunition they carried, although the judgment, discretion, and nerve of the stage driver or conductor also counted for a good deal. The stage driver who understood his business generally aimed to travel over that part of the road where there was most danger of Indian attacks at night, because, as a rule, the savages would not fight after dark. At daybreak in the morning, however, campers and travelers had to be on their guard, as that was the Indians' favorite time to commence hostilities.[89]

[89]Edward E. Ayer, the noted Chicago collector and business man, once related to the Editor his own experi-

The old Santa Fe Trail, which I think should be marked on the maps so that the line of this famous national highway could always be traced across the Plains and over the Rocky Mountains, commenced at Independence and ended at Santa Fe. It passed through Westport, now a part of Kansas City, as I have had occasion to say already, and crossing the state line at that point traversed the plains of Kansas in a direction a little south of west until it reached the great bend of the Arkansas River. Then it ran close to the river until the present western boundary line of Kansas was crossed. It cut off a corner of Colorado and a corner of the Panhandle of Texas and then passed into New Mexico and on to Santa Fe, Fort Union being left seven miles to one side.

That was the line of the original Santa Fe Trail, when the Arkansas River was crossed at

ence with Indians in crossing the Plains. After spending several years as a fortune hunter in California and as a soldier in the Southwest, in 1864 Ayer abandoned army life and returned to his boyhood home in Wisconsin. Somewhere enroute the stage coach was attacked by a band of Indians at a point several miles from the next station. While the driver drove furiously for the station, Ayer, crouched in the rear of the stage, took pot shots with his revolver at the pursuing Indians, who were armed only with bows and arrows. They drew off as the coach approached the station, else Ayer would not have survived to tell the story. Upon arrival, the rear of the coach was liberally sprinkled with arrows, fired by the baffled red men.

Fort Dodge. It was changed later so that it passed through Trinidad and crossed the Raton Mountains on the line now traversed by the Santa Fe Railroad. The Arkansas River was crossed at Fort Bent, near where La Junta is now, after this change was made.

The trail was eight hundred and twenty-five miles in length, and three hundred miles of it was certainly a rough and rugged road[90]. Crossing the streams and keeping clear of mud holes was the most difficult feature of the first five hundred miles travel. The mud holes we could fill with hay cut on the surrounding Plains, and the roads were not hard to make.

It was different, though, in going through the mountains. There the trail had to be hewn out of the steep hillsides, the ax had to be used to clear the trees and logs out of the cañons, and when the road-makers had done their best travel was difficult and dangerous. In the winter the snows would frequently drift into the cañons and keep piling up until it obliterated every trace of the Trail, and breaking a road through these deep snows was no easy matter.

It took a man of a good deal of nerve to drive six broncos over the mountains when they had to break through these immense snow-drifts, and

[90]Obviously the length depended upon the precise route followed. It is more commonly stated as 780 miles.

stage passengers needed to have about as much nerve as the driver. More dangerous drives than these even, were those which had to be made down the steep mountain sides when they were covered with ice and stopping between the crest and the base of the mountain was out of the question. Then, if the driver did not thoroughly understand his business, if he did not have a steady head and a quick eye, if he did not keep his reins well in hand and make every turn at the proper time, there was certain to be trouble. Overturning a coach under such circumstances was a frequent occurrence, and sometimes these accidents were very serious ones.

Being caught in one of our mountain snowstorms when traveling became an impossibility, and all that could be done was to sit shivering and freezing in the stage when it came to a stop, waiting for the storm to abate, was another trying experience for those who were so unfortunate as to have to travel in the winter time, but being caught out in a summer hail and thunder storm was even worse. I doubt if there is another place on the American Continent where a big electrical disturbance can be gotten up on as short notice as here in the Rocky Mountains, nor do I believe there is any other place where the hail-stones grow as large or hit as hard when they fall as they do here.

When a coach-load of passengers were caught in a storm of this kind they might expect to see the flashing lightning, almost continuous thunder, and pelting hail stones frighten their horses until they became unmanageable. Then, to escape being crippled or killed in a runaway they would have to tumble out of the stage, to be pounded by the falling ice balls as long as the storm lasted if they were not fortunate enough to find a friendly rock or tree to shelter them. Under such circumstances as these staging in the Rocky Mountains made life a good deal of a burden to those who had to travel that way, while under the most favorable circumstances a trip from Independence to Santa Fe could hardly be looked upon as a pleasure trip.

There were but two ways, however, of getting into the mountain country. One was by stage and the other by wagon train. The gold hunters who went to California could choose between the perils of an ocean voyage and those of a trip overland, but those fortune hunters who came to Colorado and New Mexico had but one route to travel over. Whether they came by stage or wagon train depended largely on their tastes and the amount of money they happened to have in their pockets when they started out.

As a rule those who came West to grow up with the country had not a surplus of ready cash, and many of the men who are now prominent in business and in professional and public life paid their passage from Independence to Santa Fe by driving an ox team across the Plains. Many of the young men who found their way into the country in this way were men of far more than average ability, and all of them had a vast amount of pluck and energy. When they got into the country they turned their hand to whatever was to be done, but most of these plucky fellows soon rose above their surroundings and to-day they are the bankers, cattle kings, merchant princes, judges, and dignitaries of the country. If you were to ask any one of the most distinguished lawyers of Santa Fe, for instance, how long he had been in the country and how he got there, he would most likely tell you that he "came West in the sixties" and on the way out filled the responsible position of engineer of a prairie schooner. I am inclined to think that the young men who traveled into the country by wagon train have made a rather better showing than those who had money enough to travel by stage.

This talk about staging has been suggested by the mention of my going into the freighting business, because staging and freighting were twin occupations. Now I must go ahead and tell you something about my experience as a freighter.

CHAPTER XXII

Mutinous Teamsters

I HAVE spoken of the systematic movement of wagon trains and the necessity which existed for perfect discipline among the men employed in the work. This was a matter of about as much importance in moving a wagon train across the Plains and over the mountains as it would have been aboard a ship on the high seas. The owner of a wagon train assumed almost as great responsibilities when he started out with a train load of goods as the vessel owner assumes when starting out on a voyage.

When we received goods for shipment we gave to the owner a bill of lading in which it was stipulated that we should be responsible for the goods if lost in transit, or for any damage to them other than such as might result from visitations of Providence, such as fire, flood, and wind storms. We were not responsible for losses resulting from Indian attacks, although we bound ourselves to do all in our power to protect our freight and prevent it from being captured or destroyed.

The value of a train load of merchandise was frequently one or two hundred thousand dollars, and with the responsibility of protecting this im-

319

mense amount of property resting upon us it was as absolutely necessary that a crew of teamsters should obey promptly and implicitly the orders of one man as it is that a crew of sailors shall obey the commands of their captain. We were governed by practically the same laws that govern men at sea, and we dealt with a mutinous or unruly band of teamsters in pretty much the same way that a mutinous crew of sailors is generally dealt with.

The temptation to mutiny for the purpose of robbery was quite as strong among teamsters as among sailors. A well-equipped wagon train was as rich a prize as an average vessel, and while the plunder could be more easily turned into money and divided among the mutineers the chances of escape were quite as good as they would be at sea under similar circumstances. I have known of a good many cases of mutiny of this sort, and in at least one that I recall now a train was taken possession of by the teamsters near Fort Kearny, the major domo was killed, the cattle and wagons were driven into Oregon and disposed of, the plunder was divided, and the conspirators escaped arrest and punishment at the time, although they may have been caught afterward.

The very first trip I made to Kansas City I had a mutiny of no small dimensions to deal with. My wagon men or teamsters were nearly all Mexicans, as it was very difficult at that time to equip a train with anything else. The bitterness growing out of the Mexican War had in great measure subsided, but it had not entirely died out. The Mexicans still had a feeling of enmity towards the Americans, and the smouldering embers of hate were easily fanned into a flame.

I had with me on this trip about thirty Mexicans and perhaps as many Americans. Nearly all the latter, however, were discharged soldiers and others who were going back to the States as passengers.

Going through by wagon train was a cheap way of getting out of the country. We charged a passenger thirty dollars fare, that amount being about sufficient to pay for what he ate on the road. They were not expected to do any work, other than guard and camp duty, and were allowed to ride on the unloaded or only partially loaded wagons. We thought it an advantage, sometimes, to have a considerable number of passengers, because it strengthened our force in case we had any Indian fighting to do and in any event gave us a more formidable appearance and diminished the chances of attack.

While I recognized the fact that some of the Mexicans entertained for me no very friendly feeling on account of war happenings, and that there was an element of danger about undertaking to enforce discipline and exact from them obedience of orders when they were as well armed as I was myself, I knew that every man had to be armed to the teeth to insure our getting safely through the Indian country, and there was nothing but Indian country to go through at that time. I supplied all of them with the best arms that could be procured and issued to each man as many rounds of ammunition as I thought him likely to have immediate use for from time to time.

We got along very well for some time, but the strict discipline which I enforced was very obnoxious to the wagon men and I began to hear half-suppressed mutterings against the major domo. That meant me, and what I overheard now and then and what was told me by the Americans traveling with us convinced me that trouble was brewing.

I did everything I could to prevent an outbreak, but at the same time I continued to enforce the same discipline that I had enforced at the start and aimed to be constantly prepared to suppress any insubordination. It is the unexpected that generally happens, however, and when trouble did come I was taken entirely by surprise.

We were just breaking camp one morning at Ash Creek near Pawnee Rock when one of the Mexicans came to me to ask for something from the commissary wagon. I told him I would attend to it by and by, and a few minutes later walked out to where he and his companions were, not dreaming of any trouble. I left all my arms behind me with the exception of a Colt's navy revolver, and this had but four shots in it.

When I came within a few feet of the group of wagon men I told the one who had been to see me that I was ready to wait on him. Without giving me any answer he wheeled around, and drawing a butcher knife from his belt advanced toward me, swearing in mixed Spanish and English that he intended to kill me. In an instant I had leveled my pistol at his head and ordered him to throw down his knife. This did not even have the effect of checking his advance, and hoping I shouldn't have to shoot I backed away from him and kept out of his reach until I ran against one of the wagons and could retreat no farther. Then it had to be his life or mine and in a second it was his.

As soon as my pistol cracked the other Mexicans, seeing their mutinous comrade fall, grabbed their guns and before I could place myself in any more advantageous position or seek any kind of shelter they commenced shooting at me. I dared not empty my pistol, because I should then have been entirely at their mercy and should have had no chance of escape. I could do little more than stand there to be shot at, hoping at the same time that my good luck and a kind Providence would let me through with a whole skin.

I don't know how many shots were fired at me, but while I stood there thirteen bullets pierced my clothing, but only one of them grazed the skin. I managed after little to get behind a tree about six or seven inches in diameter and from that shelter I fired one more shot, wounding one of my assailants in the hip. About twenty shots were fired at me after that, but the friendly tree warded off the bullets and I escaped without even a slight wound.

I think the mutineers must have reached the conclusion that I was bullet-proof, for they ceased firing and gave me time to seek a better shelter and to have my rifle and my other pistol and knife, along with a supply of ammunition, brought to me by a brother of mine who was along with the train. Thus equipped, I felt pretty safe and mounting my horse gave directions for moving the train and then went ahead as usual, leaving the wagons to follow.

This encounter had convinced me that my life was in constant peril. The Americans whom I had with me had stood as though paralyzed while I was playing target for the Mexicans, and I was satisfied that I could not look to them for any assistance in suppressing future disturbances.

The mutinous teamsters dared not leave the train because they feared the Indians and I could not discharge them because that would have been leaving them without means of subsistence, with starvation or slaughter by the savages reasonably certain to be their fate. It was necessary, therefore, that we should travel along together until we reached the end of our journey, but I had determined that it should be under somewhat different circumstances.

That day I rode ahead of the train to what was known as Bill Allison's Fort, twenty-eight miles from my battle-ground. Allison was a brave, daring fellow who had established a trading post in the heart of the Indian country.[91]

[91]Allison's trading post was on the Santa Fe Trail at the mouth of Walnut Creek, about five miles west of the Big Bend of the Arkansas. The site is several miles east of present-day Great Bend, Barton County, Kansas. In 1857, according to a member of Major Sedgwick's Cheyenne expedition of that year, it was the only outpost between Council Grove and Fort Bent. *Kansas Historical Collections*, VIII, 487, 489. Although called a "ranch," Allison's business was trading with the Indians and with white passers-by on the Santa Fe Trail. Allison is reported to have established the "fort" in 1857. He died of heart failure at Independence, and George Peacock rented the ranch. Peacock was a practical joker to his own cost, Kiowa Chief Satanta, who figures prominently in General Custer's *My Life on the Plains,* the Lakeside Classics volume for 1952, had asked Peacock to write for him a letter of introduction stating that he was a chief of importance, in order that he might receive civil treatment when he encountered

In addition to trading with the Indians he did a thriving business taking wolf skins. The gray wolf was an animal which followed the buffaloes and as you already know there were thousands of them on the Plains. Their skins were valuable and Allison was taking them by the hundred by what he called the strychnine method. He would go out and shoot a buffalo and leave the carcass lying on the Plains, thoroughly poisoned with strychnine. Before he was out of sight, perhaps, a pack of wolves would be eating the dead buffalo, and he had a big catch by the next morning.

Allison had but one arm but he handled a gun as well as anybody and wasn't afraid of anything. I rode to the fort that night, told him what had happened, and asked him to assist me in disarm-

white men. Peacock wrote as follows: "The bearer of this, Satanta, is the dirtiest, laziest, lousiest vagabond on the Plains; if he comes to your camp, kick him out." When Satanta presented this missive to the next emigrant train he encountered, he was treated with derision and abuse. Having sought and obtained from another trader a reading of the letter, Satanta swore vengeance upon its author. On September 8, 1860, he visited Peacock's ranch, where he killed the joker, along with his clerk and his Mexican herdsman. See *Kansas Hist. Collections,* X, 664–65. Although Wootton gives 1856 as the year when he had this experience (*ante,* 305) the statement that Allison founded his fort in 1857 seems to point to a later year. Satanta's tempestuous career ended March 11, 1857, when, a prisoner in the Texas State Penitentiary, he committed suicide by throwing himself from an upper story of the prison.

ing all the men I had with me. He agreed to help me out, and when the train came up next morning we rode out to meet it with four six-shooters each stuck in our belts and our rifles in our hands. As the teamsters came up we compelled them to step to one side and lay their guns, pistols, and knives in a pile. The Americans were also required to give up their arms, as I did not propose to furnish any equipment without being able to command its use in my own defense.

All these arms were stored away in Allison's fort, and we went on our way without any arms except such as were in the hands of myself and a few trusted employes. This was running a great risk, but I thought I should rather fight Indians without any assistance than run the risk of being assassinated by an armed band of insubordinate employes.

When we reached Council Grove we found the Kaw Indians about to go on the war-path.[92] Seth

---

[92]The Council Grove was at the present-day town of Council Grove, Morris County, Kansas. It is about fifty miles southwest of Topeka and some one hundred and fifty distant from Kansas City. The place took its name from a treaty negotiated here in 1825 between the Osage Indians and U.S. Commissioners charged with marking a road from Missouri to Santa Fe. The grove, in a generally treeless country, was a heavily timbered tract half a mile or so wide lying on Council Grove Creek, a tributary of the Neosho or Grand River. See Gregg, *The Commerce of the Prairies,* the Lakeside Classics volume for 1926, pp. 30–32.

Hayes, who was there as a government sutler, had gotten into some trouble with one of the Indians and killed him. The Indians swore vengeance and things looked very warlike.

I stopped there two days waiting for matters to quiet down, and helped Hayes patch up a truce. I was better acquainted with the Indians than he was and knew better how to settle a quarrel of that kind. He asked me what should be done and I told him that the way to make peace with the Indians was to pay them for the one that had been killed. I knew that this was what they expected and that they would not be satisfied until the affair was fixed up that way. He requested me to go ahead with the negotiations and I invited the chief to hold a conference with me. We sat down together and after we had had a long talk it was agreed that if the sutler would give the Indians a pony and a hundred dollars worth of goods out of his store they would be entirely satisfied and peace would be established.

My friend, the sutler, was satisfied with this arrangement; the Indians got the pony and their goods and I left them smoking the pipe of peace with Hayes when I went on my way, congratulating myself on my success as a peace commissioner. I got into Kansas City without having any more trouble of any kind, and the first thing I did was to pay off and discharge my unruly wagon men.

We were not long loading our wagons for the return trip and I started out with a new crew of teamsters. I had no trouble with them, and got along very smoothly on the whole trip. We had to build bridges here and there and had considerable difficulty crossing the Arkansas, but these difficulties were not unexpected, although they would not be looked upon nowadays as slight obstacles to overcome. In crossing the Arkansas, for instance, it took eighteen ox teams to drag one of our loaded wagons through the quicksands, and I spent the greater part of a day standing waist-deep in the water superintending the work of getting wagons and teams across safely.

Some distance this side of where we crossed the Arkansas I got a good scare, but as it turned out there was no occasion for it. I was riding along, as I usually did, some distance ahead of the train, looking up a place to camp for the night. I had not been keeping so sharp a lookout as usual, because I was thinking about the business in hand, and looked up all at once to find myself surrounded by Indians; that is to say, the Arkansas River was on one side of me and the Indians on all the other sides. The band was a large one, numbering perhaps four or five hundred, and it looked to me as though I had no chance of escape; at any rate, there was but a single chance, and that was to cross the river, run down on the opposite bank, recross the stream, and join the wagon train.

I had concluded to take this one chance and was about to make a dash for the river when the Indians hailed me and I discovered that they were Arapahoes. I knew then that I was among friends and my fears subsided. They came up to where I was and seemed to enjoy having given me a scare as much as a practical joker enjoys one of his own jokes. They said they knew me as soon as they caught sight of me, and surrounded me just to see what the Cut Hand would do. Cut Hand was the name I was always known by among the Arapahoes, and what gave me the name, was the fact that I was short two fingers on my left hand, having lost them by an accident in my childhood.

The Arapahoes were returning from a campaign against the Pawnees and they had been victorious. They were going home laden with the scalps of their enemies and driving a large number of ponies which they had captured. They were in a joyous mood, and proposed that night to have the scalp dance with which they always celebrated a victory. I gave them a barrel of hard tack, a sack of flour and a sack of sugar and they went into camp with us, or rather alongside of us.

The chief who was in command of the band, whom I had known for a long time, detailed four young Indians to herd my stock during the night and at exactly the time I had named to start in the morning they were on hand with the cattle.

They kept up the scalp dance all night, which gave some of the tenderfeet who were coming out with me a good opportunity to witness this very peculiar Indian dance, which, however, has been described so often that I need say nothing about it. Some days after that we were attacked by the Comanches, but the fight did not last long and nobody was injured, unless it was some of the Indians. They only made one dash at us and that, fortunately, was from the side which brought the wagons between them and the teamsters. This sheltered the men from a shower of arrows which were left sticking in the wagons, and gave them a chance to do their shooting from behind this breastwork.

About the time we crossed the New Mexico line I fell in with William Bent, a brother of Governor Bent, who was coming through with a wagon train, and we agreed to travel together. We kept along at about an even pace for some time until we got well towards Fort Union, when I discovered that Bent was racing me and proposed to beat me into the fort.

He got ahead of me, and fastened a bit of paper on a stick, which he stuck in the ground near the Trail. On this bit of paper he had written "good bye," and informed me that I would find him at

Fort Union when I got there. I pocketed the note and said nothing, but made up my mind that I wouldn't follow Mr. Bent into the fort. My cattle were in first-class condition and I knew they would stand several days hard driving without being injured by it.

The first thing to do, however, was to get past Bent and get a good start of him, if possible, before he found out what I was up to. He was only a couple of miles ahead of me and that night I rode down to his camp and we made an evening of it in a social way. My being in his company threw him off his guard and consequently he was not looking for me to make any effort to get my teams past him. While we were having a few games of cards and taking a few toddies together, however, my men were moving our wagon-train, by a slightly circuitous route around his camp and when we broke camp in the morning I was two miles ahead of him. Then it was my turn to say "good bye" and he gave up the race, falling so far behind that I beat him into Fort Union by a day and a half.

We used to have races of this kind very frequently in the old freighting days and sometimes a good deal of money would be staked on the result. The competition between us was not quite as strong as it is just now between Trans-Atlantic steamers, but it was worth something to a freighter to have the reputation of making quick trips. It added to his patronage and gave him a greater amount of business.

If there had been no such inducement, however, we should still have raced each other across the Plains when an opportunity presented itself, because in those days every man was more or less of a gambler and would back his judgment with his money, as the saying goes, on any proposition. The average mountain man would bet on a five-hundred-mile race between ox teams as readily as on a mile dash of Kentucky thoroughbreds or native broncos. I have seen them go into a herd of horses that they knew nothing whatever about and lay a wager on one horse beating another, just for the fun of seeing the horses run and the excitement of having something staked on the result.

Chapter XXIII

Freighting for Uncle Sam

KEEPING up military posts in this country back in the fifties was an expensive business. There was scarcely anything in the way of subsistence which did not have to be hauled from Kansas City by wagon and the cost was enormous. Fort Union was the principal distributing point for military supplies of all kinds, and as soon as I returned from my trip to Kansas City in 1856 my wagons were loaded for Albuquerque with government freight. The distance between the two points was one hundred and sixty-two and one-half miles, by the old trail; and, by the way, it was at my instance that the road was measured.

We were paid for hauling government freight so much per mile, per hundred pounds. It had been understood for some years that the distance between Fort Union and Albuquerque was one hundred and sixty miles and the government paid the freighters for hauling that distance.

My experience in driving ox teams, measuring distances, and timing the cattle, had enabled me to calculate, almost as accurately as if I had measured it, the distance traveled every day; and after I had made one or two trips over the Fort

334

Union and Albuquerque trail I was satisfied that one hundred and sixty miles did not cover it.

When I had carried about eight hundred thousand pounds of freight and got ready to settle with the authorities at the Fort I thought the distance over and above one hundred and sixty miles was worth looking after and figuring in the freight bills. I therefore proposed that the road should be measured and agreed to pay expenses of the survey provided the measurement did not show that the distance was greater than one hundred and sixty miles. As I have stated, this survey showed that the distance was two and one-half miles greater than it had been previously estimated, and that made a difference of several hundred dollars in my cash receipts for the work done.

I put in pretty much all my time on the road and rarely had more than a day or two between trips during the freighting season. When stopping over at Fort Union I was frequently very much annoyed by a gang of petty thieves who made their headquarters at a notorious place called La Plazarota, about three miles from the fort. These scoundrels would steal anything from a halter to a two-horse wagon and I hardly ever stopped over night at the fort without losing something.

The authorities were so much afraid of the gang that no officer would venture to go to the

Plazarota to arrest one of the thieves, and I finally concluded to inflict a little punishment on my own account. That's the way I happened to turn man-stealer. Now I don't want anybody to jump to the conclusion that I became a professional kidnapper or engaged in man-stealing as a regular business. I made only one expedition of that kind, but it was a very successful one.

It happened this way. One night a wagon belonging to me was stolen from my corral and the next day I found out where it was and who stole it. That night I got together a party of seven men and sometime after dark we rode into the Plazarota, where we located our man. Then I took one of my men with me and we entered the house in which the man was sleeping to bring him out, leaving the other members of the party to keep watch outside. We found the doors open and entering the house very cautiously we secured the thief and got out so quietly that although there were several other persons in the house at the time none of them knew until afterwards what had happened. The thief himself only knew of our presence a moment before we laid hands on him and a gun shoved up against either side of his body caused him to preserve as perfect silence as we could have wished. We knew that if any outcry was raised, or an alarm given, it would not be five minutes, before twenty-five or thirty desperadoes would rally to the assistance of our prisoner and then somebody was pretty sure to get killed. We rejoined our companions, who had remained some distance from the house, without having attracted any attention, and proceeded to a place two or three miles away which was well adapted to an old-fashioned hanging.

There we stopped, and after dismounting and tying our horses we organized a court and tried the prisoner for stealing. He was found guilty and sentenced to be hanged; then we got out a rope and commenced getting ready for the execution. About that time the wagon thief began to get thoroughly alarmed and begged us to spare his life. He promised to return everything he had stolen and never to steal anything more as long as he lived.

Finally we turned him loose and left him to walk home. The next day my wagon came back all right, and I think the fellow kept his promise not to steal anything more as long as he lived, because he didn't live long. He was killed in a row at a fandango only a few days afterward.

There was one member of our own party that night who looked upon the affair almost as seriously as the man who was put on trial for wagon stealing. This was William Kroenig, afterward a prominent and wealthy citizen of New Mexico, with whom I have had many a good laugh over it since[93]. Kroenig, as his name indicates, was a German, and at that time he had not been long in the country and was not familiar with our frontier ways. When the trial commenced there was an air of solemnity about the proceedings which made him feel somewhat nervous; then when the jury brought in a verdict of guilty and we began mak-

[93]William Kroenig was born in Westphalia, Germany, February 3, 1828. He migrated to America in 1847, where after sojourns in Wisconsin and elsewhere he set out for the California gold mines. The party with which he left Independence was attacked by Indians and Kroenig lost his horses. He arrived with another train at Santa Fe in August, 1849 but never went on to California. He joined as a volunteer the armed expedition which went in pursuit of the Indians who had massacred the White party, for which see *ante*, Chap. XIII. He was subsequently employed by Colonel Bell to seek to learn from the Utes the fate of Mrs. White's child. With one companion he undertook a journey in midwinter to the Ute village, where he learned from the chief that the child and its nurse were dead. For this hazardous service he was paid $5 per day. In 1850 he established a store at Rio, Colorado, engaging in further trading ventures, which he abandoned following the Christmas Day, 1854 destruction of the Pueblo settlement. He subsequently engaged in large-scale business enterprises in Colorado and New Mexico, winning and losing successive fortunes. His biographer credits him with building the first flour mill in Colorado, and the first shingle-roofed house in Pueblo. The date of his death has not been learned. Data condensed from biographical sketch of Kroenig in Charles F. Coan, *History of New Mexico* (Chicago, 1925), II, 52-54. H. H. Bancroft credits Kroenig's *Report as to Mora County* (Las Vegas, 1881) as the source of most subsequent writings about the County. See *History of Arizona and New Mexico*, 783.

ing preparations for the execution he made up his mind that we really intended to lynch the Mexican. This was going a good deal farther than his kind heart and sympathetic nature would allow, and no barrister ever pleaded more earnestly for the pardon of a condemned criminal than did the young German for annulment of the death penalty in this case.

I made four trips across the Plains in 1857–58, but as the Indians were on their good behavior at that time I had no more thrilling experience than being caught once in a Kansas blizzard. I had to abandon the wagons and drive my cattle to the sand hills for shelter and when I got back to where I had left the wagons I found the overland stage inside my corral, where the passengers were trying to keep warm around a fire made of my ox yokes.

My last trip was from Atchison, Kansas, to Salt Lake City. The distance between these two points was twelve hundred and twenty-five miles by the trail and it took me ninety-seven days to get through, although I reached Salt Lake in advance of any of the other trains which started out at the same time I did. On this trip I traveled over what was known as the Salt Lake Trail, passing near Omaha and then on by the way of Laramie, Pacific Springs, and Fort Bridger into Utah.

That was a bad year for the freighters generally, although fortune happened to favor me. Heavy rains in Kansas made a portion of the road almost impassable, while farther along the Spanish fever attacked the oxen and killed hundreds of them. In some places along the trail over which I passed I saw the dead animals lying so close together that it was almost impossible to find water which had not been polluted by their decaying carcasses. I also passed scores of wagons which had been abandoned when the owners, having lost their cattle, could move them no farther.

That was the year after the Mormon War and matters were in a very unsettled condition in Utah at that time. As I have already said in speaking of Utah, when the Mormons went there in 1847, after being driven out of Missouri and Illinois, their intention was to get out of the United States. They had hardly gotten settled down in their new location, however, when the territory was ceded to the government of the United States as a result of the Mexican War.

Then, in order that they might be able to control their own affairs in their own way and have no interference with the practice of polygamy they organized the State of Deseret, which they tried to have admitted into the Union. They failed in this, but President Fillmore made Brigham Young Governor of Utah Territory when it was organized, and this arrangement was fairly satisfactory to the Mormons.

Young didn't propose to have any other United States officials to assist him in governing the Territory unless they were in perfect sympathy with the Mormon Church and after a time he drove the United States District Judges out of Utah.

This led to his being removed from the office of Governor in 1854 and Colonel Steptoe was appointed in his place. When the new Governor reached Salt Lake he found the Mormons so hostile to the government that he never made any effort to discharge the duties of his office.[94]

In 1857 Alfred Cumming, who had an idea that he could compel the Mormons to respect his au-

[94]Edward J. Steptoe, a native of Virginia, graduated from West Point in the class of 1837. He served in the Florida and Mexican wars, and on garrison and other duties. In 1854–55 he was on a march for Washington Territory via great Salt Lake when (Dec. 21, 1854) he was appointed Governor of Utah Territory, which he declined. On May 17, 1858, after two years service in Washington he was engaged in the desperate conflict of To-hots-nim-me against the Spokane Indians on the site of present-day Rosalia. His defeat on this occasion may be ascribed in part to his own ineptitude, but in large measure also to the fact that the arms of the soldiers were markedly inferior to those possessed by the Indians. He was on sick leave thereafter until 1861, when on Nov. 1 he resigned his commission. Steptoe Butte, near Spokane bears his name. See G. W. Cullum, *Biographical Register of the Officers and Graduates of the U.S. Military Academy at West Point,* N. Y.; H. H. Bancroft, *History of Washington, Idaho and Montana* (San Francisco, 1890), 178–83; Oregon Hist. Soc. *Quarterly,* XVI, 45–47.

thority, was appointed Governor of Utah by President Buchanan, and he called upon the government for twenty-five hundred soldiers to preserve order and enforce an observance of law in the Territory.[95]

This was what led to the uprising which has sometimes been called the Mormon War. Brigham Young called upon the Saints to arm themselves and fight for what he termed their liberties, and Governor Cumming declared the Territory in a state of rebellion.

When General Albert Sidney Johnston undertook to get through to Salt Lake City the Mormons

[95]Alfred Cumming was a native of Georgia, who in 1836 as mayor of Augusta acquired credit for his measures to combat the cholera epidemic. During the Mexican War he served on General Scott's staff. Appointed Governor of Utah Territory, he accompanied the army dispatched by President Buchanan to establish the Federal authority over Utah as far as Camp Scott. From there, "anxious only that matters should be adjusted, if possible, without loss of life," he entrusted himself to a Mormon escort and proceeded to Salt Lake City, where he assumed the well-nigh impossible role of pacifying the Mormons while upholding the authority of the Federal Government. His measures had the result of winning the cordial support of the Mormon element, and of antagonizing the anti-Mormons, who demanded his removal from office. In May, 1861, two months before the expiration of his term of office, he departed from Salt Lake City. "He had entered [it] amid a forced display of welcome, but he left it with the sincere regrets of a people whose hearts he had won by kind treatment." See H. H. Bancroft, *History of Utah,* 1540–1887 (San Francisco, 1891), *passim.*

attacked and burned his wagon train and drove away eight hundred head of his cattle, so that he was compelled to go into camp at Black Forks, near Fort Bridger, in the winter of 1857–58, where the soldiers suffered greatly on account of a scarcity of provisions.

The same year John D. Lee and his band of savages killed one hundred and fifty emigrants at the Mountain Meadows and altogether there was quite a speck of war in Utah.[96]

The government finally fixed up a sort of compromise with the Mormons under which they became nominally submissive to the authorities, but

[96]The Mountain Meadows Massacre in southern Utah, September 11, 1857 was one of the most shocking crimes in American history. A party of 136 emigrants enroute from Arkansas to California was waylaid and treacherously overpowered by a band of Mormons and Indians under the leadership of John D. Lee, a Mormon elder and zealot who had held numerous offices in the Church. After the emigrants had been induced to surrender their arms all of them were slaughtered save 17 small children who were presumably too young to bear testimony against the murderers. Efforts to bring the culprits to trial proved unavailing until 1876 when Lee alone, deserted by his associates in the crime, was convicted and shot on the scene of the butchery. In 1877 his book, *Mormonism Unveiled*, written after his sentence of death, was published. Despite its understandable bias, it still remains one of the most important sources concerning the tragedy. See also Hubert H. Bancroft, *History of Utah* 1540–1887 (San Francisco, 1891), Chap. XX: M. R. Werner, *Brigham Young* (New York, 1925), Chap. XI.

the soldiers were not allowed to come into Salt Lake City. They were stationed near Utah Lake, forty miles from the capital city, and remained there until 1860, when the Civil War broke out and they were needed elsewhere.[97]

When I got to Salt Lake in 1858 I found the feeling of the Mormons toward the Gentiles, as they call all those who do not belong to their church, a great deal more bitter than it was when I visited the city in 1852 on my way to California. Whenever a train load of emigrants came in they were looked upon with suspicion and none but Mormons were encouraged to settle in the territory.

Personally I was treated very kindly while I was there. My visit was a longer one than that which I made there in 1852, and I had an op-

[97]On June 26, 1858 the army, several thousand strong, entered the city and spent practically the entire day marching through it. In advance of the army's arrival the inhabitants had deserted the city en masse, leaving behind only a score of men who were prepared to burn it. Colonel Johnston, however, was only desirous of finding a place remote from all settlements for his army to encamp. This proved impossible, since every spot where water was available was occupied. The place selected, named Camp Floyd in honor of President Buchanan's Secretary of War, John B. Floyd, was about midway between Salt Lake City and Provo, some thirty-odd miles from each: A detailed account of the entire war, here briefly summarized by Wootton, is in H. H. Bancroft, *History of Utah*, 1540–1867 (San Francisco, 1891).

portunity of forming the acquaintance of a number of the prominent Mormons.

Brigham Young was particularly kind to me. As soon as he learned that I was in the city he sent me an invitation to visit him. I called on him one afternoon and dined with him in the evening, spending the time very pleasantly. My opinion of Brigham Young then, was that he was a shrewd, in fact a very able man, who among other things was making his religion very profitable; and when he died and I learned that he had left a fortune of more than two millions of dollars I flattered myself that I had judged him correctly.

I got my wagon train unloaded and was ready to start home early in September. Doyle, my partner in the freighting business, was with me, and before we had gotten very far on the road back to New Mexico I sold out my interest to him. I returned to Salt Lake and made an effort to get a seat in the east-bound stage. This I found it impossible to do, and I then made up a small party, composed of those who were equally unfortunate in the matter of securing stage accommodations, and we started across the mountains on horseback.

There were four of us in the party, besides a little Mexican boy that we brought through with us, and I never had more agreeable traveling companions. We made good time and the only thing we had to annoy us on the trip was getting short, at one time, of something to eat. I was sent ahead to look after game and the only thing I could find was a badger. I killed the badger, dressed it, and served it to my companions as bear meat. As a bear roast they liked it first-rate, but when I told them it was badger they couldn't swallow any more of it.

One of my companions on this trip was Doctor Cavanaugh, who lived in Taos for many years and was well-known throughout New Mexico, and another was Alexander Hicklin, a noted character among the mountain men. Both Hicklin and Cavanaugh were from Missouri, and that State furnished many of the men who were most prominent in the mountain region thirty or forty years ago. Some of those who came out here in the forties are still living in the country, one of the best known being Thomas Boggs, a son of Governor Boggs of Missouri, now living at Cimarron City in New Mexico.[98]

[98]Lillburn W. Boggs, a native of Kentucky, was elected Governor of Missouri in 1836. A man of decisive temperament, he aroused public criticism over his handling of the building of the State Capitol, and over his policy toward the Mormons, whom he drove from the State. Soon after his term of office expired he became the victim of a murderous attempt at assassination, supposedly by a Mormon agent, of which his son has left a detailed and gory account. See *Missouri Hist. Review*, IV, 106-110 (January, 1910).

The reputed assassin was Porter Rockwell, reputedly a member of the band of Danites or Destroying Angels of the

Zan Hicklin, as we always called him, had a ranch on the Greenhorn River about twenty-five miles out from Pueblo, and lived there up to the time of his death some years ago. He was the best story teller and the most famous practical joker in the mountains, and whenever you run across a man in the country to-day who has been here thirty years he will tell you something about

Church. Years later some one told Rockwell that A. D. Richardson, correspondent of the New York *Tribune* had characterized him as a murderer of 150 men. Rockwell remarked that if Richardson had said it he would make it 151. It turned out that another correspondent than Richardson was the culprit: Rockwell complained to Richardson that he had been cruelly slandered, and, in his cups, affirmed that he would kill any journalist who would publish falsehoods about him. See *Beyond the Mississippi....*, 468–69.

Thomas O. Boggs, son, of Governor Boggs, was born at Harmony Mission, Indian Territory, in August, 1824. Upon attaining manhood he engaged in the fur trade and about the year 1845 arrived at Taos. He became a friend of Kit Carson and married a niece of Carson's wife. She was a step-daughter of Governor Charles Bent and along with other members of his family was present in the house when he was murdered, in January, 1847. When Kit died in 1868, leaving a small property and several dependent children, Boggs became the executor of his will and assumed the care of several of the children. He prospered in business and lived at different places in New Mexico, his final residence being at Clayton, where he died in 1894. Data condensed from Charles F. Coan, *History of New Mexico* (Chicago and New York, 1925), III, 973; E. L. Sabin, *Kit Carson Days, passim*; R. E. Twitchell, *Leading Facts of New Mexican History*, II, 234–35.

Zan Hicklin. I don't think he ever met his match as a practical joker but once, and he used to tell this story on himself with as much relish as he told any other story.

He was riding from Pueblo out to his ranch one day and had struck a very lonely part of the road when he noticed a stranger coming toward him from the opposite direction on horseback. Not knowing what might be the character of the man he was about to meet and thinking himself unobserved, he turned his horse aside and rode into a clump of bushes, intending to remain there until the stranger passed by and had gotten out of sight.

Hicklin watched the man as he rode along, and the more he looked the more he thought the fellow looked like a dangerous highwayman. He was just beginning to congratulate himself on having avoided a meeting with the suspicious-looking individual when the man suddenly wheeled his horse out of the path and rode straight toward the clump of bushes in which Hicklin had concealed himself.

He rode up alongside of the practical joker and with one hand caught his horse by the bridle while in the other he held an ugly-looking navy revolver at full cock. He ordered Hicklin to dismount, at the same time getting down off his own horse. Then he told the joker to sit down on a log which lay within a few feet of them and took a seat beside him.

By this time Hicklin said he began to feel uncertain whether he was dealing with a robber or a madman. He didn't know what to expect next, but would not have been surprised if the stranger had either made a demand for his money or informed him that he had been commanded to offer up a human sacrifice, and had found the man who had been designated by some mysterious agency as an acceptable victim. For five minutes not a word was said, and all the time Hicklin's hair was standing on end, while the perspiration rolled down his forehead and dropped off the end of his nose.

Once it occurred to him that this might be somebody who had hunted him up to settle an old score, but when he looked at the man he could not remember that he had ever seen him before. It relieved him a little to notice a sort of merry twinkle in the stranger's eye, instead of the cold glitter which characterizes the eye of a desperado or maniac, but still he expected to be either robbed or murdered and perhaps both.

Finally, the man said to him:

"Your name is Hicklin, I believe."

Hicklin, in telling the story afterward, said he was so badly scared that he wasn't quite sure what his name was, but he let the stranger have his own way about it.

"I've been looking for you, for a long time," the man went on to say. "I've got some important business with you, and I reckon you'd like to know what it is."

Hicklin thought the critical moment had come, and in spite of his effort to keep cool he started involuntarily and made a motion to get up from where he was sitting.

"Sit still," said the man with the merry twinkle in his eye, and the gun in his hand. "I won't kill you if you'll keep quiet until I get through with you. I've heard of you, and I want to tell you a story."

"I've been in this country a good many years and I've made a stake. Now I'll tell you what I propose to do. I'm going back East and shall buy me a farm. Then I'll build a nice little house and get married. When my children begin to grow up around me I'll take one of them on each knee and tell them about the hardships I have undergone in this country, and what struggles I have gone through to get money enough to buy them a home and make them comfortable. It will be a sad story of suffering and privation, as you can understand, Mr. Hicklin, and if those children don't cry when they hear it, I'll lick 'em like blazes. That's all I wanted to say to you, Mr. Hicklin, and I hope I haven't occasioned you any annoyance."

Without saying anything more the man mounted his horse and rode away, leaving Hicklin to chuckle over a good joke at his own expense. It turned out that the fellow who had scared the famous old joker nearly to death was a miner who had heard of him, and knowing him by sight had concluded to beat him at his own game of practical joking.

CHAPTER XXIV

An Infant City

WHEN I reached home, at the end of my Salt Lake trip I had been gone over seven months. I was forty-two years of age and had spent twenty-two years in the mountains. I thought then that I was getting tired of that kind of life and would enjoy getting back to the States, where I would have fewer hardships and privations to undergo and where I should find a better condition of society. The yearning to revisit the scenes of my childhood and meet again my friends and old-time associates was stronger than it had been at any time in the twenty-five years which had elapsed since I said good bye to the old folks at home and started out on my adventurous career.

While I had not amassed a great fortune I had enough to live on very comfortably, and after cogitating over the matter for some time I determined to take what I had accumulated and seek a home among the friends of my youth. With this object in view I settled up all my business at Fort Union and got ready to start back to the States.

On my way I intended to make one more trade with the Indians and that was to wind-up my affairs in the Rocky Mountain region. I loaded sev-

352

eral wagons with goods, pocketed the drafts on St. Louis in which the bulk of my fortune had been invested, and early in October found myself again on the road, but with a different object in view from what I had had when setting out on my former trips.

The snows commenced falling early in the fall that year and I had a hard time getting over the mountains. My first objective point was the upper Platte River, where I knew I should find the Arapahoe and Cheyenne Indians, and it was with them that I proposed to trade.

I followed what is now the line of the Santa Fe Railroad from Fort Union to Trinidad and from there went due north by way of the Pueblo to where Denver is now. There I came to a stop, and all my plans and I suppose the whole course of my after life was changed.

There wasn't much of Denver at that time, and I don't think anybody ever dreamed that any such city as we find there today would grow up inside of a hundred years. What is now Colorado was then a part of Kansas Territory. A few adventurers who had visited the country and returned to the East had told wonderful stories of the marvelous wealth of the Rocky Mountain region, and all at once people began to get it into their heads that the territory acquired from Mexico, was a vast gold and silver mine.

When I reached Denver a few hundred treasure hunters had located on Cherry Creek and were living in rough log cabins waiting for spring to come, when they proposed to explore the surrounding mountains. It was what they had heard about the old Spanish mines on the Platte River above Denver which probably brought the gold hunters to that point originally, and it then became headquarters for the prospectors.

The settlement was generally known as Cherry Creek, but two town sites had been laid out on opposite sides of the little stream. Auraria, now called West Denver, was the first town laid out. There must have been some classical scholars among the founders of the town, because I am told that the name has a Latin origin, the word "aura" meaning a gentle breeze. I suppose, then, that Auraria was intended to mean the town of gentle breezes, and it was rather a pretty and appropriate name.[99]

The first cabin had been built in Denver not more than two months before I got there—about the first of November, 1858, I think it was—by

[99]Whatever the classical meaning of the name may have been, Auraria obtained its name from the town of Auraria, Georgia, from which state many of the first Pike's Peak Argonauts had come. When the townsmen of Auraria and Denver determined to unite as one municipality Auraria acquired the less classical designation of West Denver.

A. H. Barker,[100] who had caught the gold fever and come out from Ohio. Barker is still living in Denver, and is a young man yet to have witnessed the birth of so large a city as the capital of Colorado is to-day. When Denver was laid out, the place was named after General James W. Denver, who was then Governor of Kansas Territory. He is still living in Ohio and I should think would be proud of his namesake.[101]

[100] Anselm H. Barker was born in Gallia County, Ohio, November 23, 1822. Following various removals in Ohio and Iowa he located at Plattsmouth, Nebraska in the spring of 1857. On October 24, 1858 he arrived at the site of future Denver with a train of six teams and fifteen men. Following the organization of Auraria he built the first cabin ever erected on the site of Denver. He brought his family from Plattsmouth to Denver in the spring of 1860. His son, Lincoln, born September 7, 1860, acquired the double distinction of being one of the first children born in the city and one of the first male offspring to whom their doting parents gave the name of Lincoln. Like Wootton, Barker in 1862 abandoned Denver to live on a ranch on Clear Creek. Five years later he returned to the city he had helped to found, subsequently engaging in mining and other activities. In 1889, when Wootton was relating his memories, Barker—born in 1822—was not exactly a young man. The date of his death has not been learned. Data condensed from W. B. Vickers, *History of the City of Denver, Arapahoe County and Colorado* (Chicago, 1880), 348-49.

[101] James W. Denver was a native of Virginia who removed with his parents to Ohio in 1830. He practiced law for a time at Xenia and subsequently moved to Platte City, Missouri. During the Mexican War he raised a company of soldiers, of which he was chosen captain. In 1850 he mi-

When I stopped my wagon train in this infant city in December of 1858 there were, as I say, but a few hundred people there, perhaps not more than five hundred all told. They were nearly all men, who had been brought there by the mining excitement, and they were of all kinds and classes. There was no such thing as a store or anything like one in the place and when I got in there with the stock of goods I had picked out for the Indian trade I was at once surrounded by the miners, who wanted flour and sugar and other merchandise that I had with me.

I should have very much preferred to carry out my original plan of trading with the Indians, because in the first place I should have made a better profit on the goods traded, and in the second place I should have been able to go East with several loads of peltry, which would have sold at a handsome profit in Kansas City. I found it im-

grated to California, where he served as Secretary of State and as a representative of California in Congress (1855–57). As chairman of the special Committee of the House on the Pacific Railway he "astonished" that body by reporting a bill advocating the construction of not one but three transcontinental railroads. Appointed Governor of Kansas Territory by President Buchanan in 1858, he acted decisively to quell the prevalent violence and lawlessness. For his role in organizing Arapahoe County, he was honored by the citizenry by giving his name to the newly-born city of Denver. He died in Washington, August 9, 1892. Data adapted from *Dictionary of American Biography*.

possible, however, to resist the importunities of the pioneer settlers of Denver, and I finally agreed to unload my goods and remain there until I traded out what merchandise I had in stock.

My first trading on the site of the present "Queen City of the West" was carried on in a style about as primitive as Indian trading. There wasn't much more style about my first store-room than there was about the average Indian lodge. I moved into a log cabin and without waiting for any such thing as shelving or counters to be put in I commenced business. I had several barrels with me which I rolled alongside of each other and used as a counter. What was in the barrels doesn't matter, but it was something that every well-regulated store kept on hand in those days. I think there are a few highly respected old gentlemen still living in Denver who will remember what it was and would be willing to testify that it was a good article, if it did come high.

Well, it did not take me a great while to sell everything I had, and then I found I had done so well that I concluded to buy a new stock of goods and go into the merchandising business regularly. So it happened that I again gave up going back to my old home and settled down to live the remainder of my life on the frontier.

The enterprising gentlemen who owned the land on which the city of Denver has since been built were exceedingly anxious to have me locate there permanently, and they were generous enough to offer some inducements in addition to that which the town afforded as a trading point. They were short of money, but had plenty of land, and they subsidized me to the extent of one hundred and sixty acres of land in consideration of my opening and carrying on a general store in the town. The land wasn't worth much at that time and did not bring me a very large amount of money when I sold it four years later, but it would be hard to estimate its value now, as it lies in the heart of a city of over one hundred thousand people.

After I had entered into this arrangement to locate permanently in Denver I put up a two-story log building in which to carry on my business and commenced merchandising on a larger scale. This was the first business block put up in the city, and in fact the first building constructed of material so expensive as hewn logs.

There was not much money in the town, or the camp, as we called it, but I got the most of what there was and when the miners didn't have money they generally had something to barter, and so we managed to keep business moving.

New men kept coming into the camp very rapidly that winter, and it seemed that about nine-tenths of all those who came were gamblers.

They would reach Denver broke, and the first thing to do, of course, was to make a raise. They nearly all came through with ox-teams and they would come to me and leave a good yoke of cattle as security for a loan of twenty-five dollars. On the day following they would bring back thirty dollars or forfeit the cattle. This was a matter of such frequent occurrence that loaning money in this way became a part of my business.

After I had completed my log store building, I built a frame house for a residence, which by the way is still standing, and was the first frame building put up in Denver.

The first newspaper published there was started in 1859, by W. N. Byers—who still lives in the city which he has done much to build up—and was printed in the second story of my log business block. It wasn't a very pretentious sheet, and was published under great difficulties. Sometimes the publishers were able to get hold of the right kind of printers' supplies, and sometimes they failed to get hold of anything better than fools-cap or wrapping paper upon which to print an issue of the old *Rocky Mountain News*, now a great metropolitan newspaper keeping pace with the growth of the city and this rapidly developing western country.

The difficulty of procuring printers' supplies was not the most serious with which the publishers of this pioneer newspaper had to contend. I remember one time, when they had been carrying on something of a warfare against the lawless element in the town, that two desperate characters made their appearance in the neighborhood of the building one morning and shot all the windows out of the printing office. The fire was returned from the inside and before the shooting ceased one of the desperadoes was killed. About the first question Byers asked of an employe in those days was whether he could handle a gun to good advantage, and a printer who was handy in this respect stood well with the proprietors of the paper, even though he had a multitude of shortcomings as a compositor.[102]

[102]Wootton does not exaggerate the exigencies of existence suffered by Denver's pioneer newspaper. The initial issues of two papers, the *Rocky Mountain News* and the *Cherry Creek Pioneer*, appeared the same day, April 23, 1859, barely half an hour apart. However, local historians affirm that the *News* appeared on the streets earlier in the day than its rival. Regardless of this distinction the *News* promptly bought out the *Pioneer*, whose initial issue was also its last. While the *News* was being printed in the night of April 22 the roof of Wootton's emporium leaked so badly that a tent cover had to be placed over the press to keep it dry. It continued publication throughout the summer with "tolerable regularity," although isolation from the East and paucity of printers' supplies rendered its publication highly uncertain. Laramie, Wyoming, over 200 miles distant, was the nearest post office, and even there arrival of the mails was irregular. Neither paucity of printing supplies or of news, however, served to daunt the

Thousands of people came to Denver in 1859. They scattered out to prospect in the mountains, or at least some of them did, while a great many after looking about for a few days would return to where they came from, declaring that there was not enough of the precious metal in the country to be worth looking after.

Among the thousands of prospectors who came to the country, of course, there were many who were law-abiding men and made good citizens, but there was a very large element which was utterly lawless. Murders were almost every-day occurrences and stealing was the only

resourceful Editor, who devoted much space to boosting the country, reporting new mining strikes, and depicting the brilliant future in store for Colorado; thereby earning, at the hands of disgruntled immigrants, the reputation of being one of the most capable and dangerous Liars in the country. Since the Editor did not hestitate to denounce the vicious element in the community, threats were made upon his life, and on at least one occasion an attack was made upon the printing office. Here the printers worked with firearms ready at hand. A. D. Richardson, a contemporary eastern reporter and traveler, who visited Denver in 1859, wrote: "The establishment was always in a state of armed neutrality. Printers and editors were moving arsenals, with revolvers at their belts and shotguns standing beside their cases and desks." On the occasion noted, they returned the fire of the desperadoes, killing one of them. See *Beyond the Mississippi* 292–93; Nolie Mumey, *History of the Early Settlements of Denver* (Glendale, Calif., 1942) *passim.* Facsimile reproductions of the initial issues of the *News* and the *Pioneer* accompany the latter work.

occupation of a considerable portion of the population. This gang of thieves was a peculiar one. They seemed to steal for the love of it, and would take anything from a pet calf or a counterfeit gold dollar up to a saw mill. It is an actual fact that the first steam saw mill set up in Denver was stolen, not by the man who put it up but before he got possession of it, from St. Joseph, Missouri.

It had been shipped to that point from St. Louis and while aboard the boat on which it had been forwarded to St. Joseph, waiting for the owner to come and claim it, it was unloaded one night on to a flatboat and pushed some distance up a small stream running into the river. Then it was taken off the flatboat, loaded on to wagons, and brought through to Colorado. The man who bought it, to go into the milling business in Denver a year or two after it was first brought to the country, hired a man to set it up for him, who identified the stolen property and it had to be paid for a second time.

The scoundrels and thieves came pretty near running the country until the vigilantes organized. Then they took a back seat, as the saying goes. I remember the first man who was hanged under this regime. He was a Hungarian named Stoefel who lived on Clear Creek, four or five miles above Denver, with his brother-in-law.

They started out together one day to come to Denver and on the way the Hungarian killed his companion and robbed him of a little sack of gold dust, which he afterward sold to me. A couple of Mexican boys discovered the body of the murdered man while the Hungarian was still in town and he was taken into custody. He confessed to having committed the murder, and we proceeded at once to a trial of the case.

A court was organized and a jury of twelve men empaneled. The prisoner was defended by an able lawyer, but according to the custom in those days his confession was admitted as evidence and the verdict of the jury was that he should be hanged at two o'clock in the afternoon of the day of trial. An executioner was appointed to carry out the sentence of the court and at the appointed time three men got into a two-horse wagon and were driven under a cottonwood tree on the bank of Cherry Creek. These three men were the prisoner, the executioner, and a minister who had found his way out from the East along with the great crowd of gold seekers.

A rope was placed around the murderer's neck and thrown over a limb of the tree. Then the minister, a good Christian man, kneeled down in the wagon to offer up a prayer and the executioner also got down on his knees. The fellow who was to be hanged didn't follow their example, but stood up until the executioner poked him in the ribs and asked him if he didn't know better than to act like a heathen.

After prayer the wagon was driven out from under the tree and the man who had murdered his friend to get possession of a few dollars worth of gold dust was left dangling from the cottonwood limb until he was pronounced dead and cut down. It was as neat and orderly an execution as ever took place anywhere, and was the first of a series which revolutionized Denver society. Within the next few months a number of notorious characters were gotten rid of in this expeditious and generally satisfactory manner, and others escaped the same treatment by heeding the warning they received and leaving the country without unnecessary delay.

So many people came into the country in the winter of 1858–59 that a strong agitation sprang up in favor of cutting loose from Kansas and organizing a new Territory. In the spring of 1859 the friends of this project got together and took steps to bring about the organization of a new Territory, to be called Jefferson Territory, and B. D. Williams was sent to Washington to lay the matter before Congress. At the same time Captain Richard Sopris represented us in the Kansas legislature, and secured the passage of an act establishing Arapahoe County.

The effort to secure the organization of Jefferson Territory was not successful, and it was not until 1861, when Kansas was admitted into the Union as a state, that we got a territorial form of government, the new Territory formed taking the name of Colorado. Colorado is a Spanish word, meaning red, and it was thought to be an appropriate name for our Territory because the country was noted for its red rocks and a soil which gives some of its hills a reddish cast. "Jefferson" was the name we had chosen for the Territory and we were somewhat disappointed when it was not given that name, but we soon got used to the new one and have always been satisfied with it.[103]

[103]There is some understandable confusion in Wootton's account of the steps taken to organize a government for Colorado. On April 11, 1859 delegates representing the several local settlements assembled in Wootton's Hall, the only structure in the settlement that could boast of having a second story, and adopted resolutions calling for the selection of delegates to a convention to be held at Denver on May 7 for the purpose of preparing a State constitution, to be submitted to the people in June, and to call for an election of State officers and representatives in Congress. On June 6 the delegates appointed formed a permanent organization and appointed a committee to draft a State constitution. Controversy over the issue whether to organize a State or a Territorial government followed, and in the election held on September 5 the State proposal was defeated. The steps leading to the organization of Jefferson Territory now quickly followed. On October 3, delegates to a constitutional convention to be held in Denver, and the election of B. D. Williams as representative in Con-

While we were endeavoring to secure recognition as a new Territory we organized a provisional government with R. W. Steele as Governor. One of the first things which we undertook to do under the provisional government was to organize a territorial militia for protection against the Indians. I had the honor of being appointed a brigadier general of militia under this arrangement, but as the resources of our government were very limited I never had any militia to command and consequently had no opportunity to distinguish myself as a general.

The Indians used to give us a good scare every now and then in Denver. Although they never attacked the town, they were killing miners, settlers and emigrants within a few miles of the place almost every day.

I suppose I came near precipitating hostilities

gress, ensued. The convention met in Denver a week later (Oct. 10) and adopted a constitution for the Territory of Jefferson, nominated Territorial officers, with R. W. Steele as Governor, and these were elected in another election held on October 24. Thus the Provincial Territorial Government began operations, with its first legislative session held November 8–December 7, 1859. Serious opposition to the governmental measures presented developed, and the new Territorial Government proved abortive. Congress now entered the picture, and after approximately a year of discussion and delay the law creating Colorado Territory was enacted February 28, 1861. Data condensed from Baker and Hafen, *History of Colorado*, II, 485–90.

one time when there were five or six hundred Comanches in and about the settlement, although I had no intention of doing so. A drunken old chief who had been terrorizing women and children and timid people generally came into my house and became very abusive. I hadn't been used to that sort of thing in the mountains and I picked up my gun and pressed the muzzle against his body to shoot just as he started to mount his horse, which was standing at the door. The gun misfired and it was a good thing it did, because if I had killed the copper-colored old vagabond it would most likely have brought the whole band of Comanches down on the town, and we might have had serious trouble.

A great many of the adventurers who came to Denver while I was there had a hard time of it. Some came without money and others had so little money when they reached there that it was soon exhausted. There was little or nothing for them to do, and as they could not obtain employment many a deserving man had to go hungry in those days, while others borrowed the wherewithal to secure an occasional meal from sympathetic friends who were more fortunately situated.

There were hundreds of bitterly disappointed men who seemed to have come to Colorado thinking they could pick up gold nuggets almost anywhere, who found it difficult to pick up a square meal once a week. I fed a great many of them and did that much, at least, towards building up the city. One of the first, if not the first hotel started in the town was one in which I was interested. That hotel enterprise failed financially for the reason that neither the manager nor myself could understand that only men who had money had a right to eat. Whenever a man came to me and said he was hungry and had no money I used to send him around to the hotel for a meal, and the manager made it a point never to turn away a man who made the same sort of appeal. Our house was well patronized, but in view of the fact that the most of our patrons were free boarders I suppose it is not surprising that we did not make a success of the hotel business.

CHAPTER XXV

The Haunted Fort

I LEFT Denver in 1862. Looking at it from a business standpoint, I can see now that this was a mistake. If I had remained there and grown up with the capital city I might have become a rich man and had a big hotel or an opera house or something of that sort named after me.

I reckon I shouldn't have felt right though, after the buildings got too thick. There would have been a lack of room and breathing space and I might have been expected to wear fine clothes. Anyhow, I should have been jostled about on the streets instead of having the road all to myself as I do now when I go out for a walk, and should have had the noise and dust of the city instead of the singing of birds and the pure air of the mountains that I have here.

I guess I'm better off as it is, but to tell the truth it wasn't the fear that Denver would become a city that drove me away from there. While I left the place at the end of a four years' stay with about twenty times the population it had when I went there, the chances seemed to me to be that it would get smaller rather than larger. The population had fluctuated continually during the four years I remained there, first going up and then

369

down, until I made up my mind that it was a good place to get away from. There's where I lacked what you call foresight, but such things all go in a life time and as I have already said I suppose I'm just as well off where I am.

The breaking out of the war in 1861 kept back immigration, and that and the following year were comparatively dull years in the mountains generally and particularly dull in Denver. I sold out my business there, and concluding to try ranch life again I started in on the Fountain River nine miles above Pueblo. That was where my farm was located, but I built a house first on the site of Pueblo near the old fort which gave the place its name.

Here again I became a squatter on the site of a future city without ever dreaming of any such thing. The town site had been laid out, but very few buildings had been erected and there were not many people in the settlement. The massacre which had occurred in 1854 had operated to keep people away from there, not only because they feared another outbreak but because they had a sort of superstitious dread of being near the old fort. The walls of the old adobe building had been stained and bespattered with the blood of the victims of the slaughter and there were stories about its being haunted, which made even some of the mountain men timid about stopping over night in it when they passed that way.

I remember an amusing thing which happened there when I was returning from my last trip to Salt Lake which illustrates how one man, at least, was affected by the stories of the haunted fort. We had with us an old fellow named Betts. Barney Betts, I think it was, but anyhow the last name is right. He had heard of the ghosts that made their appearance from time to time about the fort and protested mildly against camping near it, but the other members of the party laughed at his fears and our camp fire was kindled under some cottonwood trees not very far distant from the haunted ruins of the trappers' old headquarters.

We sat around the fire until nine or ten o'clock telling stories, and the character of the stories we told was not such as to allay nervousness on the part of a man who believed in ghosts and was afraid of them, because we wanted to have a bit of fun at the expense of our timid traveling companion.

At a reasonable hour we retired for the night. That is to say, we wrapped ourselves in our blankets, and stretched ourselves out on the ground near enough to the fire to be warmed without being burned by it. Betts lay down close to me and I noticed that he was not in a comfortable frame of mind for a good night's rest, but as I was not disturbed by the same, or similar fears, in ten minutes after I lay down I was sound asleep.

I had slept perhaps an hour or two when I felt something plucking at my blanket and in an instant I was wide awake. I raised up a little so that I could look around, and discovered Betts sitting up beside me. It was a moonlight night and I could see that his face was as pale as bleached cotton, while his teeth were chattering as I had seen men's teeth chatter when they had the old-fashioned ague down in Mississippi.

"What on earth's the matter, man!" I said to him in a whisper.

"Hear 'em?" said he.

"Hear what?"

"I've seen 'em," he whispered, crawling up so close to me that I could hear his heart beat as though it was trying to knock out some of his ribs.

"You've seen what? you old idiot," I exclaimed, thinking of Indians and beginning to get slightly alarmed myself.

"The Ghosts."

"Where?" I inquired, beginning to understand what the trouble was.

"At the fort," said he; "don't you hear 'em?"

I listened, and heard what had not attracted my attention before, the plaintive notes of two whippoorwills, which were evidently perched on the adobe wall or somewhere about the old fort. Then I burst out laughing, and this awakened my companions. We thought the joke had gone far enough, and explained to him that what he heard was not the wailing of a perturbed spirit, but the night song of a very harmless little bird.

Poor old Barney was not entirely satisfied with our explanation. The noise might be accounted for, but he still insisted that he had seen rebozo-wrapped, but headless, Mexican women wandering about the fort, and I think he really believed he had seen the ghosts of some of the senoras who had perished in the massacre.

While I am talking about ghosts I might as well tell you another ghost story, although I must tell you about some other things which lead up to it first.

I have already told you that when the war broke out there were some differences of opinion among the men who found themselves in Colorado and New Mexico as to whether the northern or the southern states were in the right. The population of the mountain towns, settlements, and mining camps had been gathered from every State in the Union, and I think it's a mean man who has no feeling of loyalty for his native State and no love for his birthplace.

Colorado was made a Territory in 1861 and with Texas in rebellion Colorado and New Mexico were border territories, and for a time there was really some uncertainty as to whether they would fall in line with the Federals or the Confederates.

When Colonel Sibley made his raid into New Mexico with his Texas Rangers in 1862, he expected to receive considerable reinforcements in the way of volunteer additions to his little army along the way and he had been promised a thousand men when he reached Colorado.

Whether the enthusiastic Southerners who made this promise would have been able to furnish that or any other considerable addition to Sibley's force must always remain a question, because he never reached Colorado and they were not put to the test.

After defeating General Canby at Valverde he came on to Santa Fe and captured that city, but the New Mexicans did not flock to his standard as he had expected. They treated him with a good deal of consideration and made his stay in Santa Fe a very pleasant one, but they didn't come up with guns in their hands, ready to enroll themselves in the Confederate army.

The hospitality which they extended to him was about as detrimental to the cause which he represented as their armed opposition would have been. Colonel Sibley had spent many years in the Territory as a regular army officer and he knew almost everybody in the country of any consequence. When he got among these old-time friends he couldn't resist the temptation to enjoy himself and have a good time, even in war times.

He seemed to forget that he wasn't doing garrison duty and had no time for dancing attendance at fandangos and holding convivial reunions with old friends. He wasted time in Santa Fe and in the meantime the Colorado First, a regiment which had been raised by Governor Gilpin for service in the Union army, was making a forced march across the mountains to head him off before he reached Fort Union, while Canby was following him up from lower New Mexico.[104]

The result was that he was cornered and defeated in the battle on Glorieta Mountain, when he should have been at Fort Union. Had he pushed on to Fort Union from Santa Fe he could have captured it without difficulty, as the small garrison

[104]William Gilpin, first Governor of Colorado Territory, was a remarkable man. He was a native of Pennsylvania and a graduate from the University of Pennsylvania in the class of 1833 (the date 1822, often given for his birth, is obviously incorrect). On July 1, 1834 he entered the U.S. Military Academy, but withdrew a few months later. This action, is perhaps symptomatic of his restless disposition. In 1838 he located at St. Louis, where he became Editor of the *Missouri Argus.* Subsequently he practiced law at Independence, and in 1843 joined Fremont's exploring expedition to the Pacific Coast. On the outbreak of the Mexican War, now returned to Missouri, he joined Colonel Doniphan's Expedition, and for a couple of years was engaged in military activities against the Indians in the Rocky Mountain area, attaining the rank of lieutenant colonel of volunteers. Subsequently he returned to Independence, and in 1861 was appointed Governor of the new Colorado Territory, whose name he may have been re-

stationed there did not expect to offer any effective resistance and would have evacuated the fort before Sibley reached it. There he could have entrenched himself so strongly that no force which could have been brought against him for a considerable time could have driven him out, and he could have remained in the country long enough to have had some influence on public sentiment and possibly he might have received material assistance from Colorado and New Mexico.[105]

As it was, he was whipped back into Texas, and the war ended so far as Colorado and New Mexico

sponsible for selecting. A man of forceful temperament, he countered Confederate efforts to establish control of the Colorado-New Mexico area by organizing the First Colorado Regiment, for whose equipment he paid with drafts which the merchants and others were compelled to accept. Although he deserves a large measure of credit for saving the Southwest for the Union, his arbitrary measures provoked complaints which led to his removal from office in the spring of 1862. He entertained fantastic visions of the future destiny of the western country, which found expression in several books, published from 1860 to 1890. See *Dictionary of American Biography*; H. H. Bancroft, *History of Nevada, Colorado, and Wyoming* (San Francisco, 1890), 413-27.

[105]Henry H. Sibley entered West Point from Louisiana in 1833 and graduated with the Class of 1838. Thereafter he served in the Florida War and in varied frontier assignments and campaigns. He was promoted from the rank of captain to major on May 13, 1861 and on the same day he resigned his commission to join the southern Confederacy. Thus he was never a colonel in the United States Army. Prior to his resignation he had served for a year or more in

were concerned. Had Sibley gained a firm foothold these Territories might have been considerable of a battle-ground, but when the Confederate Colonel was driven across the line some of the Colorado troops were sent into Missouri, while those who remained at home had nothing to do but watch hostile Indians and discipline those who manifested what was thought to be too great sympathy with the Southerners in the struggle to get out of the Union and build up a government of their own.

I was one of those looked upon by the territorial government as an erring brother and subjected to some little discipline as a consequence. Having been born in Virginia and raised in southern Kentucky, I was essentially a Southern man and naturally enough, I think, was very strongly in sympathy with the Southern States. Those who know me well know I have never hesitated to express my

New Mexico. Wootton does not exaggerate the consequences of his failure in the battle of Glorieta Pass, fought March 28, 1862. With it "Jefferson Davis' dream of revolutionizing New Mexico Sonora, and California was definitely ended." Data condensed from G. W. Cullum, *Biographical Register of the Officers and Graduates of the U.S. Military Academy....* and *Dictionary of American Biography.* For an additional and possibly over-colored account of the battle of Glorieta Pass see Baker and Hafen, *History of Colorado* (Denver, 1927), III, 967–71: see also H. H. Bancroft *History of Arizona and New Mexico* (San Francisco, 1889), 694–97.

opinions, and so I came to be looked upon as rather a pronounced Rebel.

At one time in 1863, when the war feeling was very bitter, I had occasion to go up to Denver from Pueblo on some business. Before I had been long in the city I was warned by friends that I was looked upon by the authorities there as an enemy of the government, and was likely to be taken into custody and held as a prisoner. I wasn't at all pleased with the idea of being locked up in jail. In-door life never did agree with me and besides I had a family to look after down at Pueblo.

I got through with my business as quickly as possible and started for home on horseback just as the news was brought to me that a posse had started out to hunt me up and put me under arrest. I started early in the morning and rode all day, reaching the head of Kiowa Creek at nightfall. This was one of the places which the mountain men, or at least a good many of them, avoided, and here's where my ghost story comes in.

A soldier named Fagan belonging to Captain Marcy's company had dropped dead while standing guard one night when the company was in camp here several years before, and the place had come to be known as Fagan's Camp. The lonely grave, which was miles away from any human habitation, had probably moved some superstitious hunter or trapper to start the story that the spirit of the unfortunate soldier materialized every night, and dressed in full uniform with musket in hand, tramped all night in a circle about the grave to guard the resting-place of the body which it had once inhabited.

I had heard the story, but did not know the exact location of Fagan's Camp, although it would have made no difference if I had as superstition has never been one of my weaknesses. When I got down off my horse and went into camp for the night—if I may call it going into camp for one man to build a fire and sit down by it alone—it chanced that I dismounted, without knowing it, inside the circle around which it had been alleged the ghostly sentry paced every night, and when I kindled my fire it was at the head or the foot, I don't know which, of Fagan's grave.

When I lay down to rest I stretched myself alongside of this same little mound of earth, which served to protect me to some extent from the cold, raw night wind. Tired as I was after my long hard ride, I dropped asleep and had slept something like two or three hours when I was awakened—as I always was by the slightest noise—by the tramping of horses some distance from me.

I had left my own horse secreted in a cañon not far away, and leaving my camp-fire I hastened to the horse, thinking it possible that the Denver posse had followed my trail and that there might be necessity for immediate and hasty flight.

My fire, which had not been a big one to begin with, had burned down, so that when I left it the few dying embers remaining sent up only a sort of will o' the wisp blaze which would scarcely have been noticed twenty yards away.

I stood by my horse, ready to mount and gallop away if occasion required it, but having a fancy to see who my visitors were before starting or becoming seriously alarmed. By and by they came close enough to me to enable me to hear their conversation, and although I could not make out who they were I knew there were several men in the party.

Presently I heard one of the men say: "Look sharp now for ghosts. This is Fagan's camp and they say the dead soldier's ghost stands guard over his grave every night."

"I'd a heap rather see Dick Wootton," said another member of the party, whose voice I recognized as that of a friend. "We've kept on his trail, and he must be some place in these mountains."

"We'll find him if he's here," said the first speaker, "though I tell you I don't much like prowling around a dead man's camp. If Fagan's ghost is running these parts, as I've heard lots of 'em say it is, I want to camp some place else. What the devil is that!"

They had caught sight of my little camp fire, which would blaze up now and then just enough to throw a pale glare over its surroundings and make the outlines of the grave distinctly visible, when it would apparently die out again so completely that hardly a spark could be seen.

It was really a ghostly-looking kind of manifestation and as the party stood looking at it for a minute or two without saying anything I thought the men were half inclined to stampede and run away from the place without making any further investigation.

Finally, one of them said: "Might as well see what it is."

Then they all got down off of their horses and approached the place as cautiously as though they thought themselves in danger of being at any moment impaled on the bayonet of the ghostly sentinel. Not one of them uttered a word above a whisper until they reached the grave and discovered that the light they had seen and regarded with so much superstitious dread came from a real fire. Then one of them blurted out:

"It's Dick Wootton's camp fire, and I'm a natural born liar if he haint been asleep on Fagan's grave."

"You're right, partner, as sure as I've got a front and a hind name," said another one of my midnight visitors. "That fellow would camp in a sepulcher without having any bad dreams, or risk going to sleep in a powder magazine with his pipe lit. He aint far away from here now either. Let's call him."

The discovery that I had slept in Fagan's camp seemed to dispel all their fears, and their voices rang out on the night air calling me by name. I had learned by this time that I had nothing to fear from that party, and when I joined them I found five friends who were getting away from Denver as hurriedly as I was myself, and for the same reason.

We didn't look for another camping place, but raked together the remains of my fire and piled on more fuel. Nobody cared much about sleeping, but we sat around the fire and talked over war matters and nursed our grievances until morning. Then we went on to Pueblo and never heard anything more about the proposed arrests. When it got noised around that I had not only stayed all night in Fagan's camp, but had actually kindled a fire on the grave and slept alongside of it until I was awakened by the party looking for me it spoiled a very pretty ghost story and Fagan's camp was no longer avoided by the mountain men or other travelers who had occasion to go that way. The story of my adventure was vouched for by so many witnesses that it could not be disputed, and the haunted camp sensation was exploded.

Chapter XXVI

Plains Indians on the War Path

I PUT up two cabins in Pueblo, among the first built there. I lived in one of them and ran a grocery in the other, while superintending the building of some cabins on my farm.

My farming on the Fountain River was quite extensive and I demonstrated that grain of all kinds could be raised in Colorado. I had done that before when farming on the Arkansas River, but I did still better on my new farm. Corn and wheat were the principal crops which I raised, and my hundred-acre cornfield attracted more attention than anything else in that section of the country.

I can tell a good story in connection with that big cornfield which will illustrate fairly well the hardships of another phase of frontier life, and give you an idea of what gentlemen of the learned professions had to contend with sometimes in the discharge of their duties or pursuit of their callings.

I was sitting in my cabin one night, some time after dark, when the dogs outside of the house commenced making a great fuss and I knew that some stranger, or strangers perhaps, were around. I stepped to the door with my gun in my hand and listened. Pretty soon I heard some one calling,

383

who had gotten within hailing distance but was afraid to come nearer. I couldn't make out what the man was saying, but I quieted the dogs and then answered his call, asking him who he was and what he wanted. He came up closer and informed me that he was Judge Allen Bradford; that he had gotten lost in my cornfield, and that what he wanted was to get out of it and find something to eat and a place to sleep.

I went out and brought him up to the house, because I knew of Judge Bradford, although at that time I had never seen him. When he got up to where the light shone on him I think he looked less like a judge than anybody I ever saw, unless it was a Yuma Indian. The cornfield was very muddy and the mule which he was riding, a consumptive-looking animal any way, had mired down several times and both man and mule looked like they had been made of adobe and hadn't got dry yet.

The Judge was on his way to Conejos, where he was to hold court, and had gotten lost, the result being that he landed in my big cornfield and came pretty near not getting out of it. When he got indoors that night I traded him a trapper's suit for his mud-stained judicial garments and he felt better after the change, if the clothes didn't fit him. He got a good night's rest and in the morning when I sent him on his way, riding a good horse in place of that sickly-looking mule, he looked more like a judge. Judge Bradford afterwards became one of the most distinguished men in the State, and he used to laugh over losing his way in my corn patch, every time I saw him.[106]

It was not a great while afterward that I happened to be called on to make my appearance in the Judge's court. That was while the war was going on, and as I have already said, it stirred up a good deal of controversy between the representatives of the different sections who were living at the time in Colorado. The question at issue, as the lawyers say, when my presence in Judge Bradford's court was required, was a political one and I didn't agree with the court politically.

In the course of the proceedings, which from my standpoint seemed to be a little irregular, I suppose I must have gotten somewhat excited.

[106]Allen A. Bradford was a native of Maine who studied law and migrated to Missouri in 1846. Subsequent removals were made to Iowa, where he served as judge from 1852 to 1855, to Nebraska where he served in the Territorial Legislature, and to Colorado, where on June 6, 1862 President Lincoln appointed him a member of the Territorial Supreme Court. He subsequently was twice elected to the lower house of Congress and practiced law in Pueblo until his death, March 12, 1888. Historian Bancroft characterizes him as "a man of many experiences," one of which Wootton relates. See *Biographical Directory of the American Congress*, 1774–1949; H. H. Bancroft, *History of Nevada, Colorado and Wyoming*, 1540-1888 (San Francisco, 1890), 434.

Anyhow I did some swearing which wasn't of the character that men are called upon to do in court. The Judge called me to order very mildly, but he didn't fine me for contempt of court, as everybody present expected he would, and I always thought the reason he didn't fine me was because he had not forgotten that cornfield scrape.

For three years I plowed and planted and harvested my grain, leading almost as quiet a life as the average eastern farmer. The markets were good for everything in the way of farm produce because the troops which the government kept stationed in Colorado and New Mexico required supplies, and everything that could be raised on the small amount of land under cultivation was taken at handsome prices.

We soon made up our minds that the War of the Rebellion wasn't to be fought out in Colorado and that there was no occasion for us to get greatly excited over it out here. After we had gotten into this frame of mind, Northern and Southern men got along very comfortably together, notwithstanding their differences of opinion.

It was about this time that the most serious Indian troubles ever experienced in Colorado commenced. The influx of whites into the Territory led the Indians to believe that their country would soon be overrun and they looked upon every immigrant as a trespasser. The Cheyennes, a band which the mountain men had generally been on good terms with, became for some reason or other particularly incensed against the settlers.

The Comanches, the old-time enemies of the Cheyennes, had been hostile to the whites, whether settlers, traders, or trappers, from the time they first commenced coming into the country. As soon as the Comanches learned that the Cheyennes were inclined to become alarmed over the invasion of their territory by white settlers, they made peace with them and did all they could to stir them up against their common enemy, the pale face.

The Kiowas, after being almost exterminated by the Arapahoes and Cheyennes, had joined the Comanches, as had also a fragment of the Apache tribe which became known as the Prairie Apache band.

After the alliance between the Comanches and the Cheyennes these two bands, together with the Kiowas and the Prairie Apaches scattered over a broad area of country, constituted what I think was the largest number of Indians that we ever had on the war path at one time in the Far West.

The Arapahoes joined them later, one of their principal grievances being the cutting down of a grove of timber near Fort Wallace, Kansas. This grove, which they called the Big Timber, was a favorite wintering place of the Indians. Buffaloes were numerous in the surrounding country and it was at this grove that the Indians gathered after the chase to tan the buffalo skins and prepare them for the traders.

The contractors who built Fort Wallace, cut down the fine old trees and entirely destroyed the grove, so that when the Arapahoes visited their old camping place again they found scarcely a tree standing. Then the Indians put on their war paint and declared that for every tree the white men had cut down they would kill a white man, and I reckon they did it before they were finally subdued and forced to quit the country.[107]

The Comanche and Cheyenne warfare was very shrewdly carried on. They were never all on the warpath at once, and while some of them were killing immigrants and making forays against weak settlements, the others were claiming to be good Indians and in that way managed to keep on good terms with the traders. They did all the trading for the hostiles as well as themselves and by that means secured large supplies of guns and am-

[107]Fort Wallace was established in 1865 on the south fork of Smoky Hill River, near present-day Wallace, Kansas. A reservation of 14 square miles was laid out and quarters for 500 soldiers were built. It was a place of importance while the Union Pacific Railroad, completed to this point in July, 1868, was being built and warfare with the Cheyennes was being waged. The fort was abandoned by the army in 1882. See Gen. Custer, *My Life on the Plains*, the Lakeside Classics volume for 1952, index entries, and *Dictionary of American Biography*.

munition, which were at once turned over to the Indians who were on the warpath. It was some time before we found out how it was that the Indians who were actually doing the fighting kept themselves supplied all the time with arms of as good pattern as those used by the soldiers, and also with plenty of ammunition.

When we made this discovery we very naturally came to the conclusion that all the Indians who had entered into the understanding according to which part of them furnished the ammunition for killing white men, women, and children while the others did the killing, were equally guilty.

It was the necessity for punishing all the Indians who belonged to the hostile combination, whether they were actually caught scalping their victims or only sharpening the knives for those who did the scalping, which led Colonel Chivington to march against the Cheyennes with the Colorado First and fight the first band he came across. Chivington was severely censured by the tender-hearted eastern people, whose scalp-locks were never in danger, for this action, and a great deal has been said by them about the Chivington Massacre. The most absurd and unreasonable stories were started about the affair in the East, and I shouldn't wonder if the Indian lovers didn't succeed in persuading people back there that the Comanches, Cheyennes, Apaches, and Kiowas were kind-hearted, industrious, and peace-loving creatures, while the white people of Colorado were merciless savages.

One of the stories published was to the effect that when the Colorado First got back to Denver the citizens had a sort of combined jubilee and scalp dance, at which the scalps of the slaughtered Indians were placed on exhibition.

Now the facts were that the people of central and eastern Colorado and western Kansas were very glad to learn that the savages who had for months menaced life and property, who had in cold blood killed scores of settlers and immigrants, had been severely punished by Colonel Chivington and his troops at Sand Creek. At a public meeting which was held in Denver soon after the occurrence, called for the purpose of congratulating the officers and soldiers of the First Regiment upon the success of the campaign from which they had just returned, there were scalps on exhibition, but *they were not the scalps of Indians.* They were the scalps of white victims of the savages which had been found in the possession of the alleged good and peaceable Indians. They were the scalps of immigrants who had been slain while attempting to cross the Plains in search of homes in the Far West. They were the scalps of settlers who had never wronged either Indian or white man. They were the scalps of gray-haired men and prattling children, of fair-haired and dark-haired women who had suffered a thousand deaths at the hands of the red devils.

Those were the scalps which were exhibited on that occasion, and they were exhibited for the purpose of showing that the savages who had been so severely punished deserved the punishment. I was never on very friendly terms with Colonel Chivington, and have censured some of his acts as a military officer as severely as anybody, but my opinion of this particular campaign and his action in connection with it is, that if it is any part of the business of soldiers stationed in the Indian country to protect the lives and property of settlers, he and his men did their duty and did it well.[108]

[108]The Chivington or Sand Creek Massacre still remains "the most controversial subject in Colorado history." *Dict. of American Hist.*, V, 26. At dawn, Nov. 29, 1864 Colonel J. M. Chivington led a force of about 1000 soldiers in a surprise attack upon the camp of several hundred Arapahoes and Cheyennes (chiefly the latter) in the bend of Sand Creek, a tributary of the Arkansas. Taken by surprise, the Indians were mercilessly slaughtered to the number, variously estimated, of 150 to 500. Whether the Indians were peaceful bands encamped under the pledged protection of State and Federal authorities is still a matter of confusion and dispute. Regardless of this detail, the white soldiers, who were said to be under orders to give no quarter, perpetrated a shocking massacre, and in true savage fashion mutilated the bodies of the slain. At the subsequent Federal inquiry into the affair, Lieutenant Olney swore that he witnessed Lieutenant Richmond

Nothing ever had a more salutary effect upon the Indians than the result of this campaign. While no peace was made with them at that time

coolly shoot and scalp three women and five children who had already been taken prisoners, disregarding their frantic pleas for mercy. This item is but a single detail of the entire affair, which happens to rest upon the sworn evidence of a participant and eyewitness. Despite Wootton's statement, the massacre seems not to have produced a "salutary effect" upon the Indians, who instead were enraged and embittered by it. One of the chiefs who escaped from the massacre was the same Black Kettle whose village General Custer destroyed in the battle of the Washita, almost exactly four years later (Nov. 27, 1868). For Custer's own account of this campaign see *My Life on the Plains*, the Lakeside Classics volume for 1952.

Broadly viewed, the attitude of the western settlers toward the Indians in this period was not unlike that of the settlers of New England earlier. The New Englanders ruthlessly slaughtered their Pequot and Narragansett neighbors; in like fashion their western successors slaughtered, when able, the Plains Indians. Wootton clearly expresses their attitude, and gives as good a defense of it as can be found. For a comprehensive account of the Chivington Massacre by a writer sympathetic with the Indians see George B. Grinnell, *The Fighting Cheyennes* (N. Y., 1915), Chap. XIV. For a more balanced recent account see Baker and Hafen, *History of Colorado*, I, Chap. VII.

Colonel Chivington, leader in the gory affair, seems to have imbibed some of the characteristics of Oliver Cromwell. At the outbreak of the Civil War he was a presiding elder in the Methodist Episcopal Church and he was at first appointed chaplain of the First Colorado Regiment. However, he requested a more militant role, and was given the rank of major. In the battle of Glorieta Pass he played a decisive role. His conduct at Sand Creek seems to have met with general local approval.

nor, in fact, for some years after that, and they kept on murdering weak parties of immigrants and isolated settlers, they kept their distance from the larger settlements, and particularly from Denver. Before that it was hardly safe to ride out a dozen miles in any direction without an escort of soldiers to accompany you.

I remember that just before that time I had occasion to escort the family of an old friend of mine, who had died, from Pueblo to Denver; and when I had gotten through safely, I felt that I had completed the most perilous trip of my life. People were killed along a portion of the road the day before, and others the day after I passed over it, and how I had the good fortune to escape, with the lady and her children in my charge, was always something of a mystery to me.

The lady and children, by the way, were very much shocked by a discovery which we made as we drove along the road between where the town of Colorado Springs is now and Denver. We noticed the ravens hovering about a spot not far from the road, in a small grove, and driving to one side we found there the skeletons of four men bound with ropes to as many trees. The flesh had been picked clean from the bones, but a bullet hole in each skull showed how the men had met their death. Each skeleton stood in a pair of boots, which was all that was left about them in the way of clothing, and altogether this was as ghastly a find along a lonely road as one could imagine. We learned afterwards that the skeletons were those of the notorious Jim Runnels and three of his band of robbers, who had been captured and summarily executed only a short time before.

In the summer of 1864 I again soured on farming, and I think my experience that summer would have soured a philosopher. First I had to wrestle with a water spout which rolled over my wheat and corn, and then when it made a feeble effort to stand up again a hail storm completed the work of destruction.

I shall never forget that terrible flood of 1864. It had been raining hard, and about the last of May the Fountain River and other streams were considerably swollen, but we did not think them dangerously high. I was living then on my farm on the Fountain, and had just gotten up one morning when I saw what I can only describe as a great bank of water coming down the valley. It looked to me then as though it might be a hundred feet high and a mile or two wide. Actual measurements of the water marks taken later demonstrated that it was eighteen and a half feet high, or deep perhaps I should say, in the main current, and it spread out until it made a stream between one and two miles wide.

My house stood on high ground and I felt safe so far as my family was concerned, but I had a neighbor some distance down the river whose house I knew must be swept away by the torrent. My little fourteen-year-old boy mounted a horse, and riding as fast as possible to this neighbor's place, warned him of the danger just in time to enable him to escape with his family to the hills.

We afterwards succeeded in getting some of the furniture out of the house, but the house itself went down the stream and along with it went eleven hundred dollars in gold that Dodson—that was the neighbor's name—had left behind him when he made his hurried race for the hills. The great torrent, as it came down, following the course of the Fountain River, uprooted cotton-wood trees which were four or five feet in diameter and carried them along until they lodged against some hill-side, or were piled up with other debris.

The flood subsided almost as suddenly as it came on. In an hour or two the river was but little higher than at the ordinary high water stage, but in that two hours about everything that the settlers in the valley had in the way of property had been swept away and nine lives had been lost. When the water receded so that I could look over the ground where my growing crops had stood, I found in the place of wheat and corn scores of uprooted trees, wrecks of log cabins, farm wagons, plows, and other wreckage which had been brought down from above. The wheat and corn, while it had been leveled to the ground, had not been entirely destroyed. I cleaned off the debris as best I could and in a few days the grain began to recover to some extent from the effects of the flood. I was beginning to congratulate myself on the prospect of having something of a crop after all, when the hail storm came which finished it.

The big hail-stones knocked the heads off my wheat and pounded my corn into the ground, so that when it was over I had no more show of reaping a crop of either kind of grain than I would have had if the seed had never been put into the ground. I need not say that my farming operations did not pay that year. I need not say, either, that I began to have doubts about my being able to make a fortune out of the business. With Indians on the warpath and liable at any time to sweep through the valley and drive away my stock, and hail storms and floods to destroy my crops, it didn't look to me as though the time had come to make a success of farming in Colorado and I left the ranch the next spring.

Chapter XXVII

Pathfinder and Builder

I HAD long had in mind the building of a stage road through the Raton Pass, and when I made up my mind to quit farming on the Fountain I thought it a good time to put through my road project.

I had been over the mountains so often, had in fact lived in them so many years, that I knew almost every available pass in Colorado and New Mexico and understood just about how the travel ran in various directions. I knew that the Raton Pass was a natural highway connecting settlements already in existence, and destined to be a thoroughfare for other settlements which would spring up in south-eastern Colorado and north-eastern New Mexico.

Barlow and Sanderson, the proprietors of the Santa Fe stage line, were anxious to change their route so as to pass through Trinidad, which had by this time become a point of some importance, and the freighters generally wanted to come through that way. How to get through the Pass was the problem, however, with all of them.

A trail led through the cañon it is true, but that was almost impassable for anything but saddle horses and pack animals at any time, and entirely

397

impassable for wagon trains or stages in the winter time. Nobody knew this better than I did, because I had come through the Pass on my way to Denver in 1858 and spent nearly a month travelling a distance of fifty miles with a comparatively light wagon train.

What I proposed to do was to go into this winding, rock-ribbed mountain pass and hew out a road which, barring grades, should be as good as the average turnpike. I expected to keep this road in good repair and charge toll for travelling over it, and thought I could see a good business ahead of me.

The first thing to be done was to secure a charter, or rather two charters, because the road which I intended to construct would be an inter-territorial highway, partly in Colorado and partly in New Mexico. I applied to the Colorado legislature, when it met in the winter of 1865, for a charter authorizing me to construct a toll road from Trinidad to the New Mexico line, and to the New Mexico legislature for a charter covering the distance from the New Mexico line to Red River, which was to be the southern terminus of my road. I got both charters without difficulty, although the Colorado charter bill was not passed until just before the adjournment of the legislature, which at that time met at Golden. The following spring I moved down here, picked out the spot which I have since made my home, and commenced work on my mountain road.

I had undertaken no light task, I can assure you. There were hillsides to cut down, rocks to blast and remove, and bridges to build by the score. I built the road, however, and made it a good one, too. That was what brought the Santa Fe Trail through this way, and as the same trail extended to Chihuahua in Mexico, my twenty-seven miles of turnpike constituted a portion of an international thoroughfare.[109]

After I got my road completed the next thing was to make it a paying investment. Such a thing as a toll road was unknown in this country at that time. I do not think there was one in either Colorado or New Mexico until after I built mine.

People who had come out here from the eastern states understood, of course, that the object of building a turnpike was to enable the owner to collect toll from those who travelled over it, but I

[109]For an interesting account of Wootton's toll road by a modern scholar see Bess McKinnan, "The Raton Toll Road," in *New Mexico Hist. Review*, II, 83–89 (January, 1927). Considerable uncertainty shrouds the question of Wootton gaining a New Mexico charter for the road. Miss McKinnan states that there is no record of such a charter in the early territorial laws, while a law enacted Feb. 1, 1873 declares that "said charter or so-called charter" is null and void. She also cites territorial laws authorizing two other toll roads prior to Wootton's enterprise.

had to deal with a great many people who seemed to think that they should be as free to travel over my well-graded and bridged roadway as they were to follow an ordinary cow path.

I may say that I had five classes of patrons to do business with. There was the stage company and its employes, the freighters, the military authorities who marched troops and transported supplies over the road, the Mexicans, and the Indians.

With the stage company, the military authorities, and the American freighters I had no trouble. With the Indians, when a band came through now and then I didn't care to have any controversies about so small a matter as a few dollars toll. Whenever they came along the toll gate went up, and any other little thing I could do to hurry them along was done promptly and cheerfully. While the Indians didn't understand anything about the system of collecting tolls, they seemed to recognize the fact that I had a right to control the road and they would generally ride up to the gate and ask permission to go through. Once in a while the chief of a band would think compensation for the privilege of going through was in order, and would make me a present of a buckskin or something of that sort.

My Mexican patrons were the hardest to get along with. Paying for the privilege of travelling over any road was something they were totally unused to, and they did not take to it kindly. They were pleased with my road and liked to travel over it, until they reached the toll-gate. This they seemed to look upon as an obstruction that no man had a right to place in the way of a free-born native of the mountain region. They seemed to look upon the toll-gate as a new scheme for holding up travelers for the purpose of robbery, and many of them evidently thought me a kind of freebooter who ought to be suppressed by law. Holding these views, when I asked them for a certain amount of money before raising the toll-gate, they naturally differed with me very frequently about the propriety of complying with the request.

In other words, there would be at such times probably an honest difference of opinion between the man who kept the toll-gate and the man who wanted to get through it. Anyhow, there was a difference, and such differences had to be adjusted. Sometimes I adjusted these matters through diplomacy and sometimes I did it with a club. They were always settled one way, however, and that was in accordance with the toll schedule, so that I could never have been charged with unjust discrimination in rates. Only the Indians were exempted from paying the fixed rates, but collecting turnpike tolls in the Far West twenty years ago was a lively business.

I did make one other exception to the rule, too, now that I come to think about it, and that was in favor of officers and parties who were in pursuit of horse and cattle thieves. Stealing cattle and horses in Colorado and running them into New Mexico got to be a business about that time, and the same band of thieves that drove stolen Colorado stock into New Mexico would recross the line with stock stolen from the Mexicans.

There was one gang of robbers in the country at that time headed by Jim Gray, a notorious scoundrel, which was carrying on a very extensive cattle and horse-stealing business in this region. Gray was the most daring horse-thief I have ever known. He came to my place once in broad daylight when a large party of soldiers were stopping here, stole the best mule they had, rode it away, and escaped. Jack Ross was at the head of another notorious gang of thieves, and members of both gangs used to pass through here frequently.

One morning, I remember, just as I was starting out to work I met a young fellow riding a fine-looking horse, without either saddle or bridle. I suspected it was stolen, but was not sure of it until half an hour later when a pursuing party came along and gave me the information. Learning that the man they were looking for was not far ahead they galloped along, and in the afternoon of the same day they came back, bringing with them the stolen horse. I asked them if they had captured the thief, and they said: "Yes, we captured him, and if anybody inquires for him you can tell them that they can find his remains over in New Mexico, where his career as a horse-thief ended."

Members of these bands would sometimes come along and hire to me for the purpose of getting an opportunity to steal, and I had to be continually on the lookout for them. On one occasion a government wagon train with an escort of soldiers stopped here over night, and in the middle of the night they came to my room, woke me up, and informed me that all their horses and mules had been stolen. I got up, and after looking about for some time we found all the stock with the exception of a fine black horse.

I had in my employ a fellow of whom I had been somewhat suspicious for some time, and when I went to the cabin in which the men were sleeping I found him gone. He was on hand, however, the next morning and I set him at work in the garden. I was satisfied that he was the horse-thief and by and by I walked down to where he was at work, leveled a pistol at his head, and ordered him to throw up his hands. He had a pistol sticking in his belt, but he made no attempt to use it and promptly obeyed my order. I then told him that I knew he had stolen the missing horse and that I wanted to know where it could be found. The fellow weakened, confessed that he was the thief, and agreed to return the stolen animal, which he did later in the day.

Just about the close of the war, and in fact in 1866-67, the Indians were so bad that all wagon trains passing over the Santa Fe Trail had to be accompanied by escorts of soldiers. These escorts joined west-bound trains at Fort Larned, which was located at the eastern edge of the Comanche country.

In 1865, a company composed partly of Californians and partly of Mexicans and commanded by Captain Haley passed through here, escorting a train of perhaps a hundred and fifty wagons. While they were stopping here, one of the non-commissioned officers of the company was brutally murdered by three soldiers and I came near being a witness of the murder. The officer was a Mexican corporal and the soldiers were also Mexicans. There was a feud between the corporal and the privates which originated at Las Vegas, where the men had been bound and gagged by order of the corporal for engaging in a disturbance at a fandango.

The soldiers were camped near the summit of the mountain at the time they stopped here, but some of them would come down to my place every little while. The corporal, whose name was Juan

Torres, came down one evening with the three men who, although he did not suspect it, had plotted to kill him.

They left at an early hour, going in an opposite direction from their camp, and I closed my doors soon after for the night. They had not been gone more than half an hour when I heard them talking, not far from my house, and a few seconds later I heard the half-suppressed cry of a man who had, I was satisfied, received his death blow. I had gone to bed, and lay for a minute or two thinking whether I should get up and go to the rescue of the man whose cry I had heard, or insure my own safety by remaining where I was.

A little reflection convinced me that the murderers were undoubtedly watching my house to prevent any interference with the carrying out of their plot and that if I ventured out I should only endanger my own life, while there was scarcely a possibility of my being able to save the life of the man who had been assailed.

In the morning, when I got up, I found the dead body of the corporal stretched across Raton Creek not more than a hundred yards from my house. As I surmised, he had been struck with a heavy club or stone, and it was at that time that I heard him cry out. After that his brains had been beaten out and the body left where I found it.

I at once notified Captain Haley of the occurrence, and identified the men who had been in company with the corporal and who were undoubtedly his murderers. They were taken into custody and made a full confession, in which they stated that one of their number had stood at my door on the night of the murder to shoot me if I had ventured out to assist the corporal.

Two of the scoundrels were hanged afterwards at Las Vegas and the third was sent to prison for life. The corporal was buried near where the soldiers were encamped at the time of the tragedy, and it is his lonely grave which frequently attracts the attention of passengers on the Santa Fe trains, just before they reach Raton Tunnel, as they travel southward.

Notwithstanding the fact that there were frequent quarrels and now and then a bloody fight between the teamsters and others who passed over the road, that was the only murder ever committed in this neighborhood, so far as I know, since I have lived here.

My toll-road was a success financially from the time I completed it up to the time it was paralleled by the Santa Fe Railroad. Then I got out of the way of the locomotive and turned my business over to the railroad company.

I have but one objection to railroads, by the way, and that is they drive the game out of the country. Cutting down the timber which must necessarily be used in the construction of a railroad frightens away the deer and other game in the first place, and then when the road gets into operation the whistling of the locomotives and the noise of the trains drives the timid animals still farther away. Before the railroad was built I used to sit on the front porch of my house and shoot deer, but since that time I have had to get out and skirmish around a good deal to find even a jack rabbit.

Speaking of the disappearance of the game reminds me that I have heard recently of a novel complaint being made by the white settlers of western Colorado. The Ute Indians have a reservation over there and the settlers complain that they are exterminating the game, hundreds of deer being killed for their skins alone. This is a charge which the Indians have preferred against the Whites a great many times, but I don't think I ever knew before of the white men complaining of the Indians driving the game out of the country. They have generally been willing to see the game disappear, hoping that the Indians would disappear at the same time.

When I first located where I am living now the Utes were about the only neighbors I had. They were always scattered around in the mountains and I had some of them about me pretty much all the time for several years.

When they got to using guns they would come in here very frequently and challenge me to shoot with them. I had to humor them and the shooting always had to be for some kind of stake, as an Indian never missed an opportunity to gamble. I could always beat them shooting, because I have seen but very few Indians who handled a gun well; but they would try over and over again to get the best of me in a match.

Old Conniach, a famous Ute chief, who used to come to see me very often, was more chagrined than any of the other Indians over his failure to beat me in a shooting match. He came in one day and insisted on wagering five buckskins against five Mexican silver dollars that he could beat me shooting at a mark, each of us to take a single shot.

I won, and then up went another pack of buckskins against another five dollars. I won the second pack as easily as I had the first, and then I wanted to make Conniach a present of the buckskins. I came pretty near offending the old fellow by making this proposition and he very curtly informed me that "Ute Indian always paid his debts."

He wasn't satisfied with that trial of our skill as marksmen, but tried it again a few days later. The result was the same that it had been before, and when I brought up one of my boys, "Little Dick" the Indians called him, and he too had beaten the old Chief, it took all the conceit out of him.

He had boasted that no white man could beat him shooting and he honestly believed what he said. As a matter of fact, there were few white men in the country who knew anything about handling a gun who could not have done better shooting than old Conniach under any circumstances, although he was one of the best shots among the Indians.

The mountain men always had a great advantage in fighting the Indians. While they were using the bow and arrow we had the advantage of being able to shoot a much greater distance than they could, and after they got to using guns we could shoot more accurately and handle our guns a great deal quicker. To shoot with any accuracy whatever, the Indian had to have a rest for his gun and he was always slow about taking sight, while the mountain men all shot off hand and lost no time in drawing a bead on an enemy.

At hunting game with the rifle the Indians were no match for the white hunters. They were experts at finding the game, it is true, but anybody could do that in this country twenty years ago. When the game was discovered, however, such as deer or bears for instance, the hunter had not, as a rule, much time to hunt up a tree or a rock to rest his gun on before shooting. The game usually saw the hunter about as soon as the hunter saw the game, and was up and away if he was not quick in his movements.

It was the habit of the Indian hunter, when using the rifle, to carry a couple of gun rods in his hand and when he got ready to shoot at anything down would go the rods on the ground in the form of the letter X. With one hand the hunter held the rods together while with the other he managed his gun, resting it between the two rods. Sometimes he would make a single rod answer the purpose, holding it with his hand in the same manner, but he never had sufficient confidence in himself as a marksman to risk a shot at game without some sort of a rest. That was when the Indians first commenced using rifles. Of late years they have learned to use them to better advantage.

Chapter XXVIII

Stage Coach Stories

WHEN the stage company commenced running its coaches through by way of Trinidad and over my toll-road my place was made a stage station. Of course I had to keep a hotel then in connection with my other business and I entertained guests of all grades and stations, from the Vice-President of the United States down to plain stage robbers and horse thieves.

Tavern keepers in those days couldn't choose their guests and we entertained them just as they came along. The knights of the road would come by now and then, order a meal, eat it hurriedly, pay for it, and move on to where they had arranged to hold up a stage that night. Sometimes they didn't wait for it to get dark, but halted the stage, went through the passengers' pockets and the treasure box in broad daylight, and then ordered the stage driver to move on in one direction while they went off in another.

One of the most daring and successful daylight stage robberies that I remember was perpetrated by two men when the east-bound stage was coming up on the south side of the Raton Mountains one day about ten o'clock in the forenoon.

On the morning of the same day, a little after

411

sunrise two rather genteel-looking fellows mounted on fine horses rode up to my house and ordered breakfast. Being informed that breakfast would be ready in a few minutes they dismounted, hitched their horses near the door, and came into the house. I knew then just as well as I know now that they were robbers, but I had no warrant for their arrest, and I should have hesitated about serving it if I had, because they looked like very unpleasant men to transact that kind of business with.

Each of them had four pistols sticking in his belt and a repeating rifle strapped onto his saddle. When they dismounted they left the rifles with the horses, but they walked into the house and sat down at the table without laying aside the arsenal which they carried in their belts. They had little to say while eating, but were courteous in their behavior and very polite to the waiters. When they had finished breakfast they paid their bills and rode leisurely up the mountain.

It did not occur to me that they would take chances on stopping the stage in daylight or I should have sent some one to meet the incoming coach, which I knew would be along shortly, to warn the driver and passengers to be on the lookout for the robbers. It turned out, however, that a daylight robbery was just what they had in mind, and they made a success of it.

About half way down the New Mexico side of the mountain, where the cañon is very narrow, and was then heavily wooded on either side, the robbers stopped and waited for the coach. It came lumbering along by and by, neither the driver nor the passengers dreaming of such a thing as a hold-up.

The first intimation they had of the presence of stage robbers was when they saw two men step into the road, one on each side of the stage, each of them holding two cocked revolvers, one of which was brought to bear on the passengers and the other on the driver. Both the driver and the passengers were politely but very positively told that they must throw up their hands without any unnecessary delay, and the stage came to a stand-still.

There were four passengers in the coach, all men, but their hands went up at the same instant that the driver dropped his reins, and struck an attitude that suited the robbers. Then, while one of the men stood guard the other stepped up to the stage and ordered the treasure box thrown off. This demand was complied with and the box was broken open and rifled of its contents, which fortunately were not of very great value.

The passengers were compelled to hand out their watches and other jewelry, as well as what money they had in their pockets, and then the driver was directed to move on up the road. In a minute after the robbery had been completed the robbers had disappeared with their booty, and that was the last seen of them by that particular coach-load of passengers.

The men who planned and executed that robbery were two cool, level-headed and daring scoundrels known as Chuck-a-luck and Magpie. They were killed soon after this occurrence by a member of their own band whose name was Steward. A reward of a thousand dollars had been offered for their capture and this tempted Steward to kill them one night when they were asleep in camp. He then secured a wagon, into which he loaded the dead robbers and hauled them to Cimarron City, where he turned them over to the authorities and received his reward.

On one occasion I had a notorious horse-thief and murderer and the man who was in pursuit of him in my house at the same time. The man who was hunted was a half-breed Cherokee Indian who went by the name of Chunk, and the man hunting him was Porter Stockdon, himself a great rascal and all-round desperado, who was killed afterward while resisting arrest for some one of his numerous crimes.

Chunk rode up to my place early one morning, hitched his horse, and went in to breakfast. After breakfast he rode away without manifesting any uneasiness or indicating by his manner that he had any fear of being pursued. Stockdon was in the house at the time, but he had said nothing to me about his business and if he saw Chunk he must have been afraid to undertake to arrest him. He went away by and by, and I saw no more of him until that night.

I was sitting by the fire talking with guests, of whom there were perhaps ten or a dozen in the room, when I heard a knock at the door. Without getting up, I called out "come in," and turned about in my chair to see who the visitor was. The door opened and a man stepped inside with a cocked six-shooter in each hand. We were all taken by surprise, and my guests didn't know whether they were to be held up or had a desperado to deal with who would want them to stand on their heads for his amusement, and they looked mighty uncomfortable.

I recognized Stockdon in a moment and asked him what he wanted. He had sense enough to tell me then that he was looking for Chunk, who had killed a man at a fandango near Trinidad the night before.

I told him the man he was looking for had left the house shortly before he left it himself in the morning, and that he would have had no trouble in finding him at that time. I then told him which way the murderer had gone and requested him to put up his pistols before he hurt somebody, reminding him that it wasn't a very genteel performance to come into a public house flourishing a couple of guns and frightening people until their hair stood on end, when there was no occasion for it.

He had several men with him who had been left outside the house and they all went on together in the direction that the man they were after had taken. They killed an innocent young man over in New Mexico by mistake, but came back without having seen anything of Chunk, the murderer.

This fellow was killed afterward at the Clifton House near Raton by Clay Allison, whom the young people about here can remember as something of a man killer and desperado. Allison and Chunk met at the Clifton House and as their meeting was a peculiar encounter between what we called bad men I will tell you about it.

They had been together half a day or more, had quarreled more or less, and each was watching for an opportunity to get the drop on the other. They went into dinner together and sat down at the same table, Allison laying his pistol on the table alongside his plate, while Chunk held his weapon, at full cock, in his lap. They had hardly seated themselves at the table when Chunk made a grab for Allison's pistol with one hand, at the same time that he attempted to fire his own pistol with the other hand. His pistol struck the table and was discharged without injuring his antagonist, and before he could shoot again Allison blew his brains out.

I was never bothered by the bands of road agents who infested the country at that time, but once. That is, they made but one attempt to rob me, and they didn't get any satisfaction out of that. That robbery was planned by Jack Ross and his gang, and after robbing me they were to go on and meet the stage, which was to be held up, and altogether they expected to make a pretty good night's work of it.

To get through with me and meet the stage before it reached my house they had to commence operations pretty early in the evening, and so it happened that although I had gone to bed I had not yet gone to sleep when four men rode very quietly up to a little thicket near the house, dismounted, and hitched their horses.

In those days you couldn't run a stage station without a bar, and like every other keeper of a stage station I had one. The robbers had to pass the building in which the liquors were kept, on their way up to my sleeping apartments, and the temptation to break in and help thmselves was too strong to be resisted. They did this very quietly, but I heard them, and looking out of a window near my bed I saw them when they came out of the bar room.

I always slept with a couple of pistols under my pillow and my rifle near enough to the bed so that I could put my hand on it without getting up. When I saw the four men come out of the bar room and start toward the building in which I was sleeping, I picked up my rifle and poking the muzzle out through the open space left by the breaking out of a pane of glass, waited until the leader of the gang was within ten feet of the window. I pushed my gun out of the window a little farther, so that the foremost robber could get a good look into the muzzle of it, and called a halt, threatening to shoot if they advanced an inch farther.

Ross himself was at the head of the party, and he undertook to explain to me that all they wanted was a night's lodging, and asked me to get up and let them in. I told him that I wasn't opening my house to robbers at that hour of the night; that I knew who they were and what they wanted, and would shoot in two seconds if they didn't clear out.

They evidently didn't like the situation, because they lost no time in getting away. Just as they turned back we heard the stage, which happened to be ahead of time, rattling down the mountain not more than two hundred yards distant, and as they knew that I would give the alarm they did not meet the stage, but rode down the road in the opposite direction.

When the stage came in I found there were eight passengers aboard, and they were well armed. They examined their weapons carefully to see that they were all in good order, borrowed a few guns from me, and started on towards Trinidad, prepared to give the road agents, of whose presence along the road I had informed them, about as warm a reception as robbers of any kind ever met with.

They had no occasion, however, to use their weapons, because the robbers, knowing that I would inform the stage driver and his passengers of the danger ahead of them, and that in consequence they would be on their guard and prepared for a fight, were not seen along the road.

When a stage-load of people came along and stopped with me over night they generally had some good stories to tell of their adventures on the road, which had sometimes been perilous and sometimes only amusing. Sometimes they would tell of having been chased by the Indians, when it was a race for life, and at other times they had met with nothing more serious than being held up by the genteel brigands and losing their money and such valuables as they happened to have along with them.

I remember one time John Chisum, the famous ranchman who owned the cattle on a thousand hills, or at any rate had thousands of cattle, came along with a good story about his having been robbed on his way through by stage from some point in Arizona to Santa Fe, where he took the overland stage for the East.

He had a big contract for furnishing supplies for the Indians down in Arizona, and had gone there a short time before with a large band of cattle, which he turned over to the agency. He stopped there until he got paid for them, and then took the precaution to send nearly all of his money and drafts ahead of him to Santa Fe. When he got into the stage to leave for home he had with him a thousand dollars in greenbacks and some small change, which he expected to use along the road.

The first night out they were stopped by stage robbers, who had evidently been shadowing Chisum and expected to capture the proceeds of his cattle sale. When the stage came to a stop he knew what was up, and had just time enough to get hold of his roll of greenbacks and drop it down the leg of his pants before the robbers opened the door of the stage and ordered him to get out and turn over to them what money he had with him.

He told them they could search him and take what they found, but he was not prepared to contribute very handsomely on that occasion. They had no trouble in finding his watch, which they appropriated without ceremony, and then they began a thorough search for the money they supposed he had concealed about him. He said he expected every minute they would find that roll of bills hidden away in his pants leg; but they didn't, and all they got was a two-dollar bill, which they found in his vest pocket.

He told them that two-dollar bill was all the money he had to pay for something to eat on the road to Santa Fe, and he thought they ought to let him keep it. One of the robbers finally pulled a silver dollar out of his pocket and handed it to him, remarking that a man who was mean enough to travel in a stage coach with only two dollars in his pocket ought to starve, but he would give him that dollar just to let him know that he was dealing with a gentleman. Chisum told this story every time he made a stop at a stage station, and chuckled over the way he fooled the stage robbers and saved his thousand dollars.[110]

[110]John S. Chisum was born in Tennessee in 1824. In boyhood he was taken by his parents to Texas. In 1854 he engaged in the cattle business, in which he attained great prosperity, becoming known eventually as the "cattle king of America," owning herds variously estimated at 60,000 to 100,000 cattle. For several years subsequent to the Civil War he engaged, along with his partner Charles Goodnight, in driving cattle from Texas to New Mexico, Colorado, and Wyoming. Data condensed from R.E.Twitchell, *Leading Facts of New Mexican History*,V, 281–85: *Dictionary of American Biography*.

A west-bound stage came in one night just at dark with as much as a hundred arrow points and broken arrows sticking in the sides and running-gear of the coach, and the passengers told a story which is but a sample of scores of stories I have heard as I sat by the fire with my guests on an evening when we had had a lot of fresh arrivals.

There were five men, one woman, and a child in the party that arrived in the battle-scarred stage, and they were all on their way to Santa Fe. In coming through the Comanche country they had had a military escort most of the way, but as they saw no Indians the escort turned back, leaving the stage to go on its way alone. They were making good time over a perfectly level prairie and the stage driver was beginning to congratulate himself on having made another trip over the most dangerous portion of the old trail without having an Indian fight, when a passenger who sat beside him on the box called his attention to what looked like a huge ant hill not more than two hundred yards distant, near the road side.

Scanning the little mound closely, the driver at once reached the conclusion that what he saw was an Indian covered up in the sand, where he could see the roadway and give the signal for an attack on the stage at the proper time.

That a band of Indians was concealed in the long grass and an ambush lay just ahead of him he was certain, and how to avoid it was the question. He dared not turn back, and turning out on either side might be to plunge into the very midst of the band of savages.

He was not long in deciding what course he would pursue, because there was no time to lose. The man who sat beside him was informed that there were Indians ahead and he was directed to swing himself into the coach and notify the other passengers. He did so without being told a second time, and the men gathered up their guns and held them at the coach windows, ready to fire the moment they caught sight of the Indians.

Meantime the driver, who was as brave a fellow as ever cracked a whip over a stage team, had tightened his hold on the reins, shook out his long whip lash, and touching up his six broncos just enough to put them on their mettle, held them in check so that they would appear to the Indians to be jogging along at the regulation pace until he got ready to make his contemplated dash through the ambuscade.

He waited until he got within forty yards of the sand-covered Indian, when he cracked his whip over the horses and uttered a series of yells which started them at once on a dead run. At the same moment the suspicous-looking sand pile resolved itself into an Indian, who sprang to his feet and gave a war whoop which brought a score or more of the Comanches up out of the grass, where they had been lying on either side of the road.

The driver's tactics had taken the Indians by surprise and he was through the ambuscade before they could fairly bend their bows. The next moment, however, the arrows fell thick as hailstones about the stage and a rifle ball cut a hole through the broad brim of the driver's hat. The passengers returned the fire; but with what effect they could not tell, as they were going at terrific speed and the stage was rolling from side to side like a ship in a storm.

They were soon out of reach of the arrows for the time being, but within two hundred yards of the place where they ran into the ambuscade they caught sight of the Indians' horses, which had been hidden in a ravine, and they knew that pursuit was certain. Realizing that there was but one chance for him to save the lives of his passengers and his own as well, the stage driver kept his broncos forging along at the top of their speed, hoping to reach the next stage station, four miles away, before the Comanches should overtake them.

It took the Indians some little time to get to their horses and mount them, and the stage had gotten a good start in the race, but before half the distance to the station had been covered the arrows again commenced whistling past the driver and pelting the stage. Fortunately the men who were inside knew how to use their guns, and although it was difficult to shoot with any degree of accuracy on account of the rolling motion of the stage, they managed to hit one or two of the Indians and that caused the red-skins to fall back. They followed the stage almost to the station, however, and were in sight of it when the panting, foaming, and almost exhausted ponies dashed into the big stage barn, the doors of which were closed behind the coach load of thoroughly frightened passengers.

The stage station was by no means well-garrisoned, and would hardly have withstood much of a siege, but the Indians knew well enough that there were a few determined men there, and they knew also that to make an assault on the station meant the killing of some of their number. For some time they hovered about, apparently waiting for the stage to resume its journey. Not until after night-fall, however, and some time after the Indians had been seen riding away in an opposite direction, did the plucky stage driver assure his passengers that it was safe to start again on their trip to Santa Fe, to which place he carried them in due time without any more thrilling adventures.

The only one of the passengers who received any injury more serious than the terrible shaking up they got was the child, a little girl about four years old, whose cheek was grazed by an arrow. The wound was little more than a scratch, however, and could only have left a slight scar to remind her in after years of her narrow escape from death at the hands of the savages. The driver had his clothes torn in several places by the arrows and there was a bullet-hole through his coat, as well as his hat, but he escaped like the rest without injury.

Chapter XXIX

Farewell Visits of the Red Men

THE railroad took the place of the stage line in 1878, and since that time I have lived in a different atmosphere from that in which I formerly lived. I almost feel that I am no longer on the frontier, and that there is no frontier to go to. In my old age I have been brought back into civilization, and I find just one unpleasant feature about it.

While I am not so foolish as to lose sight of the fact that I have grown old and as a consequence am no longer suited to an adventurous life myself, I still fancy that I should like to live amidst such surroundings as we had in this country twenty-five years ago, so that visitors could drop in every day or two to see me who would have something to talk about. If buffaloes had not all been killed, if there were more deer and bears in the mountains, if the stage lines were still running and the Indians had not been driven out of the country, the young fellows who visit me would now and then be able to tell a story worth hearing.

As it is, I have to do pretty much all the story telling myself, except when I happen to meet somebody who tells me about the cities that have grown up on the Plains where I used to hunt buffaloes, and along the streams where I used to set my beaver traps. Every once in a while I meet a man, too, who tells me about the gold or silver that has been dug out of the mountains that I used to tramp over when trading with the Indians, and that interests me almost as much as if I had found it myself.

Then another man comes along who happened to know one of the old-timers with whom I had slept in camp perhaps a hundred times, and when I inquire about my old friend I hear something which has a sort of melancholy interest for me. I learn that my old-time companion is dead and that the lawyers are dividing up his estate among themselves; or in other words, that the heirs are engaged in a legal dispute over the disposition to be made of his property, which amounts to the same thing as dividing it among the lawyers. I don't feel very old, but when I look about me for my associates of the forties I find that only the mountains and I are left, and before long it will be only the mountains.

The Indians disappeared from this portion of Colorado a few years before the railroad came, and since that time I have seen as little of them as if I had been living in one of the New England States. The Utes used to claim the land on which I am now living, and a large area of surrounding country. They disliked to give it up but they had to go, because, as they said, "the white men wanted more room."

They were terribly whipped by a party of soldiers under command of Colonel Fauntleroy and a party of volunteers under Colonel St. Vrain only a year or two before I came here, just over the mountain on Sugarite Creek. They had killed some people and stolen some stock in the neighborhood of Abiquiu, and the soldiers followed them over four hundred miles before they came up with them.

The Indians, believing they had distanced their pursuers, lay down at night to sleep in brush-covered booths, some of which were standing not many years ago and may yet be for all I know, never dreaming that before morning half their number would be lying dead on the banks of the little creek beside which they were encamped.

The soldiers came on them in the middle of the night, and at once attacked the camp. The Indians were taken completely by surprise. For once they were caught napping and that very soundly. Bewildered by the sudden and unexpected attack, they could offer but little resistance and something like a hundred of them were killed, only a remnant of the band escaping.[111]

[111]The massacre of the Mexicans at Pueblo described by Wootton *ante*, 284–89, occurred on Christmas Day, 1854. About the same time the Apaches were conducting hostile

The last fight the whites had with the Utes in this part of Colorado, in fact the last serious trouble they had with any of the Indians, was at Trinidad in 1867.[112] It was early in the fall when quite a large band of the Utes came along past my house, and as usual stopped to pay me a visit. I

raids in which the Utes joined. Since the regular army in the Territory was too weak to restrain them, General Garland appealed to the Governor of New Mexico for help, who responded by promptly levying six companies of militia which he placed under the command of Cerain St. Vrain. In March, 1855 Colonel Fauntleroy of the First U.S. Dragoon Regiment led 500 troops, comprising regular contingents and St. Vrain's militia, in pursuit of the hostile Utes. The pursuit was pushed relentlessly until the hostiles were overtaken, much as Wootton relates. In the last 24 hours before the attack the artillery company marched 52 miles "without complaint," over mountain roads in extremely cold weather. At dawn, April 28, the Indians were surprised and quickly defeated with a loss of 40 warriors killed and an "incredible quantity" of buffalo robes and other camp baggage captured. The loss of the attacking soldiers was 2 men wounded, one of whom subsequently died of his wound. *Kit Carson's Autobiography*, pp. 161–67, the Lakeside Classics volume for 1935, gives a rather brief account of the campaign and of St. Vrain's subsequent operations. A much better account is in Sabin, *Kit Carson Days*, II, 666–70. For the contemporary official reports of General Garland and Colonel Fauntleroy see *House Exec. Docs.*, 34 Cong., 1st and 2nd Sessions, Vol. I, Pt. 2, pp. 56–72. (U.S. Serial, 841). Once more Wootton's sequence of events is confused. His own account *ante*, pp. 284–94, shows that he was living on his ranch in 1855, the year of Fauntleroy's campaign.

[112]Although the hostilities narrated by Wootton may have been the last Indian warfare in southeastern Colorado,

knew a good many of them, and among others I recognized a good-looking chief who was about fifty years old as an Indian I had seen at some time, but I couldn't remember when or where it was.

After asking him a good many questions I learned that he had been with the band of Utes that gave me so much trouble near the Uncompahgre River when I was on my way to California in 1852. We talked over my encounter with old Uncotash, whose life I had threatened when I didn't think my own was worth a farthing, and whom I succeeded in frightening into good behavior. The chief with whom I had this talk, more than fifteen years after the occurrence, gave me credit for being "heap brave" and "heap fool," by which he meant that I took desperate risks.

The Indians told me that they were going to Trinidad to have "big horse-race with the white men." They said "Indian horses run fast, beat white men's horses; Indian win heap bets." I thought it altogether likely that they might have

a serious outbreak of the Utes, with consequent massacres and battles, occurred in northern Colorado in 1879. For comprehensive accounts of the hostilities see Baker and Hafen, *History of Colorado,* I, 414–28, and H. H. Bancroft, *History of Nevada, Colorado and Wyoming,* 471–81. A contemporary and more detailed narrative is in W. B. Vickers, *History of the City of Denver, Arapahoe County and Colorado* (Chicago, 1880), 122–75.

as good luck as they expected, but I knew that those horse-races generally led to trouble, and I tried to persuade them not to go to Trinidad. The chief who had charge of the band promised me, however, that they would behave well, and assured me that they would not quarrel with the white men.

For some days after they got to Trinidad everything went along smoothly, and they were quite as fortunate in winning horse-races as they had expected to be, but just as I had anticipated, the affair wound up in a quarrel. There were but few people at Trinidad in 1867, and when the hot-tempered Utes began to make some hostile demonstrations the settlers became alarmed and appealed to the military forces for protection.

There were no troops stationed at Trinidad, but Major Alexander got there soon after the Indians began to talk about going on the warpath, with one company of soldiers. He made an effort to patch up a truce, but it was unsuccessful, and seeing that the situation was critical he notified the settlers scattered about in the surrounding country to come into town and place themselves under his protection.

I was informed that an Indian outbreak was almost certain, and that when the hostilities once commenced I would be in very great danger if I remained at my home in the mountains. I thanked

Major Alexander for giving me this warning, but at the same time informed him that my interests were here and that I should stay here and protect them as far as possible. We learned afterward that while the parleying and threatening was going on at Trinidad the Indians had sent couriers back into the mountains to stir up some of the larger bands of Utes, and an effort was being made to bring about a general Ute uprising. I will tell you farther along how this uprising was prevented.

What precipitated hostilities at Trinidad was a quarrel between Indians and Mexicans. The Indians were encamped about two miles above the town on the Purgatoire River, near a small Mexican settlement. They charged the Mexicans with having stolen some of their horses, and finally, as a result of the quarrel, one of the Indians was shot and killed by a Mexican.

That happened about ten o'clock in the morning, just as the Indians were getting ready to leave their camp. Of course, they at once commenced a warfare on the Mexicans and Major Alexander with his company of soldiers and a few volunteers picked up in Trinidad marched out to suppress the savages.

They retreated about two miles up the river, sent their women and children into the mountains, and having formed the usual ambuscade, waited for the soldiers to come up. Their first fire killed and wounded several of Major Alexander's men, but as soon as the fire was returned they scattered in the mountains and made their escape. The Indians always insisted that they did not lose a man in the fight, aside from the one killed by the Mexican early in the morning, and they claimed a victory for that reason.

Two of the Utes came to my house immediately after the fight and complained bitterly of the way they had been treated at Trinidad. They were loud in their threats of vengeance, and declared that the big bands of Utes would soon be on the warpath, and that much blood would be shed before their anger would be appeased.

Before the fight occurred, L. B. Maxwell, who had for years been on very friendly terms with the Utes, had learned of the trouble at Trinidad and the contemplated general uprising of the Indians, and had sent a messenger to Kit Carson, who was stationed at Fort Garland, giving him full information in regard to the plans of the Indians. Maxwell advised him to go out and hold a conference with a large band of hostiles then on their way to meet the retreating Indians, and see if he could not make peace with them.

Kit acted on this advice, and in doing so probably saved Major Alexander's company from being entirely destroyed. Major Alexander was in pursuit of the band that had been driven away from Trinidad when Kit met him and induced him to turn back. Had he kept up the pursuit twenty-four hours longer he would have met a band of several hundred Ute warriors and could hardly have escaped a disastrous defeat.

Kit Carson spoke the Ute language well, had been among them for years, and had a great deal of influence with them. When he met the hostiles he held a long conference with them, listened to all their complaints, and promised them that everything should be arranged to suit them if they would turn back and abandon the idea of going on the warpath. The result of this interview was that several of the Ute chiefs agreed to go to Cimarron City, the home of L. B. Maxwell, where a peace conference was to be held.

They sent for me to come over there, and I was present at the conference and did what I could to aid Carson and Maxwell in fixing up a peace arrangement. Maxwell made the Indians a present of a lot of ponies, and that put them again in good humor, and sent them back to their hunting grounds. He had established a peace with them on his own account some years before this by doing them a good turn when they were at war with the Comanches and Kiowas.

A band of the Utes met a band of the Comanches and Kiowas near Cimarron City and were badly defeated in the fight which followed. The Utes lost all their horses, and Maxwell, taking advantage of the opportunity to place them under an obligation to him, called them in and gave them a fresh lot of ponies out of his own herd. They never forgot that favor, and when the old chief who had been the recipient of the gift was about to die he called all the other chiefs in reach around him and exacted from them a promise that they would never harm "Maxwell, the friend of the Utes." Some time after the peace had been made at Cimarron, the Utes agreed to give up this country and they never came in here afterward.

The Arapahoes and Cheyennes used to pay me visits occasionally for several years after I came here. Once a large band of Arapahoes came through on their way into the Ute country. Roman Nose was the chief of the band, and he said he came out of his way to see me. He gave as an excuse for coming that he wanted to talk to me about the old hunters and trappers, and learn what had become of them.

The whole band stayed with me half a day or more and I talked over early experiences with the old chief very much as I would have talked with an old *Compadre.*

The Arapahoes, Cheyennes, Comanches, and Kiowas, and other remnants of tribes which had roamed over Kansas and eastern Colorado were removed to the Indian Territory early in the seventies, some of them in fact before that time, and we saw no more of them after that.

About the time the Indians disappeared the game began to get scarce in the country, particularly the buffaloes. I think it was in 1874 that I had my last buffalo hunt. I drove down into the Panhandle of Texas with a two-horse wagon and loaded it with buffalo meat before I came back, but it cost me more labor than any load of meat I had ever taken before.

I found the buffaloes getting scarce, and noticed that the temper of the animals had changed very materially. They had been hunted and harrassed so much that they would fight on slight provocation, and a wounded buffalo was about as vicious and ugly as a wounded bear.

I narrowly escaped being killed by a wounded bull that I supposed was dead, when I was getting ready to butcher him. When I shot the bull he dropped to the ground as though he had received a death wound. I laid my gun aside, and rolling up my sleeves walked up to the apparently dead buffalo with my butcher knife in my hand, to begin skinning him. When I got within about ten feet of him the buffalo seemed to realize all at once that he wasn't dead, and he sprang up and charged straight toward me.

You never saw a man make a quicker turn than I did, or make better time in a race of twenty yards.

As a matter of fact, there was never a time in my life when there was greater necessity for my doing my level best in a short-distance foot race. The maddened animal behind me would have made short work of me if I had had the misfortune to stumble or had met with any similar mishap. The charge was made so suddenly and unexpectedly that I was given no opportunity to call for assistance or to secure any arms other than my butcher knife, and this would have been a poor weapon to use in a fight with the kind of animal I had to contend with. My horse was so far away that I could not reach him, and there was but one direction for me to take in trying to get away.

It happened that I had to run toward a deep ravine which I knew was too wide for me to leap across, and so deep that I should be killed, or at least seriously hurt, if I fell into it. I headed for a tree which was growing up out of the ravine, with its top sticking up a few feet above the bank. The buffalo was mighty close to me when I reached the bank, and I had no time to pick out a place to light when I made a jump for the tree, just as the bull plowed up the ground behind me as he came to a stop at the edge of the ravine.

I caught in the branches of the tree, a good deal scratched and bruised to be sure, but not seriously injured. The buffalo stood on the bank snorting and bellowing, apparently not at all inclined to abandon the fight and move off. I climbed down the tree after a little while and went down the ravine some distance before I could get out. Then I beckoned to a boy, who accompanied me on the trip, to bring my horse and gun, and mounted on the horse it did not take me long to finish the wounded but not seriously injured animal.

I found it necessary to exercise a great deal more care to be successful in hunting the buffaloes at that time than was necessary a few years earlier, and it took me longer to load my one wagon with meat then than it would have taken to load a dozen wagons ten years before. I realized then for the first time how rapidly this splendid game was being exterminated, and my boys claim that the tears stood in my eyes when I came home and told them about it.

With the removal of the Indians from the country, the disappearance of the game, the abandonment of the stage lines, and the transfer of the freighting business from wagons to railroad trains the era of adventure, I mean real, stirring, thrilling adventure, ended in this portion of the mountain region.

The whole country has thrown off its wildness, so far as the character of its inhabitants is concerned, although eastern people still speak of it as the frontier. Outside of its rugged mountain peaks, its thickly wooded cañons, and its natural scenery, the Wild West is no longer wild.

The wildest thing we see out here now-a-days is a cow-boy, and about the most thrilling experience of a cow-boy's life is getting pitched off a bucking pony before he learns to ride. Pleasure parties roam about over the mountains, and instead of being loaded down with firearms and ammunition, as we used to be when we ventured into the same localities, they carry lunch baskets and amateur photographing outfits. We no longer see walking arsenals on the streets of our little towns and cities, and like older States we have a law on our statute books which prohibits persons from carrying concealed weapons.

Of all the changes, the improvements, and the advance in civilization which have been made in the vast western half of the United States within the past fifty years, I have been a witness. I trust I have contributed my share toward bringing about the condition of affairs which exists to-day, but at any rate I have led an active and stirring life and have told you pretty much all about it.

What I have told you will, I think, interest those who care to know something more than is generally known about what was going on in this country before it was connected with the Eastern and Middle States by railroads and telegraph lines, as well as those who are always entertained by stories of adventure. You can say to those who care to know more about me than I have already said about myself that you left me taking the rest to which an old man is entitled, and which I flatter myself I have richly earned.[113]

[113] The original edition of Uncle Dick's narrative contains a final chapter of editorial comments by Mr. Conard which is omitted from the present edition.

Index

INDEX

445

450   *Index*

Gold, discovery at Denver, 9–10; prospectors seek, 353–55, 361; in California, 220; search for lost mines, 221–26.

Grand River, sheep herd crosses, 241–42.

Gray, Jim, outlaw leader, 402.

Great Britain, territorial claims, 52–53.

Green River, trappers visit, 53–54; sheep herd crosses, 248.

Grier, Major William N., leads White rescue expedition, 189–98; career, 194; races Wootton, 231.

Grizzly bears, encounters with, 137–50, 215–16.

Guides, for Col. Doniphan's army, 171–80; for Fremont expedition, 181–83; rescue of White family, 190–95; of L. B. Maxwell party, 198–202; for Col. Newby's expedition, 204–19; advice ignored, 207–208. See also Bill Williams, Kit Carson, and Richens L. Wootton.

HAIL-STORMS, 315–16, 396.

Haley, Captain ——, 404–405.

Half-breed Indians, characterized, 130; encounter with trappers, 131–34.

Hardtack, 312, 330.

Harrison, Gov. William Henry, generalship at Tippecanoe, 194.

Hayes, Seth, quarrel with Kaw Indians, 327–28.

Heredia, Gen. ——, 174.

Hicklin, Alexander (Zan), practical joker, 346–51.

Holladay, Ben, career, 248–49.

Hornaday, Dr. Wm. T., conducts buffalo censuses, 70.

Horses, fear Indians, 37; bears, 149; eaten, 42; stolen, 92–93, 107, 199–200, 402–404; raced, 122–23, 231, 431-34; trappers use, 44–45; government uses, 198–99; pull stage-coaches, 311.

Huerfano River, ranching activities on, 279–81, 299.

Hughes, John T., narrative cited, 259.

INDEPENDENCE, terminus of Santa Fe Trail, 19, 314.

New Mexico, American occupation, 153–80; Civil War activities, 373–77. See also Mexicans, Indians, and the several Indian tribes.

Nez Percé Indians, habitat, 99; religious beliefs, 119.

OKLAHOMA Territory, organized, 99.

Oregon Country, question of ownership, 50, 52–53.

Ortebees, Charles, career 281; Indian raid, 288.

Ortebees, John, 281.

Ortiz, Tomas, plans Taos rebellion, 154–55.

Owens Dick, fight with grizzly bear, 140–42; career, 140; guides John C. Fremont, 183.

Oxen, pull wagon trains, 305, 307, 310, 332; Spanish fever kills, 340. See also Cattle.

PAH-UTE (Piute) Indians, hostilities with trappers, 40, 64–65; use poisoned arrows, 64–65, 124; degraded, 107–108; courtship methods, 116. See also Ute Indians.

Pawnee Fork, Indian hostilities at, 26–28, 36–39.

Pawnee Indians, hostilities with, 36–39, 77–80, 277; habitat, 99; Arapahoes defeat, 79–80, 330.

Pawnee Rock, scene of Indian hostilities, 26–28, 37–38; teamsters mutiny, 322. See also Fort Larned.

Peacock, George, practical joker, 325–26.

Picking Bones Woman, squaw-wife, 281.

Pike, Zebulon M., route of captors, 259.

Pike's Peak Gold Rush, 10.

Pima Indians, habitat, 100; characterized, 108; kindness, 262–63.

Point of Rocks, Massacre of James M. White party, 188–98.

Poisoned arrows, Indians use, 64–65, 124–25.

Polk, President James K., role in Oregon controversy, 53.

Polygamy, Indians practice, 113.

Pony Express, founded, 248–49.

Prairie Apache Indians. See Apache Indians.

Prairie schooners, history, 305–306. See also Freighting.

458 *Index*

Roman Nose, career, 76, 436.
Rosebud, battle, 27.
Ross, Jack, outlaw, 402, 417–19.
Ruins Leroux, visited, 205; described, 206–207.
Runnels, Jim, outlaw gang executed, 393–94.
Runnells (Reynolds?), service in Col. Newby's Navahoe
    campaign, 204–19; identity, 204.
Russell, Wm. H., founder of Pony Express, 249.
Russell, Majors, and Waddell, freighting firm, 249.
Russia, territorial claims, 52.
Ruxton, Geo. F. narrative cited, 91–92, 160.

Sabin, E. L., narrative cited, 181–82.
Sac and Fox Indians, habitat, 98.
Sacramento, battle, 172, 174–75.
Sacramento (Calif.), Wootton visits, 254–56; fires, 255–56.
St. Charles River, traders settle on, 280; massacred, 285–87.
St. Vrain, Cerain, career, 14–15; trading activities, 28;
    leads rescue party, 33–34; role in Taos rebellion, 163–
    68; commands militia, 430. See also Gov. Charles Bent,
    Fort Bent, and Bent and St. Vrain.
Salmon River, trappers traverse, 53.
Salt Lake City, Wootton visits, 248–51, 339–46.
Salt Lake Trail, route described, 339.
San Bernardino, visited, 256.
Sand Creek (Chivington) massacre, 389–93.
San Francisco, visited, 256.
Sangre de Christo Mountains, bandit resort, 273.
San Luis (Col.), pioneer farmers at, 299.
San Pasquale, battle, 27.
Santa Fe, Americans occupy, 153; role in Taos rebellion,
    153–70; in Col. Doniphan's campaign, 171–79; horse-
    back record to Kansas City, 231; Col. Sibley captures,
    310, 374–75; terminus of Santa Fe Trail, 314. See also
    New Mexico.
Santa Fe Railroad, route of, 5–6, 353; built, 406–407.

Ute Indians, burial customs, 88–89, 112; trading experiences with, 88–90, 126–28; habitat, 99–100; intertribal warfare, 104, 107–108; marriage customs, 115–16; warfare with, 179–80, 187–90, 198–202, 280–89, 429–36; Wootton encounters, 225–26; prey on sheep herd, 238–47; neighbors, 407–10; kill Bill Williams' party, 184. See also Pah-Utes.

VALVERDE, terminus of Jornada del Muerto, 259; battle, 310, 374.
Vancouver, trappers visit, 54.
Verne, Jules, author, 55–56.
Vigil, Cornelio, murdered, 158.
Vigilantes, in early Denver, 362.

WAGON trains, across Plains, journey described, 19–28. See also Freighting.
Walters, ——, trapper, Indian shoots, 128–29.
Washington, George, raises buffaloes, 73.
Water, scarcity, 172, 257–60; floods, 237, 256, 394–96.
Watrous, sheep purchased, 235.
Weightman, Col. Richard H., kills Francis X. Aubre, 232.
West Denver, 354.
Whetstone Springs, massacre of J. M. White party, 188; rescue-party visits, 191–92.
White, James M., family, massacred, 188–98, 202; efforts to rescue prisoners, 338.
Williams, B. D. Territorial Delegate, 364–65.
Williams. Bill, member of trapping expedition, 128; guides John C. Fremont 181–82; last trip, 184–86; career, 186.
Wolves, destroy buffaloes, 74–75; encounter with mad, 135–36; poisoned, 326.
Wool, Gen. John E., campaign, 172.
Wootton, Richens Lacy (Uncle Dick), career, 11–16; narrative characterized, 16–18; trapping activities, 39–67, 130–34; residence described, 7–10; blindness, 10–11;